TOWARD A
THEOLOGY OF
INCULTURATION

AYLWARD SHORTER

ORBIS BOOKS
Maryknoll, New York 10545

The Catholic Foreign Mission Society of America (Maryknoll) recruits and trains people for overseas missionary service. Through Orbis Books Maryknoll aims to foster the international dialogue that is essential to mission. The books published, however, reflect the opinions of their authors and are not meant to represent the official position of the society.

Orbis/ISBN 0-88344-536-0
Geoffrey Chapman/ISBN 0 225 66502 6

Contents

For
Hugo Kamya

Abbreviations

AAS	*Acta Apostolicae Sedis*
AFER	*African Ecclesial Review*
AMECEA	Association of Member Episcopal Conferences in Eastern Africa
CAMEC	Catholic Mission Education Centre (London)
CHIEA	Catholic Higher Institute of Eastern Africa
DIA	*Documentation et Informations Africaines*
IRM	*International Review of Mission*
JAH	*Journal of African History*
NRT	*Nouvelle Revue Théologique*
SECAM	Symposium of Episcopal Conferences of Africa and Madagascar

Introduction

The Church, through its missionary expansion to Third World countries, has had much to do with the twentieth-century 'discovery' of culture as a plural phenomenon. As the centre of ecclesial gravity shifts inexorably from the North Atlantic to the Third World, this new, empirical understanding of culture is forcing a revision of Christian theology, Bible reading and Church history. It also imposes the vision and incipient reality of a multicultural Catholic Church.

The theology of this multicultural Church is Inculturation Theology, the recognition that faith must become culture, if it is to be fully received and lived. It is a concept related to, though not identical with, Liberation Theology, and it is cherished especially by Christians in Africa and recently decolonized countries in other continents. The concept of inculturation (and the term itself) gained currency in the 1970s, very largely because of the efforts of African bishops and theologians who saw in it an ally against the consequences of cultural alienation and a guarantee of a genuinely African Christianity.

The last ten years have seen a growing number of articles, working papers and even official statements on aspects of inculturation, after the stimulus of the 1974 Synod of Bishops and the Synodal document, *Evangelii Nuntiandi*, drawn up by Paul VI in the following year. The contrast, on the other hand, between theological progress on the subject and official reluctance to sanction cultural diversity in practice, remains a feature of the contemporary Catholic Church. Perhaps the time has arrived when some of the strands in the Church's present thinking and praxis can be drawn together, and that is the purpose of this book.

The first part describes the language of inculturation and the sociological data on which theology is brought to bear. This entails tracing the Church's own changing approaches to culture, noting the fundamental link between religion and culture and making a fuller analysis of the theological concept of inculturation. In the second, more strictly theological, part of the book, the various Christological and soteriological concepts, which have contributed to an understanding of inculturation, are discussed, and the biblical background is examined.

The discussion of culture and evangelization in the New Testament leads naturally, in Part Three, to an account of the Church's attitude to cultures in its missionary history, both before and after the Reformation and in the nineteenth century. Part Four presents the actual teaching of the twentieth-century Catholic Church on inculturation, and the evolution of its thought and practice, before, during and after the Second Vatican Council. The final part of the book looks at the present and future prospects for inculturation in the Catholic Church, taking three main topics: the relevance of inculturation for socio-economic liberation and development, the problem of ecclesial communion in a multicultural Church and the potential contributions of basic communities to the implementation of inculturation in practice.

Ever since publishing my book *African Culture and the Christian Church* in 1972, I have followed the inculturation debate with great interest. I have recently been giving courses on aspects of inculturation at the Catholic Higher Institute of Eastern Africa and the Theological Centre for Religious, Nairobi, as well as at the Jesuit Theological Centre, Hekima College, also at Nairobi. I have discussed the project of this book with staff-members and students of these institutions, and many things have become clearer in the process. I wish to record my gratitude to Fr Yves Gaudreault WF of CHIEA for reading several of the chapters and making suggestions, and also to Dr Hermann Hauser WF of the Institut Catholique, Toulouse, for many suggestions in connection with the biblical background. With him I have given pastoral sessions to missionaries in 1985 and 1986 on the subject of inculturation. I wish also to thank Mr John Wachira for help in making the bibliography. This is the first full-length work produced with the help of a word-processor donated by MISSIO Munich to whom, finally, I wish to express my gratitude.

Aylward Shorter
Missionary of Africa

Catholic Higher Institute of Eastern Africa
Nairobi, Kenya   *September 1987*

xii

PART ONE

INCULTURATION, ITS NATURE AND FUNCTION

1

Understanding the terms

The mid-second-century document known as the *Epistle to Diognetus* is an apologetic treatise in the form of a letter. Nothing is really known of its origins or authorship, but this anonymous epistle seems to usher in the era of the Fathers who are called Apologists and with them the beginnings of inculturation as a historical reality in the Church of the Gentiles. It is worth beginning this exploration of the concept and practice of inculturation with a celebrated passage from Diognetus.

> Christians are not distinguished from the rest of mankind by country or language or customs . . . While they live in cities both Greek and oriental, as falls to the lot of each, and follow the customs of the country in dress, food and general manner of life, they display the remarkable and confessedly surprising status of their citizenship. They live in countries of their own, but as sojourners. They share all things as citizens; they suffer all things as foreigners. Every foreign land is their native place, every native place is foreign . . . They pass their life on earth; but they are citizens in heaven. They obey the established laws, but they outdo the laws in their own lives . . . In general we may say that Christians are in the world what the soul is in the body.[1]

Allowing for the Platonic dualism of soul and body reflected in this passage — a doubtful model for inculturation, as we shall see — the author nevertheless makes a clear distinction between the religious faith of Christians which makes them citizens of heaven and the various forms taken by their manner of life, language and customs in the cities and countries where they live. Diognetus is therefore witness to the distinction and interaction between faith and culture on which the notion of inculturation rests.

3

Before we examine the phenomenon of inculturation and its theological implications, the interaction, as we have called it, between faith and culture, our terms have to be clarified. The Human Sciences are young and their vocabulary is still somewhat fluid. When this vocabulary is used by theologians there is further room for misunderstanding. In offering the reader some initial definitions there is no intention of artificially halting the development of sociological or theological language, of 'freezing' the terminology, as it were. Much of the history of our thinking about inculturation in recent years has consisted in the search for a more adequate terminology. The purpose is simply to establish meanings and to ensure that we know what we are talking about.

Culture

Inculturation has to do with the interaction of what, for the present, may be referred to as 'faith', on the one hand, and culture, on the other. The identity of this 'faith', the Christian term of the process of interaction, will be discussed at length in Chapter 5. We begin here with the other term, culture. There are many definitions of culture, one of the most celebrated being Sir Edward Tylor's: 'that complex whole which includes knowledge, belief, art, morals, law, custom and any other capabilities and habits acquired by man as a member of society'.[2] In this fundamentally descriptive definition, human society becomes the criterion of culture. Culture is what a human being learns, or acquires, as a member of society. It comprises the learned aspects — as opposed to the inherited aspects — of human thinking and human behaviour. A more modern tendency is to reverse the order and to define human society in terms of culture. According to this way of thinking, it is what human beings share culturally, their customs, values and distinctive way of living, that constitutes them as a recognizably distinct human group or society. Human societies not only possess a culture, but are distinguished by it from other human societies.

Human individuals interact with one another according to preconceived mental patterns, and they continue to reflect mentally about their interactions. Culture is therefore not simply about behaviour. It is also about ideas. The mental basis of culture is commonly stressed in modern definitions. For example, Clifford Geertz defines culture as:

4

> A system of inherited conceptions expressed in symbolic forms by means of which human beings communicate, perpetuate and develop their knowledge about, and their attitudes towards, life.[3]

Other definitions take the same approach, for example:

> A set of symbols, stories, myths and norms for conduct that orient a society or group cognitively, affectively and behaviorally to the world in which it lives.[4]

Culture is therefore essentially a transmitted pattern of meanings embodied in symbols, a pattern capable of development and change, and it belongs to the concept of humanness itself. It follows that, if religion is a human phenomenon or human activity, it must affect, and be affected by, culture.

Enculturation

Enculturation (sometimes spelt 'inculturation') is a sociological concept which has been used analogously by theologians for the theological notion of inculturation. In order to differentiate between the sociological and theological uses of this term, it is better to preserve the spelling 'enculturation' for the sociological context, and 'inculturation' for the theological context.

Enculturation, then, refers to the cultural learning process of the individual, the process by which a person is inserted into his or her culture. It is a concept that is closely related to that of socialization, another term employed by social scientists to refer to the education of an individual by society. While the process obviously includes formal teaching and learning, it is very largely an informal, and even an unconscious, experience. To a great extent the individual teaches himself through a process of adaptive learning, the rules of which are given by society. The images or symbols of a culture are in themselves didactic, and they teach the individual to construct his own categories and even to transcend them in the very act of constructing them. Thus the manner in which an individual apprehends experience is essentially culture-bound. Borrowing Wordsworth's phrase, culture causes the eye and ear of the individual to 'half create' what they perceive:

> Therefore am I still
> A lover of the meadows and the woods,

5

And mountains; and of all that we behold
From this green earth; of all the mighty world
Of eye and ear, — both what they half create,
And what perceive; well pleased to recognize
In nature and the language of the sense
The anchor of my purest thoughts, the nurse,
The guide, the guardian of my heart and soul,
Of all my moral being.[5]

Culture is therefore a psycho-social phenomenon which exploits psychological factors that favour the adoption of certain symbols and certain conceptions. Dan Sperber has even employed a medical analogy in this connection, calling culture an 'epidemiology of representations'. Just as an epidemiology is the study of the factors which favour the spread of an epidemic, so the study of culture examines the factors that explain the generality of a society's collective representations.[6]

Another useful cultural learning model is provided by Cardinal John Henry Newman's use of the word 'grammar'.[7] It is not only language that has grammar. There is also the imaginative grammar of culture. Each culture is a universe of signs comparable to language, a configuration of images, concepts and interpretations. Through the process of enculturation, this grammar is acquired unconsciously by the individual member of society.

In so far as there is a useful analogy between enculturation and inculturation, it consists in the parallel between the insertion of an individual into his or her own culture and the insertion of the Christian faith into a culture where Christians were not previously present. Although this parallel may be responsible for the adoption of the term inculturation by theologians, it must be said at once that the analogy does not cover the whole theological concept by any stretch of the imagination. Inculturation is not limited in its application to the first insertion of faith into a culture.

Acculturation

The word acculturation is closely associated with the theological concept of inculturation. So much so, in fact, that it is sometimes confused with it, and it is difficult to know whether authors think the two terms are interchangeable. It must be made clear from the outset

that, although acculturation is a necessary condition of inculturation, it is a distinct sociological concept.

By acculturation is meant the encounter between one culture and
another, or the encounter between cultures. This is perhaps the
principal cause of cultural change. It is a process which is a necessary
concomitant of culture itself. Human beings possess the collective
freedom to modify their particular cultural traditions through
contact with people of other cultures. Culture itself comes into existence through collective processes, and the encounter between
cultures is likewise a collective process largely beyond the scope of
individual human choice. It is, of course, an encounter between two
different sets of symbols and conceptions, two different interpretations of experience, two different social identities. Unreflective and
unprogrammed though it may be, the encounter is fraught with
complexity. Its consequences can be discerned *post factum* at the
conscious level, but many of the conflicts it engenders are worked out
at the subconscious level.

More will be said about acculturation in Chapter 4, but it is useful
to make one point now. Culture being made up of intercommunicat-
ing ideas and forms of behaviour, the introduction of new behaviour
entails an eventual change in ideas, and vice versa. On the other
hand, a shared form of behaviour may be interpreted differently, and
a shared idea may be expressed in differing forms of behaviour.
Whatever may be the case, behaviour and ideas cannot be separated
from one another. There is nothing comparable in acculturation to
the dualistic Platonic model of soul and body where ideas and behaviour are concerned.

Perhaps another point that needs to be retained throughout the
discussion is that acculturation is a historical process, and that, in
dealing with culture and the encounter between cultures, we are
confronting a dynamic and diachronic phenomenon, and not a
static, unchanging one.

In view of what has been said about acculturation, what it is and
how it comes about, it is clear that any internal manipulation of
culture is an abuse. Sometimes governments try to politicize culture,
even to seal it off from the external influence of foreign cultures.
There is talk of cultural 'purity' and 'authenticity'. Several African
countries have experienced policies of this kind. Much of the contemporary revolution of Islamic fundamentalism consists in a violent
reaction against the influence of alien, Western culture. Governments that adopt manipulative cultural policies may be justified in so

far as they seek to redress a situation of cultural domination. Generally, their refusal does not extend to alien science and technology and these are a cultural 'Trojan horse'. Once again, they fall into the trap of Platonic dualism.

Acculturation, the communication between cultures on a footing of mutual respect and tolerance, is a necessary condition of Catholicism, of a Church that claims to be universal. One of the teachings of Catholic Christianity, which this book will attempt to explore, is that every culture has a vocation to cross its own border, to transcend its own limits, as it were. Being human demands, not only insertion into one's own culture, but openness towards other cultures. The Christian faith is able to pass from culture to culture, from history to history, in the ministry of worldwide reconciliation.

Cultural Domination

The concept of cultural domination is readily intelligible after what has been said above about the manipulation of culture. Various terms are used, e.g. 'transculturation', 'cultural imperialism', 'cultural alienation' and so on. All of them express the idea of one culture dominating another culture, or other cultures. Domination implies the unwelcome transference of foreign cultural traits: symbols, meanings, values and behaviour, from one culture to another.

The transference may occur simply because one culture overwhelms another. Its technology is superior, for example, or its ideas are compelling, or its media of communication irresistible. Initially for the whole population, or thereafter for a large proportion of the people, the transference may not be wholly unwelcome. People in Britain sometimes grumble about 'Americanisms' in everyday speech, about too many American films on television, about the 'brain drain' to America, or about Americans buying up British companies. This is because the powerful culture of North America is difficult to resist. The cultural 'incapsulation' of Britain is neither desirable nor possible. French culture and language are in a similar position with regard to the Anglo-Saxon cultures. The importation of English words into French (*Franglais*) or French interest in the British Royal Family cannot be stopped by force, because the French wish their country to remain free and democratic. However, the cultural truculence of foreigners may be resented, and there is always the possibility of an ultimate tide of reaction against them.

The use of moral and physical force to impose a foreign culture is a violation of human rights, since people have a right to their own culture and a right to develop it in the way they wish. The peoples of the so-called Third World, and especially Africa, have in recent decades experienced cultural domination by force. Although Africans very often put up armed resistance against the annexation of their homelands by the colonial powers of Europe, they were initially fascinated by Western culture and technology. When modern states were carved out of the continent and Western education and Western institutions were imposed on them without any alternative, Africans were at first docile. It was only later that they began to rediscover their original culture and to realize the extent to which they had become culturally alienated. This explains, for example, the hatred of an African writer like Ngugi wa Thiong'o for Shakespeare. The Western world continues to exert an immense economic and technological pressure on countries like those of Africa, and such pressure carries with it an overwhelming mass of cultural traits. Even after political independence Africans find cultural liberation elusive. They are striving to take control of their own cultural development against enormous odds. In this confused situation their original, historical culture, while it cannot be restored in its entirety, remains an important resource for national and social indentity. This, of course, explains the immense interest of African theologians in the concept and practice of inculturation.

Cultural domination may be characterized by an ethnocentric posture on the part of the dominating culture that is so strong as to amount to the claim to be a 'world culture'. At various periods of their history, British and Americans have deemed their own culture to be superior because their wealth commanded the respect of other nations. We are all familiar with the stereotype of the Englishman on the Grand Tour, or the American tourist on the continent of Europe, expecting the nationals of other countries to speak English. At a more extensive cultural level, Europeans and North Americans advanced their own interests all over the world under the spurious pretext that they were raising the poorer peoples of the earth to a higher level of culture. Even theologians and philosophers of history defended this outlook, and writers such as Christopher Dawson and Arnold Toynbee saw the hand of Providence in the historical conjuction of Christianity and Western culture.[8] In the next chapter the monoculturalism of the Church up to the middle of the twentieth century will be examined.

Inculturation

It is time now to introduce the theological concept of inculturation. Most of this book will be devoted to describing the reality of inculturation and the development of the Church's thinking and teaching about it. For the moment it is only necessary to introduce the basic ideas.

First of all, the term itself. The introduction and popularization of the term 'inculturation' seems to be very largely due to members of the Society of Jesus. The very first recorded use of the work in a theological sense seems to be by Fr Joseph Masson SJ, professor at the Gregorian University in Rome, shortly before the opening of the Second Vatican Council in 1962. He wrote:

> Today there is a more urgent need for a Catholicism that is *inculturated* in a variety of forms (*d'une façon polymorphe*).[9]

Although the Bishops of Africa and Madagascar made a very strong statement to the Rome Synod on Evangelization in 1974 about the reality of inculturation, they did not use the term. The first assembly of the Federation of Asian Episcopal Conferences in April of that year spoke of 'an indigenous and inculturated Church', while the 32nd Congregation of the Society of Jesus which took place from December 1974 to April 1975 used the actual word 'inculturation' fairly frequently in its texts, and included a decree on inculturation. In response to this decree, the Jesuit Superior General, Fr Pedro Arrupe, issued a letter to the whole Society on the subject of inculturation on 15 April 1978.[10] As a consequence of these developments seminars on inculturation were held at the Gregorian University (1977–78), Jerusalem (1981) and Yogyakarta (1983).[11] The word 'inculturation' first appeared in a papal document in 1979.[12]

Although the word 'inculturation' has gained a worldwide currency at the present time, this is not to say that it is the most accurate term possible. Pope John Paul II has described it as a 'neologism' (which, of course, it is), and many people find it an ugly and uninspiring word.[13] For the time being, it is difficult to improve on it, and that is why it is adopted here. Other terms, however, continue to be used, which cover more or less the same meaning. One still hears the obsolescent 'indigenization', and the term 'contextualization' favoured by organs of the World Council of Churches which has, perhaps, a more extended and less precise meaning. The terms 'accommodation' and 'adaptation' were popular before Vatican II. They refer to a conception which is now considered inadequate, but which was, as we shall see, an important stage in the Church's thinking. There remains the highly theological and imaginative use, in the context, of the word 'incarnation', adopted by the Second Vatican Council. This usage still occurs, and although it has various drawbacks which will be pointed out later on, it remains a dynamic and stimulating analogy. The incarnation analogy will be fully discussed in Chapter 6 (in Part Two) when the Christological foundations of inculturation are examined.

A short definition of inculturation is: the on-going dialogue between faith and culture or cultures. More fully, it is the creative and dynamic relationship between the Christian message and a culture or cultures. Fr Pedro Arrup SJ defines it as:

> The incarnation of Christian life and of the Christian message in a particular cultural context, in such a way that this experience not only finds expression through elements proper to the culture in question (this alone would be no more than a superficial adaptation) but becomes a principle that animates, directs and unifies the culture, transforming it and remaking it so as to bring about a 'new creation'.[14]

The first point to note about inculturation, arising from these definitions, is that we are not only talking about the first insertion of the Christian message into a hitherto non-Christian culture or cultures. Many writers appear to limit the scope of inculturation in this way. Of course, the first insertion of the Faith into a culture is an extremely important and significant moment in the process. On it depends practically all that follows. It is a stage of inculturation that is unique for each historical instance. Without any doubt, the already Christianized culture represented by the messengers of the Gospel, the missionaries, must influence the *tertium quid*, the so-called 'new creation' of the culture they evangelize. It inevitably affects the response from the evangelized culture. However, inculturation is not limited to this initial stage only. Culture, as we have seen, is a developing process, and there must be, therefore, a continuous dialogue between Faith and culture. Inculturation is as relevant to the countries of Europe and North America, for example,

11

which have been Christianized and now de-Christianized, as it is to the cultures of the Third World in which the Gospel has only recently been proclaimed for the first time. Indeed, there are times when the dialogue may be suspended, and culture gains, as it were, the upper hand, undermining or distorting the values of the Gospel. This is the situation dubbed by theologians as 'culturalism'. At such moments it is obviously vital to re-start the dialogue. As long as faith is present to a culture, the dialogue must take place. It is a process that never comes to an end.

The second point to notice is one that has already been implied, viz. that the Christian Faith cannot exist except in a cultural form. When we speak of Christian faith or Christian life, we are necessarily speaking of a cultural phenomenon. It is a distinctive way of life that can only operate culturally. Chapter 3 will examine the cultural aspect of religion in general and Christianity in particular, the fact that religion is necessarily a cultural system. All of this means that when we describe inculturation as a dialogue between faith and culture, we are really speaking of a dialogue between a culture and the faith in cultural form, in the first instance a dialogue between the Christianized culture of the missionary and the hitherto un-Christianized culture to which he comes. In other words, we are speaking about acculturation or the interaction between cultures. Before the 'new creation', of which Fr Arrupe speaks, can take place there has to be an acculturation stage in which Christianity (in a previous cultural form) seeks expression through elements proper to the new culture. It follows that Christian evangelization can only take place through the ordinary human process of acculturation, and that the message of the Gospel passes from culture to culture, and from history to history, as we have said above.

In the third place, when we speak of inculturation, we are referring to a phenomenon that transcends mere acculturation. It is the stage when a human culture is enlivened by the Gospel from within, a stage which presupposes a measure of reformulation or, more accurately, reinterpretation. Jean-Marie Aubert has some helpful insights on this point.[15] Acculturation may lead merely to a juxtaposition of unassimilated cultural expressions, coming from various directions or origins. This may lead, further on, to a form of syncretism, in which an illegitimate symbiosis occurs that is harmful to authentic Christian meaning. It is only when there is a truly critical symbiosis, and the Christian experience is really integrated, or — to

12

use the term favoured by Pope Paul VI — 'transposed', within the local culture, that we can speak of inculturation in the strict sense. It remains perfectly true, of course, that in many of the particular churches which make up the Church Universal evangelization has reached only the level of acculturation, and has not succeeded, or perhaps even sought, to attain the deeper level of inculturation.

The reciprocal and critical interaction between the Christian Faith and culture is a historical process. It is to be identified with the transfer of religious meaning between cultures which, in Christian terms is called 'mission' or 'evangelization'. As such, it is closely connected with the concept of conversion and of religious renewal. It is also intimately associated with the development of doctrine, since culture evolves on the vertical plane and proliferates on the horizontal. Christianity is itself enriched upon entering new cultural phases and regions, acquiring surplus meaning in loyalty and conformity to its tradition. This, however, touches upon our discussion of yet another term.

Interculturation

It cannot be denied that the word 'inculturation' by itself suggests merely the transfer of faith from one culture to another, the insertion of the Christian message into a given culture. In short, it seems to suggest that the process of mission or evangelization is a one-way process. To create such an impression is unfortunate, and it is the reason why some missiologists are dissatisfied with the term. Mission, as we have seen, operates through the ordinary historical interaction of cultures, and it would be altogether short-sighted to maintain that only the recipient culture benefits by the operation.

In 1980 Bishop Joseph Blomjous coined the term 'interculturation' precisely in order to safeguard the reciprocal character of mission. He wrote:

> The period 1960–1980 can be considered as the main transition period from the traditional Mission to the new Mission of the future. It has been characterised as the period of 'inculturation', though the better term would be that of 'interculturation', in order to express that the process of inculturation must be lived in partnership and mutuality. It seems that we are now living at the peak of this movement, the critical phase which demands from us a real decision for profound and courageous reform.[16]

13

The word 'interculturation' correctly expresses the sociological and the theological reality, both at the individual and collective, cultural levels. Inculturation is carried out in partnership by individuals who represent different cultures. This is true, even though the final, authentic symbiosis can only be the work of indigenous people belonging to the evangelized culture. In a situation of acculturation, missionaries begin to accommodate or adapt the Christian message, seeking local cultural expressions in order to make the message understood. They use elements from the local culture simply in order to communicate meaning and to enable their hearers to grasp that meaning according to their own cultural categories. In itself this facilitates the process of inculturation carried out by the local people. It is naturally an enriching experience for the missionary, as any culturally 'bilingual' person will confirm.

However, it is not only enriching at the personal level, it is also enriching at the collective, cultural level. Inculturation implies that the Christian message transforms a culture. It is also the case that Christianity is transformed by culture, not in a way that falsifies the message, but in the way in which the message is formulated and interpreted anew. When offical Church statements declare, as they often do, that Christianity is enriched by the values of the culture that is being evangelized, it means that the Christian way of life is finding new scope and fuller understanding. It also means — and this is made explicit by Pope Paul VI in *Evangelii Nuntiandi* — that the particular churches of other cultures which make up the Church Universal are invigorated and enriched by the missionary process of intercultural communication.[17]

It is a commonplace of contemporary ecclesiology that the primary reality of the Church is the relatively autonomous particular church. As the Fathers of Vatican II declared: 'It is in these (particular churches) and formed out of them that the one and unique Catholic Church exists'.[18] The Catholic Church is not only a hierarchical Church, it is also a communion, and this community dimension appears both within and between the particular churches. Within a particular church are found communities, some of which are culturally distinct. This is especially true of culturally heterogeneous churches like those of many African countries. Within the Church Universal the particular churches also constitute a communion, and they interact with one another in a mutually enriching manner. Thus contributions are made by particular churches at the World Church level, through the hierarchical structures of communication

14

which exist within the Church, but also horizontally and often in an unstructured manner through the 'contagion' of example. It is understandable that cultural interests should surface more readily at continental and regional assemblies of bishops than at Synods of the whole Church, for example. On the other hand the bishops of an entire region are capable of making an impact at World Church level, as happened in the case of the Latin Americans at Vatican II, or in the case of the Bishops of Africa and Madagascar at the 1974 Rome Synod.

It is not only through episcopal assemblies that particular churches communicate with one another. Especially because of the rapidity of modern travel and communication, there are many other means of contact, formal and informal. By these means new currents of theology, new forms of spirituality, new movements in the Church are exchanged at the widest possible level. Missionaries play a significant role in such exchanges, particularly when they realize their obligation to share their experience of missionary inculturation with the particular church of their home culture.

While it is true that the profound evangelization of a culture may be a lengthy process, it is understood that inculturation is an ongoing phenomenon, and that there are bound to be periods of recession in the history of any particular church, periods when cultural interests obscure aspects of Gospel truth. If that is understood, it becomes more difficult to speak of particular churches as 'young churches', or as 'immature' or 'adolescent' churches. In theory, if not in practice, there is no seniority and juniority among particular churches, except in so far as the particular church of Rome serves as the principle of visible unity in the whole communion. There should be a coexistence in equality among particular churches that are definitively established and recognized as such. The age of a church should not be a disadvantage in the process of mutual exchange.

It has been stated above that openness to other cultures is a mark of Catholicism. This implies being ready to learn from strangers. It is God who speaks through strangers, and this 'conditioning by strangers' is an important theme in the history of divine revelation. In the history of Christian mission, the message has always been brought by strangers in the first place, and the chain of tradition goes back ultimately to the original 'stranger' who is Jesus Christ. One of the most valuable insights of the Second Vatican Council was that God's all-encompassing grace and activity is not limited by the visible institutions of the Church. With this truth in mind, it is easier to accept that missionary activity is a two-way process, and that inculturation is really an intercultural activity with intercultural benefits.

This first chapter has looked at some of the basic vocabulary of inculturation. Before entering more fully into a theological discussion, more attention must be paid to the sociological notions and assumptions involved, and the Church's understanding of them. A question of fundamental importance is the evolution of the Church's own thinking about culture and cultures.

References

1 Bettenson 1956, pp. 74–5.

2 Tylor 1891, Vol.1, p. 1.

3 Geertz 1975, p. 89.

4 Schineller 1983, pp. 1–14.

5 Wordsworth, from 'Tintern Abbey' (Thomas 1971, p. 24).

6 Sperber 1985, pp. 73–89.

7 Newman 1870 (1947 edn).

8 Cf. Dawson 1950; Toynbee 1961.

9 Masson 1962, p. 1038.

10 Arrupe 1978.

11 Crollius 1984.

12 *Catechesi Tradendae*, 53.

13 *Ibid.*

14 Arrupe 1978, p. 172.

15 Aubert 1986, pp. 13 and 25.

16 Blomjous 1980, p. 393.

17 *Evangelii Nuntiandi*, 63.

18 *Lumen Gentium*, 23.

2

Evolution of the Church's understanding of culture

Classicist and Modern Views of Culture

There is a popular use of the word 'culture' which applies exclusively to what may be called 'highbrow culture', to classical music, opera, serious theatre, literature, poetry and art. Being 'a vulture for culture' means belonging to the educated classes that appreciate the arts, and culture itself is regarded as the patrimony of an élite that possesses superior taste. Even in countries of the so-called Third World, 'culture' may be used in a similarly restricted way. In many countries of Africa, when people speak of 'culture' — *utamaduni*, let us say, in Swahili — they are referring to traditional dances and rituals, to ancient crafts and artefacts, the products of specialized troupes and craft schools, displayed at 'cultural centres' and museums. Such cultural activity plays an important role in keeping traditions alive and exerts an influence on modern artistic creativity. However, it remains a specialization, an ideal, an aspiration for the individuals who appreciate its importance.

The concept of culture as an ideal, or as normative in society, is not in itself incorrect. However, it does not exhaust the notion of culture by any means. Culture is a considerably more complex and more comprehensive phenomenon. Within a single culture there are cultural levels, and some of these levels may enjoy sufficient autonomy to justify being called 'sub-cultures'. They may be, in fact, variants of the total culture to which they belong. We find this, not only in the industrialized societies of the Western world, but also in the ethnic mosaic of Third World countries, where an ethnic group often represents a subtle variant of a shared national or regional culture. From the way in which the word 'culture' is being used, it will also be obvious to the reader that it is essentially a plural

17

phenomenon, conferring a distinctive identity on distinct social groupings throughout the world.

The pluralistic view of culture is relatively recent, and the Catholic Church did not adopt it until the middle of the twentieth century. The first glimmerings of a pluralistic or modern view of culture to be found in a papal document, for example, date from 1944.[1] For nearly sixteen centuries, from late Roman times until our own, a monocultural view of the world held sway among bishops, theologians and thinkers of the Catholic Church. It was a view not unlike the restricted 'highbrow' view of culture that we have just been discussing, but it was applied to the entire human race. Culture, during these centuries, was a single, universal, normative concept.

When, in the fourth century, Christianity became the official religion of the Roman Empire and the Roman Emperor himself became a Christian, the Church adopted the imperial, Roman view of culture. This view was even more strongly reinforced when the Pope, in the fifth century, effectively became heir to the extinct line of western emperors, and the eastern, Byzantine branch of Empire was increasingly isolated from its western tradition of origin.

The Roman view of culture was of a universal ideal of civilization. Its opposite was 'barbarism', the modern equivalents of which are terms like 'savagery' or 'primitiveness'. Although the word 'barbarian' disappeared from ordinary speech, except as a term of abuse, 'savage' and 'primitive' became part of the terminology of modern political philosophy and social science. The Roman understanding of culture was of a universal system of values and laws that could be elicited through philosophical reflection and imposed through education. Thus the entire human race could be divided into two camps: the civilized and the barbarian, the cultured and the uncultured.

When Church and Empire united to become the politico-religious system known to history as 'Christendom', Roman monoculturalism received a powerful reinforcement. The superior world culture was identified with Christianity. In other words, it was assumed that the Gospel must be proclaimed everywhere in a single, 'perfect', cultural form. Any variation was deemed to be either a deviation or a stage of development towards the, as yet, unrealized ideal. When classical Graeco-Roman philosophy came to be applied to the truths of revelation during the high Middle Ages, the immutability of the Christian cultural ideal was sealed.

The late Bernard Lonergan has described very well the older, classicist view of culture that was held by the Church at this time:

On the older view, culture was conceived not empirically but normatively. It was the opposite of barbarism. It was a matter of acquiring and assimilating the tastes and skills, the ideals, virtues and ideas, that were pressed upon one in a good home and through a curriculum in the liberal arts. It stressed not facts but values. It could not but claim to be universalist. Its classics were immortal works of art, its philosophy was the perennial philosophy, its laws and structures were the deposit of the wisdom and the prudence of mankind. Classicist education was a matter of models to be imitated, of ideal characters to be emulated, of eternal verities and universal laws. It sought to produce not the mere specialist but the *uomo universale* that could turn his hand to anything and do it brilliantly.[2]

According to Lonergan the classicist theologian often assumed that the Church's dogmas were permanent, not so much because they represented revealed truths, but because he believed in a universal, permanent culture and in the existence of fixed, immutable substances and meanings. Now the meaning of dogmatic statements actually depends on historical contexts, and such contexts are, in reality ongoing and multiple. The classicist theologian similarly tended to defend the unity of the Christian faith by an appeal to the unity of culture. Lonergan again:

> On classicist assumptions there is just one culture. That one culture is not attained by the simple faithful, the people, the natives, the barbarians. Nonetheless, career is always open to talent. One enters upon such a career by diligent study of the ancient Latin and Greek authors. One pursues such a career by learning Scholastic philosophy and theology. One aims at high office by becoming proficient in canon law. One succeeds by winning the approbation and favour of the right personages. Within this set-up the unity of faith is a matter of everyone subscribing to the correct formulae.[3]

Before classicist assumptions were ended by the findings of critical history, the political and technological domination of Western culture over the entire world was being justified by an ultimate appeal to Christian classicism. In the reconsiderations of his *A Study of History*, which Arnold Toynbee published in 1961, we find the following:

> Just as Western technology involves Western science, so Western political systems imply Western moral ideals — con-

19

flicting ideals reflected in conflicting systems. Ideologies and
ideals cannot be appraised without taking some account of their
history. The spiritual history of the West had therefore to be
taken into consideration in any twentieth-century estimate of
the prospects of the World as a whole.[4]

In Toynbee's vision of things, the world is being unified under the
aegis of Western culture, the origins of which are to be found — after
a Graeco-Roman 'overture' — in Christianity. Of course it is undeniable that science, technology and ideologies originating in the West
are having worldwide repercussions. It is also undeniable that these
things have cultural implications, and we shall study these in
Chapter 4. However, if this means that Western culture is being
turned into a world culture, then such a supposition is demonstrably
false.

Nevertheless the Church clung to the notion of a Christian world
culture for sixteen centuries, and this world culture was, in practice,
identifiable with the culture of Europe. Hilaire Belloc's assertion that
'the Faith is Europe and Europe is the Faith' was almost geographically true. In the minds of European Christians it was also culturally
true, since it was assumed that the spread of the Gospel entailed the
spread of European culture.

The classicist, normative view of culture inhibited the Church's
missionary activity. It also prejudiced relations between Latin Christianity and the ecclesially and culturally pluralistic East. Perhaps
worst of all, it distorted the Church's own understanding of itself.
Christians failed to recognize cultural changes and developments and
the ways in which they affected the Church's interpretation of the
Christian message through history. It is because of this that the
adoption of a modern view of culture is so traumatic for the Church.
Inculturation does not just mean that an empirical view of culture
and cultures must now be taken. It means that the whole of Church
history and the history of theology must be rewritten.

The socio-political philosophers of the seventeenth and eighteenth
centuries, thinkers and writers such as Hobbes, Locke, Rousseau and
Hume, all took the basically classicist, universal view of human
culture. Only Charles Secondat, Baron de Montesquieu (1689–1755)
began to take a more empirical approach. Montesquieu recognized
that social laws and cultural institutions were affected by social needs
and social ecology, and that factors such as these accounted for their
diversity. Even climate, he believed, could affect human sensibility.

> In cold countries they have very little sensibility for pleasure; in temperate countries, they have more; in warm countries, their sensibility is exquisite. As climates are distinguished by degrees of latitude, we might distinguish them also in some measure by those of sensibility. I have been at the opera in England and in Italy, where I have seen the same pieces and the same performers; and yet the same music produces such different effects on the two nations: one is so cold and phlegmatic, and the other so lively and enraptured, that it seems almost inconceivable.[5]

Montesquieu's comparison of opera audiences in England and Italy may appear faintly comical, yet this was the beginning of the modern, empirical approach to cultures.

The earlier political philosophers shared the Church's universalist approach to cultures, and both took the same ethnocentric attitude to the American Indians and to the peoples of Africa. If such newly discovered peoples could be conquered and enslaved, it was not because they were outside the human race, but because they were outside the universal culture of Christendom. Later on, it was their potentiality for culture and civilization, rather than their *de facto* lack of these things, that was made the basis for Rome's condemnation of the slave trade. The newly discovered peoples were 'true men' capable of cultural development, of civilization and of salvation. Pope Paul III had this to say in 1537:

> The enemy of the human race has suggested to some of his followers the idea of spreading through the world the opinion that the inhabitants of the West Indies and the southern continents, of whose existence we have but recently learnt, should be employed solely for our profit and our service, on the pretext that they have no part in the Catholic faith and are incapable of adopting it.
>
> We, the unworthy Vicar of Our Lord, have to do all that lies within our power to preserve the flock committed to our care, and to bring into safety the lost sheep. We regard the Indians as true men, being not only capable of adopting the Christian faith but desirous of doing so.
>
> Therefore, in the desire of remedying the ill which has been caused, we decide and declare by this Our letter (whose translation shall be authenticated with his seal by every priest) that the aforesaid Indians, and all other peoples which may, in future, become known to Christendom, shall not be deprived of their

freedom and their goods — notwithstanding contrary assertions — even if they be not Christians; but that, on the contrary, they shall be left in the enjoyment of their freedom and their property.

The Indians and other peoples which may yet be discovered in the future shall be converted only by the example of a good and holy life.[6]

After Montesquieu, political philosophers began to adopt the verifiable view of culture as a plural, rather than a universal concept. This understanding of culture developed as a result of empirical studies and of the experience of accelerated cultural change during the nineteenth and twentieth centuries, as well as of the development of history as a critical, if not a scientific, discipline. Although the imperialist expansion of Europe during the nineteenth century found its justification in a faith in a universal, superior culture — a faith which provided the inspiration for the imposing intellectual edifice of Toynbee — this ethnocentrism was eventually submerged by the complex process of acculturation which was the consequence of imperialism. Paradoxically, Western expansion brought European and American thinkers face to face with the reality of cultural pluralism, and this pluralism was recognized in theory, if not entirely in practice, when political independence was granted by the colonial powers to their subject peoples. Decolonization was understood by the latter, to a great extent, as a form of cultural affirmation or cultural liberation.

The modern, empirical approach to culture demanded a dramatic reappraisal by the Church of such concepts as mission and evangelization. The variety of human social and cultural arrangements was now seen to be extremely complex, and ecclesiology had to come to terms with this pluralism. The universality of the Church could no longer be seen in terms of a monocultural uniformity, but of a cultural diversity in a bond of communion. The universal truth of revealed religion was now seen to demand a capacity for unlimited cultural re-expression.

Perhaps the most significant and most visible contribution to the Church's multiculturalism made by the Second Vatican Council was the virtual abolition of Latin as the language of the Catholic liturgy. The Constitution on the Sacred Liturgy allowed a very restricted use of the vernacular, but left the way open for hierarchies to request further concessions.[7] However, the restrictions were gradually lifted in the face of representations by episcopal conferences, until by 1971,

22

barely eight years after the promulgation of the Constitution, the use of the vernacular at public celebrations was left entirely in the hands of the local bishops. Everywhere in the world the business of translation began. Even though the point of departure was a typical edition in Latin to which the translators were expected to be rigidly faithful, the procedure could never hope to remain at a purely semantic level. Language is too closely tied to culture, and a transverbalized liturgy eventually fails to satisfy. Once the use of the vernacular was approved, further concessions to cultural pluralism would inevitably have to be made.

The Problem of Cultural Relativism

Recognition of cultural diversity immediately raises the question of cultural relativism. If the right of every human grouping to its own culture is affirmed, we have to ask how far cultures differ from one another; whether a transfer of meaning can occur between them and whether cultures do not in fact cancel each other out? These are questions of extreme importance for a Church that claims to be Catholic, because they call into question the very possibility of a multicultural communion.

In trying to answer these questions we often tend to think of cultures as isolated entities. Indeed, philosophical criticism of anthropological methodology has sometimes centred on the specificity of cultures and on the allegation that intercultural translation is impossible.[8] Cultures are visualized as mutually exclusive 'language-games' which have arisen in concrete, task-oriented contexts. One simply has to learn the language and leave it at that, since translation, in this view, is *ipso facto* treason.

Whether, and to whatever extent, a culture is isolated, it is also a category of interaction. Experience proves that acculturation really takes place, that cultures mutually interpenetrate, that they borrow images, meanings, behaviour from each other. If a semantically bilingual person finds it difficult to keep the languages he or she has learnt in watertight mental compartments, then it must be even more true that the culturally bilingual person acts as a bridge between cultures — a bridge across which cultural traffic flows in both directions. All of this, however, is not to say that acculturation is not an extremely complex process, nor that cultural translation is not fraught with dangers and pitfalls.

Obviously cultures differ from one another, otherwise the question of cultural pluralism would not arise. However, they do not all differ from one another in the same way, to the same degree, or on the same level. Usually it is not the degree of isolation of cultures from one another that inhibits communication. Problems of diversity arise from their interaction, problems of discordance or divergence of interest, for example. On the other hand, there may be an overlapping of interests and an ability to acquire new interests from the representatives of other cultures. Culture-shock is seldom, if ever, a chronic condition. Cultures, as we have seen, are not static entities. They change and develop, especially through mutual contact. Moreover, when we speak of a transfer of meaning between cultures, we are not speaking in the purely notional terms of abstract, philosophical language, remote from immediate experience. We are speaking of the more real impact of an imaginative language that instances experience itself. Meanings become credible to the imagination before they are translated into exclusive — or relatively exclusive — notional language. That is why modern definitions of culture emphasize its symbolic character, and why conflicts of meaning tend to be worked out in the mythology of the subconscious — the private mythology of the individual that nevertheless reflects the patterns and interactions of cultures.

Another fact that mitigates the pessimistic view of cultural relativism is that cultures not only do not stand alone, but also tend to appear in groups. One of the insights of the Second Vatican Council was to recognize 'socio-cultural regions'.[9] Cultural anthropologists are notoriously wary of identifying cultural regions, because cultures have a way of shading into one another on the map. It is often extremely difficult to decide in practice whether differences outweigh similarities, and whether there are grounds for comparison or contrast between human groupings that are geographically contiguous or historically linked. On the other hand, there are obvious differences at either end of the cultural spectrum, and it is clear, for example, that the Bantu-speaking Lake Kingdoms of East Africa have more in common with one another today than with the Nilotic, cattle-keeping peoples of southern Sudan, even if there is historical evidence that Nilotic invaders were at the origins of their monarchical traditions. The differences and divisions tend to lie, not between individual cultures, but between groups of cultures.

Relations between cultures or between groups of cultures are not necessarily relations of conflict. We have already noted the possibility of an overlapping of interests and of learning new interests. Very often there is a substantial measure of collaboration between cultures, and most of our problems arise from the desire of mutual interaction, rather than the reverse. Of course there are marginalized cultures which find collaboration difficult, if not impossible. It is not that they are necessarily conservative. They have their own internal processes of change and development, and they are extremely selective in admitting external cultural influences. Usually their cultural system is one that tolerates very little variation. It is essentially cohesive, and for this reason appears to resist change. An example of such a culture is that of the six million or so pastoral nomads who inhabit the great plains of the East African Rift Valley. It may have come as a shock to TV audiences in Britain, watching an ethnographic series on the Maasai of Kenya, to hear an elderly pastoralist describe a man who sent his son to school as 'mad'.[10] Yet this apparent reversal of values makes perfect sense within a social system that closely co-ordinates the enculturation of its own young members, and which identifies the goals of education as being within, rather than outside, the ethnic group and its concerns.

The classicist view of culture held that there are propositions or formulations of meaning which are everywhere and at all times valid. Without falling back into this error, it must nevertheless be acknowledged that there are constituents of human nature and human activity that are common to the human race. The structure of the human mind and spirit is one of them. The demands of reason, intelligence and responsibility, the basic experiences of birth, stages of physical and psychological growth, procreation, sickness, disability and dying are also experiences common to humanity. However, it is also human to err. Particular cultural traditions can preserve erroneous interpretations of biological processes, for example. Certain island peoples in the Pacific Ocean believe that conception occurs as a result of the action of sea-foam when women go bathing. This is a question of factual truth or falsity, and as such, it cannot be relativized.

Even more vital questions of truth or falsity arise in the religious sphere, particularly when we are concerned with historical or prophetical religions like Christianity, religions in which revelation is held to have occurred in the order of objective knowledge. There is a limit, therefore, to cultural relativism, and to the relativization of religious truth. Our fear of being judgemental must not impede legitimate comparative analysis. Even the human sciences cannot advance without comparison.

We may even go so far as to say that a culture can be unfaithful to the insights of its own tradition. After all, a culture may be in decline, or it may actually tend to dehumanize its own adepts, rather than affirm them as human beings. Cultural facts and institutions may be dysfunctional, tending to destroy, to promote conflict and violence, or to deprave. Such a judgement cannot, of course, be arrived at independently of the views of the people whose culture it is, but even then the extent to which they may be living under an illusion may have to be recognized. Within the culture of the Western world, there are many people who lament its materialism, its permissiveness or its intrinsic lack of justice. Equally, there are many who are oblivious to such a critique, or who would vigorously deny it.

Furthermore, in asserting the pluralistic nature of human culture, a moral relativism cannot be conceded any more than a relativism where ultimate religious truth (as distinct from its knowability) is concerned. Religion, as we have already seen, cannot exist independently of a cultural expression. This fact will be examined in greater detail in Chapter 3. Nevertheless, in spite of a pluralism of expression, the truth of religious traditions does require that general moral principles be held in common. Within the various cultural systems the traditions differ in the detailed application of these principles, but all would subscribe to values such as the necessity to safeguard the lives and property of fellow members of one's group, or the need for respect towards parents and elders, the avoidance of incest or the rejection of indiscriminate killing. Even where there is an apparent conflict of moral values between cultures, this is commonly due to a perplexed social conscience, striving to reconcile one value with another, rather than to a denial of fundamental moral principles. Moral relativism thus turns out to be more apparent than real.

Religion and the Relativization of Culture

The modern pluralistic view of culture, therefore, does not imply absolute cultural relativism, or, in other words, the absolutization of culture. Cultures appear to need one another to a greater or lesser degree. Moreover, even according to their own standards, they stand in need of redemption. If religion proposes to redeem cultures, in the same act in which it evangelizes the adepts of those cultures, then it must transcend every culture. Culture cannot be invoked against ultimate truth. On the contrary, ultimate truth relativizes all cultures.

There are two important corollaries to this statement. The first is that, in saying that religion relativizes culture, we are not saying that religion can dispense with culture. Far from it. Human beings are deeply tied to culture and cannot be evangelized unless they are addressed in terms of their culture. The Gospel itself cannot be known except through the medium of culture. The paradox is that, while religion needs a cultural formulation, it cannot be reduced to the mere forms of culture. It must, by definition, transcend the purely cultural.

The second corollary is, of course, that a universally true religion cannot be identified exclusively with any one culture or group of cultures. In the case of Christianity, this is true even for European or Western culture, with which the history and development of the Church is so closely linked. It is not until 1959 that we find a clear acknowledgement of this important truth in a papal document.[11] This is not to deny the crucial importance of historical development. The past cannot be denied. On the contrary, the historic cultural forms taken by Christianity are an indispensable element in every valid symbiosis of faith and culture that takes place today, or will take place in the future.

Let us explore more deeply this transcendence by religion — Christianity in particular — of any and every culture. It stems both from the *terminus a quo* and the *terminus ad quem*, so to speak, of faith. The Christian message originates in the revelation of a mystery hidden in God. It is not a merely human truth. In the light of this divinely revealed truth, all human cultures are judged. They are not judged only by their own criteria. Every culture has, in some degree, been misread by its own adepts, misunderstood by them, disbelieved by them, perhaps betrayed by them. Christian evangelization claims to revitalize culture, to enliven it from within. If it is correctly carried out, evangelization should help people, not to despise their own culture, but to reappraise it in the light of Gospel values. It should give them a new appreciation of their cultural heritage, and it does this because of the divine character of the criteria it introduces.

It also does this because of the divine destiny of human cultures. Christian evangelization stresses the common destiny of human cultures in God. Through it, people of every culture are invited to collaborate in Christ and to enter into communion with one another through him. This communion will find its fulfilment in the final recapitulation of all things in Christ, when God will be all in all. This is the goal, the *terminus ad quem*, to which we are all directed by the Gospel. In striving towards this goal, the ordinary processes of acculturation and the interpenetration of cultures are heightened and given definitive meaning. In a word, Catholicity is constructed.

The work of evangelization should be carried out without detriment to any particular culture, and without the loss of any element that is essential to it. It goes without saying that it should not be a vehicle for cultural domination, or the equally ethnocentric attitude of cultural incapsulation. In becoming Christian, people are not invited to abandon their cultural identity. Rather, that identity is challenged and enhanced.

In saying all of this, the reader must be aware that we are speaking in terms of imperatives — of what 'should' or what 'ought to' be done, in order to be consistent with a true understanding of the Gospel. In view of the fact that the Church has only recently acquired an empirical understanding of culture, it is obvious that these imperatives have not always been borne in mind, especially during the last century-and-a-half of missionary expansion from Europe and the North Atlantic to the whole of the Third World. It must also be admitted that Christian evangelization is obliged, as we have seen, to operate via the ordinary processes of intercultural contact that are taking place in the world. Some of these processes may be detrimental to particular cultures. They may even result in what is known as 'ethnocide', or the death of a culture. If the Church has been an accomplice in such destructive actions, then this is clearly contrary to the spirit of its evangelizing mission.

Many charges are laid by newly Christianized peoples of Third World countries at the door of the first missionaries, accusations of a disregard for, even a destructive attitude towards, their culture. Some, perhaps the majority, of these charges are true. In pleading that the early missionaries were children of their times, that neither theology nor human sciences were sufficiently advanced to make them more understanding or tolerant, we are not exonerating them completely. There is a measure in which the heralds of the Gospel must redeem the times. If faith transcends culture, then surely the protagonists of the faith must transcend the processes of contact between cultures? On the other hand, the early missionaries learned from experience, and we, in turn, learn from their experience. The great movement of missionary expansion that began during the nineteenth century taught the Church that its understanding of culture was inadequate, and that evangelization applies not only to individuals but to their culture. Thus, the missionary movement added immeasurably to our understanding in more than one department of theology.

Cultural pluralism is not a scandal to the Church, but it *is* a challenge. Becoming a truly multicultural Church is not a question of resolving cultural differences or ironing out diversities. It is not even merely a question of adjudicating the rights and wrongs of cultural conflicts in the past, although the Church must necessarily face up to the challenge of rewriting its history in multicultural, instead of monocultural, terms. The Church is the 'sacrament of the world', the mirror of the world's destiny. It issues a call to conversion and communion with God in Christ. It is much more an orientation towards the future, a call to convergence, than a resolution of past divergences. Yet this convergence is destined to take place — and indeed begins to take place here and now — at a supracultural level. The love that constitutes the bond of communion between the various cultural forms of Christianity presupposes diversity.

Multiculturalism — inculturation, in other words — constitutes a challenge to the contemporary Church. Bishop Joseph Blomjous has listed some of the different aspects of this challenge:

> Inculturation (or interculturation) ultimately means: facing up to the total reality of the present Mission situation, which includes elements like: the fundamental change in Mission thinking, return to the Bible and early Christianity, development of ecclesiology, search for spiritual values, the reality and appreciation of pluralism and of human community, an increasing sense of history, the recent historical facts of colonisation and decolonisation, secularisation, the recognition of Non-Western cultural values, etc.[12]

This is a full programme indeed, but it is one on which the Church is embarked and which is reflected to a large extent in this book which deals with the theological implications of cultural pluralism. Before, however, entering upon the strictly theological analysis, there are other empirical aspects of inculturation to be studied. The first of these is the relationship of religion to culture, and its character as a cultural system.

References

1 Pius XII, Allocution to the Pontifical Mission Aid Societies *AAS* 1944, p. 210, also cited in *Evangelii Praecones* 1951.

2 Lonergan 1973, p. 301.

3 *Ibid.*, pp. 326–7.

4 Toynbee 1961, p. 528.

5 Montesquieu 1748 (1949 edn), p. 223.

6 Paul III, *Sublimis Deus* 1537, quoted in Congar 1953, pp. 36–7.

7 *Sacrosanctum Concilium*, 36.

8 Cf. Winch 1970.

9 *Ad Gentes*, 22.

10 'Diary of a Masai Village' presented on BBC2 in 1984 by Melissa Llewellyn-Davies.

11 John XXIII, *Princeps Pastorum*, Part 2, No. 4, quoting Discourse to 2nd International Congress of Negro Writers and Artists (*AAS* 51, 1959, p. 260) in Hickey 1982, pp. 132–63.

12 Blomjous 1980, p. 393.

3

Culture
and religion

Culture as a Social Phenomenon

In Part One of this book our aim is to study the nature and working of inculturation. In order to do this it is necessary to look at all the elements which enter into the notion of inculturation and its application. Having introduced some of the key terms in the first chapter, and having examined the pluralistic character of culture and the implications of this pluralism in Chapter 2, it is necessary now to examine the intimate connection between culture and religion. To do justice to this crucial fact we must first consider culture as a social phenomenon. Then the different levels of culture in society must be discerned. Finally, it must be asked whether or not religion is situated at the deepest level and is its most deep-seated element, the core of culture, as it were. In the course of this discussion it will begin to be seen how religion and culture are capable of transforming one another.

In the various definitions of culture that were cited in Chapter 1, an indispensable element was that of society, either as the criterion or as the outcome of culture. It is equally true to say that culture is learned by individuals as members of society and that society is the consequence of individuals sharing a culture. The notions are inseparable, whichever way one chooses to enter the circle. What, in fact, do we mean by society?

Human beings interact. Their behaviour consists, largely if not entirely, of such interactions. Being human, they do not interact blindly or on mere instinct, they reflect mentally about their interaction. Society is the mental picture which human beings have of their behaviour, the representation of their interaction. It is the recognition in practice that ideas influence behaviour and that behaviour

31

generates ideas. Human interactions develop into enduring relationships or institutions, as they are called. These social facts are the components of the whole mental picture called society. Situating society thus, in the logical order, does not make it any less real. The fact that we cannot see, smell, hear or feel society is not an argument for its non-existence. Society is there, but it is a law to itself.

According to Durkheim's classic definition, social facts have three basic characteristics. They are:

(a) general: that is to say, they are common to many individuals;
(b) transmissible: that is to say, they can be transmitted vertically from generation to generation and horizontally from one contemporary human group to another;
(c) compulsory: that is to say, human beings have to take account of them, whether they like them or not — they cannot be ignored.

To take an example of a social fact from Eastern Africa: in ethnic groups that follow the patrilineal family system, a bridegroom is obliged to pay the bride's family an agreed amount of livestock, other goods or money. This marriage custom is known to anthropologists as 'bridewealth' and is also known locally in English as 'dowry' or 'brideprice'. It obeys all three of Durkheim's criteria:

(a) it is a generalized practice;
(b) it is imposed by the parental generation on the younger generation, and it has even been adopted by ethnic groups that did not traditionally have the practice;
(c) young people find it difficult to evade this obligation. In spite of current abuse of the custom and frequent calls for its abolition, it is still there as a bone of contention.

Members of society see social facts as having functions towards each other in the time-space dimension. Thus the custom of paying bridewealth clearly has a function as evidence for the legality of a marriage and for the legitimation of children born of the union. Bridewealth, marriage, legitimacy are social facts connected to one another by functions. But people go further in their mental picture. They do not stop at the one-to-one links between social facts; they attribute a structure to collections of interrelated social facts. A social structure comes into existence when individual social facts are deemed to possess a teleological or end-purpose function towards an overall, integrating model, theory or ideal.

The notion of structure is extremely important in any discussion of the social character of culture, because structural change, or the change that originates in people's minds concerning their society, is often the basis of cultural development and the outcome of intercultural exchange. It is undeniable that inculturation entails structural change. In the case of the social facts cited above as examples, the structure or model may concern the mental picture people have of the family and its purpose. Thus, bridewealth, marriage and legitimacy all serve the structure of the family and are related to it as parts to a whole. If the family structure undergoes a change, then a whole collection of social facts and the relationships between them are called into question.

Social structure can be discerned by systematic observers who take into account what we have called the people's mental picture. This picture is what Claude Lévi-Strauss terms 'the mechanical model', because an individual learns it by enculturation from his or her society, and because individuals are only intermittently conscious of it. Observed systematically, the mechanical model becomes, in Lévi-Strauss's terminology, 'the statistical model'. Structuralism in anthropology thus consists in the discernment of such structures. Taken as a whole, society consists of a multitude of overlapping or interconnected structures.

Social structures develop from within an original physical environment, and from the interaction of society with this environment. Now a physical environment offers a limited number of choices to a population for solving the material problems of feeding, clothing and housing itself. The way in which the environment limits society's choice, and the way in which a society chooses, arranges and modifies what the environment provides, are called the economy of a society. The contribution of the environment can be modified by communications, trade and the diffusion of produce, artefacts and techniques. On top of all this, society creates its own environment, its own way of adapting to the chosen economy, with its own social mechanisms such as patterns of movement and settlement, forms of communication, administrative institutions and so on.

It is easy to see, therefore, that the history of a society is the history of a succession and accumulation of choices, in other words a tradition. It is the particular tradition of a society interacting with all the levels of its environment, the land it inhabits and the world at large. Tradition constitutes an inherited body of meanings and conceptions clothed in symbolic forms and this inheritance is called a culture. The symbols of a culture usually derive from its original, physical environment and from its historical experience in that environment. The bond that exists between a land and a people is always strong, but the tradition that arises out of this bond acquires an independent existence, and can even survive a national exile or diaspora. The most famous instance of such survival is that of the Jewish culture and religion.

Symbols are essential to a culture, and it would be as well to say something about them before moving on to a discussion of the levels of culture. Symbols are a species of sign. Any object, event or experience can serve as an image and so become a vehicle for a concept or a meaning. Such vehicles of meaning are called signs. It was already noted in Chapter 1 that the individual's apprehension of reality is itself culture-bound. The signs that an individual deploys and adapts in accordance with his cultural tradition may be more or less close to his actual experience. A rough-and-ready classification would be to call those which are obviously close to the experience 'natural signs', and those which are remote from it 'conventional signs'. It is, in fact, a difference of degree rather than of kind. Natural signs, therefore, include the phenomena of sense experience, while conventional signs are constructs upon that experience. Thus, the apprehension of a red-coloured flame warns the observer of the presence and the danger of fire, while the use of the colour red in, let us say, a traffic light, warns the motorist of the danger in crossing a highway. In the second case, human convention imparts a further meaning to the experience of the colour red, and it requires instruction in the highway code to appreciate the meaning of the sign. By itself, its appropriateness does not suffice as an explanation.

The symbol creates a link between two different experiences or sets of experience in order to convey a conventional meaning. Typically, there is no instruction. The observer or, better, the participant, discovers a further range of meaning through an overlapping of contexts, and so enlarges his or her experience of reality and makes it more real. Thus, in the Christian liturgy of the Easter Vigil, actual fire, light and water combine, against a background of Old Testament readings concerning the crossing of the Red Sea and the guidance by a pillar of fire, to explore the meaning of Christ's resurrection in relation to the sacrament of Baptism. Fire, light and water participate in this further reality and convey its meaning concretely.

Symbols are far from arbitrary, but are instances of experience which we cannot gainsay. We are not wholly free in front of them. Very often they encourage a critique of the conscious by the unconscious. Unlike analogies, which simply affirm the likeness and difference between the analogues, symbols express the relationship

34

between them. Through the actual experiencing of reality, further meaning is discovered.

The symbols of a cultural system are the products of society. They are the components of the mental patterns and pictures through which a society understands and orients itself to life in the world. Inculturation is all about a symbiosis of different symbol-systems.

The Levels of Culture

We have spoken about the correlation of behaviour and ideas in the social phenomenon we call culture. At this phenomenological level it is usual to distinguish the practical from the symbolical. The practical or material aspect of culture includes all that has to do with material life, technology and behaviour, and this is the proper object of the science of ethnology. The symbolical relates to the realm of ideas, and it is this realm which governs the practical order and orients human behaviour. Social anthropology is the discipline that is the most attentive to the symbolical level.

Beneath this twofold phenomenological level of culture lies the deeper cognitive level, the level of underlying meanings and values. In dealing with religion and the theological concept of inculturation we have to do with this inner level. Scholars often like to picture the levels of culture as a series of concentric circles, representing a progressive interiority. Here are two examples.

Bishop Donald Jacobs of the Mennonite Church used to present a scheme of four concentric circles.[1] The two outer circles relate to the practical sphere; the two inner circles to the underlying cognitive level expressed by symbols. (The symbolical level did not itself appear in the scheme.) The outermost circle he dubbed 'the industrial technical' and this referred to the relatively superficial level of industrial technology, techniques of manufacture, communications and travel, and the worlds of sport and fashion. It is a level that does not affect human beings deeply or permanently, a level that is in a constant state of flux. This is not to say that it does not belong to culture or does not reflect cultural values, but it is a level that can be attached to any culture. People of different cultures all over the world drive cars, play football and wear trousers, without being obliged to surrender their commitment to a distinct culture. On the other hand, as we shall see in the next chapter, there is a degree of technological efficacity that we call 'modernization' which destroys the underlying values of a culture and gives to the technological level a cultural importance which it would not otherwise enjoy. Superficial though it may be, the industrial technical may be the thin end of the wedge of materialism. It can result in people preferring to live constantly at the level of the superficial and trivial.

Jacobs' second level of culture was called 'the domestic technical'. This refers to the culture of the home and of leisure pursuits, when a person is free to be himself or herself, when one's time is one's own. It is the culture of family conventions and etiquette, of cooking and taste in food. Obviously it is a level that affects an individual more profoundly and that is more difficult to change. It is a level that has more to do with cultural tradition.

The third cultural level in this scheme is that of values. Values have to do with priorities and with characteristic choices when confronted with alternatives. Conservation and consumption, for example, are opposed values. Conjugal love and procreation are values which represent different emphases in marriage. Cultures possess their own typical values. The people of a particular culture may be obsessed with the value of honour, or purity, or prestige, or family loyalty to a greater degree than those of other cultures. Such values are instilled into the members of society through their cultural education or enculturation, and they stem from a deeper, underlying cultural level.

This fourth and final level of culture is identified by Jacobs as its worldview. In every culture there is a particular way of understanding, and acting towards, the world. By 'world' is understood the whole range of human experience, the experience of other human beings in one's own society and other societies, the experience of the physical environment immediate and remote, and the experience that we call religious. Religious experience is the encounter with ultimate reality, the intuition of a truth or power that transcends the evidence of one's senses. Culture renders faith in such a reality imaginatively credible and provides the psycho-social terrain for such a faith-encounter. Religious faith endows all experience with a new dimension. It imparts conviction and motivation, and is, according to this view, at the root of culture itself.

It can be seen, then, that this proposed fourth level of culture is remarkably rich and diverse. In fact the whole scheme of four levels, helpful and suggestive as it is, can only be a thumbnail sketch of the complex reality of culture. What it does for us is to suggest that there *are* levels of culture and that there is a hierarchy of importance among the levels. It also proposes the view that a religious under-standing of reality is at the heart of culture. As one descends more and more deeply to the innermost levels of the cultural personality, one encounters more and more resistance to change. While the outer, practical levels are reasonably susceptible of change, it is much harder to change people's values, harder still to change their world-view. It now becomes clear why evangelization constitutes a funda-mental challenge to culture. This challenge is, perhaps, greater when it is more subtle, when it is not part of a process of cultural domina-tion or alienation. This is true inculturation.

Another scheme of concentric circles is presented by T. F. Zuern in connection with a discussion of American Indian culture.[2] This three-tier scheme is a corrective to the scheme we have just con-sidered. An outer circumference of tangibles contains an inner circle of structures and a final centre of intangibles. The tangibles are all the practical aspects of culture through which society (according to J. Gritti) humanizes the world, a humanization that has four sub-levels: arts, language, industry, technology.[3] The circle of structures contains the symbols through which meaning is communicated, and the inner centre of intangibles represents the body of meanings which a culture communicates through its symbol system.

The question we may now ask is: whether religion is essential to this body of meanings? Is religion really the root of culture? Much depends on how religion is defined. Later in this chapter we shall look at the essentially cultural character of religion. What is now at issue is the essentially religious character of culture. Does a religious faith provide the final cultural coding of the human person?[4] If religion is defined in terms of 'ultimates': faith in an ultimate reality, having an area of ultimate concern, it is not difficult to ascribe an implicitly religious character to culture, provided the 'ultimate' is sufficiently comprehensive. If a person's ultimate concern lies in the practical, material level, we are obviously not in the realm of religion, but we *are* in the presence of an impoverished culture. Religion, however, is not simply about cognition or explanation. It is about communion and the efficacious, or good, life. Its essential concern is with relation-ships, and with destiny.

It is not enough to know, or to speculate about, ultimates; one has to enter into communion with the ultimately real, shaping oneself to the reality and the reality to oneself. Religion not only interrogates existence, it offers the believer a rule of life. It helps him or her to walk the tightrope between hope and despair, hovering between affirmation and negation and helping to intensify and unify the believer's experience.

Does the truly atheistic culture exist? What, indeed *is* atheism? We have spoken about secularism and materialism as an impoverishment of culture, that is to say, as a tendency to remain satisfied with a superficial level of culture, dodging all the ultimate questions. But is it possible for a cultural worldview to be atheistic? The answer is 'yes', in so far as a culture is transformed by an atheistic ideology. An ideology is a set of beliefs and values, held by the dominant group in a society, that justifies and rationalizes a programme which is being carried forward. An ideology is a total system of truth and conduct, and as such, it resembles religion. Do religion and ideology belong to the same logical category? In theory they do not, but in practice they often do. That is why they are so often in conflict. The religious view of the world includes the divine order, the ultimate reality which is the object of faith and worship and which is not empirically knowable. Ideology claims to be scientific, to be an action-oriented theory based on observable facts. However, in practice, ideologies demand a commitment to ideals which transcend the empirical and the scientific.

One such commitment may be — as it is in the case of Communism — to atheism. Explicit atheism is a kind of negative evidence for God's existence, as if faith in God is too important to ignore or to leave undenied. And just as the existence of God defies demonstrable proof, so does the non-existence of God. In practice, atheism is analogous to religious faith. This is even more clear when atheistic ideologies are utopian, that is to say, when they direct human activity towards an unattained ideal, perhaps an ideal that is in itself unattainable in terms of science, technology and social history. The Marxist utopia of revolution, with its picture of a regenerated human race, what Karl Marx himself called 'the total redemption of humanity', is really an eschatological concept, the belief that the final liberation has begun but has not yet been fully realized. Nicholas Lash has this to say about popular Marxism.

> As the doctrine of a mass movement which combined revolutionary fervour with a sense of history and the conviction that it held the key to the explanation of patterns of social change, Marxism (or, rather, what Stalin christened 'Marxism-Leninism': a simplified amalgam of aspects of the thought of Marx, Engels and Lenin) became the 'official teaching' of Soviet Communism and of those political parties which took the USSR

as their model. This teaching, complete, self-sufficient and contained in a canon of sacred texts, the masses took on faith. Its exposition was reserved to officially approved interpreters.[5]

Thus an atheistic ideology took on the characteristics of a religious faith and system. Indeed, the last two sentences of the above quotation could be a description of the Catholic Church. True atheism, even when it puts the human being in the place of God, is a thirst for the absolute, an eloquent spokesman for the divine transcendence. From the Christian standpoint, any man or woman of goodwill who strives to lead a good life according to the dictates of conscience, even without an explicit knowledge of God, is not denied the assistance necessary for salvation.[6] It does not seem, therefore, that the level of culture that is concerned with ultimate values can be removed from the religious sphere. Even when religion and faith in God are cast aside, we are dealing at this level with a religious category. Culture is therefore always in some sense religious or potentially religious.

There is, however, another question to which we shall return several times in the course of this book. Are there cultures which are essentially impervious to Christianity, essentially irredeemable? In an intervention during the final session of the Second Vatican Council, Bishop Donal Lamont declared:

No people are so primitive as to be unfit for the Gospel: none are so civilized as not to need it.[7]

In other words, the Gospel is relevant to every human culture. This relevance is both a need on the part of the culture and a recognition of truth in the culture on the part of the Gospel. A theological argument for inculturation which we shall consider in Part Two proposes that God's creative Word is at the heart of every culture, but this does not mean, as Bishop Lamont reminded the Fathers of Vatican II, that a culture has no need of the Gospel, or that the presence of God's creative Word cannot be forgotten or obscured, nor yet that forces of modernization may not be working to undermine such 'seeds of the Gospel'. The answer, then, to the question whether there are cultures that are essentially impervious to the Gospel is that, as they stand, they may be impervious for all practical purposes. However, it would be the first task of evangelization to correct such maldevelopment and to bring a culture into line with its original ideals.

Having looked at the religious character or potentiality of culture, it is time to turn to the cultural character of religion.

Religion as a Cultural System

If religion is a fundamental mode of cultural behaviour, it must be part of the interpretation of life that a culture offers its adepts. It must operate in and through a culture. In other words, the beliefs and practices of religion must themselves form a cultural system. The intangible level of culture consists of meanings and conceptions which are translated firstly into symbolic form and then into practical behaviour. A cultural system is therefore a configuration of symbols that acts as a bridge between ideas and behaviour. Religion itself is such a cultural system.

Clifford Geertz was among the first social scientists to take religion seriously as an object of study in its own right. For him it is primarily a system of symbols inherited culturally within which divine reality is rendered imaginatively credible, or, to use Geertz' phrase, made 'uniquely realistic'.

> A religion is a system of symbols which acts to establish powerful, pervasive, and long-lasting moods and motivations in men by formulating conceptions of a general order of existence and clothing these conceptions with such an aura of factuality that the moods and motivations seem uniquely realistic.[8]

Geertz does not, of course, enter into the theological question of the truth or falsity of religion. His is a purely empirical approach. A system of symbols is a model *of* an already apprehensible reality, but it is also a model *for* a reality that is coming into existence. Such a model, therefore, invites the believer, not only to conform to reality, but to transform it. It also creates religious dispositions in the believer which are powerful and long-lasting. It does this by unifying and intensifying human experience, 'formulating conceptions of a general order of existence'. Geertz cites the problem of how to make suffering bearable and the problem of evil as examples of such general conceptions. These are primarily problems of meaning, but the way in which they are formulated by religion contrives to relate human existence to a wider sphere. Religion affirms and denies at the same time. It affirms that evils are inescapable but denies that they are characteristic of the ultimate world order.

Geertz then goes on to ask Newman's question: How is it that this denial comes to be believed? How can one be convinced of a truth that cannot be demonstrated? The answer is that religious symbolism creates such an aura of factuality that the truth appears uniquely realistic. Religious symbols have the power to render the real more real. They induce faith, conviction, commitment because they act upon the creative power of the human intellect and galvanize the will towards action. This action is, of course, a common action, an action in concert with and for other members of society. No religion can exercise this power if its symbols are not inseparable from those of culture. As a cultural system, religion acts upon cultural data and within the sphere of culture.

Just as there are levels of culture, so there are levels of religion in relation to culture. Michael Amaladoss distinguishes between what he calls the 'cosmic' level and the 'metacosmic' level.[9] The cosmic is simply the popular level. At this level religion supports the view of the world that is current in society. It acts as a conservative force, challenging all deviations from the norm. The metacosmic level concerns those whom Peter Berger calls the 'religious *virtuosi*', those who enjoy a special revelation or illumination or who are especially well versed in sacred scriptures or liturgical lore.[10] This is the 'highbrow' level of religious culture. Such individuals tend to be the guardians and censors of religious faith and practice, the repositories of religious tradition.

When traditional cultural structures begin to disintegrate under the onslaught of external forces, and especially as a result of cultural pluralism, religion at the popular level may become an important vehicle of mass cultural identity. Religious loyalty becomes a crucial means of reaffirming one's loyalty to cultural values which are under threat. This gives rise to the movement known as Fundamentalism, a conservative reaction to cultural change in which religious criteria are invoked. Fundamentalism appeals to original sources and originating experiences in an oversimplified and literal way. It commands allegiance by its deceptive simplicity. As a result, it encourages religious and cultural incapsulation and often a fanatical opposition towards other religious and cultural systems. Fundamentalism is commonplace in the second half of the twentieth century, not only among Christians, but perhaps especially among Muslims, for whom it is an important ingredient of the current Islamic revolution against Western influence.

Fundamentalism has no future in terms of cultural reality. Like secularism, it is content to remain at a superficial level. It is perforce an impoverishment of religion. Moreover, its programme of incapsulation runs counter to the ordinary processes of intercultural contact. Realism demands that religion should come to terms with other cultures and with the forces of cultural change.

A particular religious system may be conterminous with a given culture. This was typically the case of the traditional religions of ethnic groups in Africa and other parts of the Third World. Before the arrival of the so-called 'immigrant religions' of Islam and Christianity, an individual who was born into a particular ethnic group was obliged to adopt the religion of that group. Religious beliefs and practices were taught as part of the general enculturation of its members. There was, therefore, no possibility of choosing a religious affiliation. There was no 'baptism' or basic initiation into the religious community. One was born into a religion. One sometimes hears African Christians ask why it should be necessary to baptize the children of Christian parents. Do they not become Christians at birth? Perhaps this kind of question reflects the mentality of traditional ethnic religion.

Experience shows, however, that it is possible for a given culture to accommodate several religions at the same time. All of them may be in perfect harmony with the host-culture, but they are each of them a variant. Each within its own tradition places a different emphasis on the cultural elements that all share. Each makes its own selection of these elements and combines them, perhaps, with elements of a tradition that originated in an alien culture. In this way, such religions become sub-cultures of the host-culture, reinforcing its essential values in their own way.

The third possibility is that a given religion may be expressed through many different cultures. This is the case of the so-called 'world religions' and even of some religions which are not usually so described. Buddhism, for example, originated in India but it takes different cultural forms in Tibet, Sri Lanka and China. The same can be said of Islam in Pakistan, Arabia and West Africa. Even African traditional religions have spread with the trans-Atlantic slave-trade from West Africa to Brazil and the Caribbean, where thay have effected a new marriage with Christianity and with the cultures of Europe and the New World. It is the fundamental claim of Christianity that it is at home in every culture which underlies the concept of inculturation.

Inculturation of a religion into many cultures assumes that the religion in question retains its essential identity. If a religion is radically transformed through its contact with a culture, then we are not speaking of inculturation, but of culturalism — the absolutization of culture, or at any rate, in a given instance, the triumph of culture. In the case of Buddhism and Islam, it is not always clear that these religions have transformed the cultures to which they came. They may have received more than they gave. Buddhism, for example, transformed the cultures of Indo-China, but was itself transformed by ancient Chinese culture. Even in the history of Christianity, schisms have arisen for cultural reasons, and cultural differences have prompted theological deviations.

However, the principle of inculturation stands or falls by the integrity of the Christian faith. Its cultural expression may vary, but its essential meaning cannot be contradicted. At the level of meaning, the Christian faith may develop, but there can be no loss of content. Proponents of culture, particularly where culture has been traditionally identified with a single religious tradition, may oppose Christianity's programme of cultural transformation. They may be unwilling, as, for example, Wole Soyinka of Nigeria appears to be, to allow that Christianity could ever find a valid expression in the culture of the Yoruba.[11] Yet a Yoruba-inculturated Christianity would not claim to be the only valid expression of Yoruba culture. Inculturation should not mean a cultural monopoly for the Church. Perhaps the objection centres on the question of cultural authenticity, and on the fear of acculturation which is a necessary condition for inculturation. This objection will be more fully countered in the chapters that follow. First we must take a look at cultural change in Chapter 4. Then in the following chapter we shall examine the Christian expectations of inculturation.

References

1 Lectures given by Bishop Donald Jacobs at the AMECEA Pastoral Institute, Gaba, Uganda in 1968. I am not aware of his having published these ideas, but I have used them myself in published work, e.g. Shorter 1973, pp. 20–21.

2 Zuern 1983, p. 3.

3 Gritti quoted in Crollius 1984, p. 35.

4 i.e. faith as distinct from beliefs.

5 Lash 1983.

6 Cf. *Lumen Gentium*, 16.

7 *Nulla gens tam fera est ut Christi Evangelii capax non sit, neque tam culta ut Evangelio non indigeat.* Lamont in Stacpoole 1986, p. 282.

8 Geertz 1966, p. 4.

9 Amaladoss 1985, p. 171.

10 Berger 1980, pp. 33–4.

11 Soyinka 1976, pp. 121–2.

4

Cultural change

Types of Cultural Change

Any discussion of inculturation demands an understanding of cultural pluralism and of the relationship between religion and culture. These basic ideas have been examined in the last two chapters. Another notion that is fundamental to an understanding of inculturation is that of cultural change.

As we have already seen, culture is itself the product of change. It is a tradition of accumulated choices in which the selection and acceptance of external ideas and behaviour play a part. This is equally true of the Church in the culturally conditioned formulation and development of its teaching. The interaction of cultures is part of the normal pattern of cultural development, but as long as cultures remained relatively isolated from one another, the effects of cultural pluralism were not strongly felt. With the development of modern travel and communications, the actual pluralism of cultures may become a threat to cultural identity and precipitate a much more radical form of change.

All cultures, therefore, throughout history have undergone a form of regular change in which the structures of society and its patterns of thought have remained intact. There are, however, developing and varying emphases within the structures. If Christian classicist assumptions prevented the perception of cultural pluralism, they were equally opposed to ideas of historical change. With the development of history as a critical discipline, it now becomes possible to take a fresh look at the Christian culture of Europe, for example, and to follow the cultural transformations of the image of Jesus Christ himself and the impact of Western culture of these different Christ images.

This is what Jaroslav Pelikan has done in a recently published study.[1] Pelikan follows the path taken by spirituality, mysticism and Christology throughout the centuries of Christendom. The triumph of the Christian Empire in the fourth century coincided with the presentation of Christ as 'King of Kings'. At the same time the development of a Christianized Platonic philosophy resulted in the idea of the 'Cosmic Christ', the mind, reason and word of God. In the fifth century St Augustine worked out a Christian anthropology that placed the emphasis on the 'Son of Man'. The popularization of Byzantine icons in the eighth and ninth centuries led theologians to explore the concept of Christ as true image of God, while in the literature and art of the tenth and eleventh centuries emphasis was placed on the saving power of the Cross, as against the demonic power of evil. The interaction of monasticism and politics in the medieval world produced the picture of Christ as the ideal of the monk, the ascetic who denied the world in order to conquer it. Traditions of neo-Platonic mysticism also encouraged the image of 'Christ, the Bridegroom of the Soul', while medieval concepts of chivalry coloured the Franciscan rediscovery of the full humanity of Christ.

The humanism of the sixteenth-century Renaissance produced the concept of 'the universal man' which was applied to Christ, while the Reformation gave birth to several images of Christ which Pelikan designates collectively as 'the Mirror of the Eternal'. The painful experience of the Wars of Religion in Europe led to a theological interest in peace and war and to the appearance of Christian pacifism in the spirit of Christ 'the Prince of Peace'. The philosophy of the Enlightenment in the eighteenth century sought to go beyond the Christ of dogma to discover a rational system of morals, while the nineteenth-century Romantic movement depicted Christ in aesthetic terms as 'the Poet of the Spirit'. Finally, at the turn of the century, with the expansion of Christianity to the Third World and with the response of leaders like Tolstoy, Gandhi and Martin Luther King to the social injustices of the time, Jesus emerged as a world liberator, and the stage was set for inculturation on a multicultural scale.

As Pelikan is at pains to demonstrate, all of these images of Christ are to be found in the authentic tradition of Christianity, but different images corresponded to different socio-cultural demands at different times. It may have been the case that in the sixteenth and eighteenth centuries structural changes in European culture occurred which were reflected in these Christian images, but on the whole the latter represent simultaneous strands of cultural tradition within an unchanging structure. These elements received varying emphasis in accordance with internal political, social and cultural developments. Most of this, therefore, is a record of regular, internal change, although from time to time selected external influences such as Byzantine art or neo-Platonism played their part. Pelikan's study provides us with a classic instance of on-going inculturation, of the dialogue between faith and culture, which, having begun through intercultural contact in the first place, is continued thereafter through a history of regular cultural change.

Intercultural contact, especially when it is multiple and rapid, as is the case at the present day, precipitates structural change, and structural change is typically associated with inculturation in its first stage, the first insertion of a faith into a given culture. Inculturation has acquired its great importance today because it is an aspect of a worldwide experience of structural change. The Christian faith is not simply being inserted into a single culture, as happened at the beginning of the history of Christian Europe, it is now being inserted simultaneously into a multiplicity of cultures all over the world. There is, as it were, a worldwide explosion of inculturation. The overwhelming nature of this experience is related to the misgivings about inculturation which are clearly felt at official levels in the Church today, misgivings which we shall be obliged to confront in the final part of this book.

In the previous chapter social structure was described as the integrating theory, model or ideal which gives meaning to social facts. Structural change, as the name implies, means a change in these integrating theories, a change in meaning or in the patterns of thought. Truly radical change occurs firstly in the mind. When long-cherished ideals of family and community life, of co-operation and authority, for example, are changed, human cultures undergo a fundamental transformation; even more so when religious beliefs and conceptions are changed.

Structural change can become acute when numerous cultures are interacting at the same time. This is the case with many countries of the Third World, particularly in Africa. In such countries ethnic cultures, or groups of ethnic cultures, are in the process of being welded into a modern nation-state. Such cultures are interacting with one another as well as with foreign cultures, such as those of the Western world. In these cases there is a cultural pluralism which is internal to the country, as well as an experience of pluralism which is a result of contact with external cultures.

In the countries of North America and Western Europe, the United

States, Canada, Britain, France and others, immigrant cultures from the Third World are jostling one another, and seeking a relative autonomy from the host-culture that is absorbing them. In other so-called 'Western' countries, such as Australia and New Zealand, a Western host-culture is grappling with a residual indigenous culture as well as with representatives of immigrant non-Western cultures. In this way many countries in the modern world are experiencing cultural pluralism and are becoming multicultural nations.

Structural change is therefore a very widespread phenomenon in the contemporary world. It is a phenomenon that can induce a certain measure of cultural disorientation, of 'culture shock'. It favours transient and superficial relationships. It tends to drive religion into the purely private sphere, and to relativize religious beliefs. From such religious relativization, it is a short step to secularism and to the massive loss of cultural meaning that we have already deplored.

Peter Berger has suggested that there are three options confronting cultural and religious traditions in this situation.[2] The deductive option is the refusal to communicate. It is, in effect, cultural incapsulation, a reaffirmation of the old certainties in a neo-traditional manner. Such a course dooms a culture or a religious tradition to irrelevance and ultimate extinction. It is an option which aptly characterizes a particular model of the Catholic Church.[3] The reductive option implies drift and an acceptance of cultural and religious impoverishment. Finally the inductive option, the only possible condition for cultural and religious survival, implies dialogue. It takes conviction, cultural loyalty and religious faith as its starting-points and seeks to strengthen and clarify these through the evidence it discovers in other traditions. The inductive option operates through intercultural experience and structural change. In a word, its characteristic procedure is inculturation.

Cultural pluralism carries with it tremendous risks, especially when it is accompanied (as it is in the modern world) by the process of modernization, but it also offers us a challenge full of hope, the possibility of a cultural and religious renaissance. Cohen and Middleton, writing about the interaction of ethnic cultures in Africa, identified three probabl{ outcomes, not necessarily exclusive of one another.[4] The first outcome is the discovery of interdependence between people of diverse cultures and religions. People of diverse cultural and religious communities often specialize in providing a service to the whole community. A church may specialize in providing medical or educational services. People of a given ethnic culture may specialize in a particular form of employment, like West Indians in London Transport, for example. Or an ethnic homeland in a multicultural state may make a specialized contribution to the national economy, for example coffee-growing among the Haya and Chagga of Tanzania.

The second outcome is that of cultural overlap or congruence. People of different cultures who come into contact with one another may discover very soon that there is an area of agreement or concord between their images and conceptions. Of course, there is room for a lack of realism here, as there is in any form of dialogue, and congruence has to be balanced by attention to the contradictions that exist, to understand them and, where possible, reduce them to a minimum. There is, however, the third outcome of incorporation: the experience of, and interest in, divergence. People of diverse cultural and religious traditions learn new interests from one another. A dialectical interchange takes place between them. Catholic ritual, for example, may be adopted by Protestant Fundamentalist sects in Africa. Pentecostalism spreads from Evangelical churches to the Catholic and Anglican communions. An African independent church in Kenya adopts the distinctive turban of the Sikh culture and religion. Authority structures of traditional cultures in Third World countries are introduced into Western forms of Christianity. A traditional cultural interest in, say, dreams or integral healing finds its way into the immigrant faiths of Christianity and Islam. Incorporation takes innumerable forms. Analytical concepts such as interdependence, congruence and incorporation help to fill out our understanding of Berger's third option, induction.

Structural change is a radical form of cultural change, and it is a worldwide prospect at the end of the twentieth century and the beginning of the twenty-first. However, it is not an instantaneous change that occurs overnight, as it were. Most of the world is probably experiencing an incipient form of structural change. Following Beattie, Firth, and Wilson, we may call this intermediate stage 'organizational change'.[5] Organizational change is present when there is a change in the scale of relationships between individuals, groups and cultures. This change of scale is fundamentally due to the increased mobility of populations brought about by modern forms of travel and communication. During the phase of organizational change, people tend to cling to their traditional values and conceptions. Cultural structures are still for the most part precariously intact. What has changed is the mode of application. People are struggling to apply traditional conceptions within a much wider field of experience. Beattie describes the process thus:

> Organizational changes are changes in ways of doing things, which themselves continue to be done, and in the extent and range of particular complexes of social relationships which remain formally unaltered . . . A decision as to the point at which organizational change, which may be gradual and cumulative, becomes important enough to qualify as structural change must be to some extent arbitrary. But sometimes distinctions in degree are as important as differences in kind, and even if Firth's distinction be regarded as marking two stages in the same process, it provides the student of social change with a useful half-way house between ordinary, 'built-in' change and conflict on the one hand, and that severer type of change which we call structural or radical, on the other.[6]

With a change in the scale or range of relationships goes also a wider range of choices, and an increasing power of choice is accompanied by a growth in the relative autonomy of individuals. This in turn facilitates personal commitment and the ability to bridge cultures or become culturally 'bilingual'. It goes without saying that organizational change is not a phase that anyone would wish to see unduly protracted, since it consists in clinging to outmoded, or at any rate unadapted concepts — concepts which are on the brink of being abandoned or reinterpreted. On the other hand, a traditional ethnic culture which is no longer relevant to a modern style of life is able to linger on as a cultural resource in a time of disorientation. This is certainly the case in contemporary Africa, where the cultural memory has almost an independent existence, and possesses the normative function to which we referred in Chapter 2. This function of an otherwise outmoded tradition may serve to prolong the organizational phase of change — to suspend its operation, as it were, pending a final reinterpretation. Writers and theorists speak not only of a radical transformation of African culture but also of a continuity that can be described by Wole Soyinka as an 'authentic cultural retrieval'.[7] The validity of such an idea is accepted by the theologians of inculturation, even if they themselves are rejected by writers such as Soyinka or Ngugi wa Thiong'o.[8] However, it is an idea that is increasingly challenged by the fruits of modernization and technological change. Up to this point we have hardly alluded to the forces of modernization in this discussion of cultural change. The truth is that it remains the most potent force which inculturation has to reckon with.

Modernization and Technological Change

The world in which we live is experiencing a rapid growth in scientific knowledge. This progress has been achieved through a long series of revolutions in which the scientific community has repeatedly reached a consensus about how to practise science. The end result has been to produce a body of scientific knowledge that is increasingly well articulated and specialized, wonderfully adapted to its purpose.[9] This body of scientific knowledge is dynamically translated into a technology that is transforming the world.

This process is referred to as 'modernization' or 'modernity'. It is a process that is concerned with the effects of technological change as well as with the development of technology itself. Developing technology has far-reaching repercussions on social, political and economic life.[10] This means that it also profoundly affects cultural realities, human relationships, human institutions, human values and ideals. In the first place, it has brought about the accelerated pace of structural change that we have been discussing above. Exploration, imperialist expansion, colonial settlement and the facile subjugation of peoples with inferior technology and weaponry have all been the results of modernization. International diplomacy, trade and tourism, rapid travel and almost instantaneous communication, have brought cultural pluralism home to every individual. These, more than anything, have increased the pace, and extended the range, of structural change in the world.

In the second place, modernization strongly enhances material values and material culture in general. It encourages the grossest forms of materialism and creates the so-called 'consumer-society'. Society 'consumes' technology, as it were, and places the highest possible value on material products. As a result, non-material values are relegated to a secondary or private sphere. Modernization, therefore, is intrinsically secularizing in its effect. Not only can it undermine religious beliefs and values, faith in God and the sense of sin, but it is capable of diminishing human sensibility itself and of promoting violence and vice.

The materialist culture brought about by modernization is not interested in altruism, let alone religion. It creates its own cultural

51

myth of success. Its values are what Kavanaugh calls 'reality principles' which relate to possessions, power, prestige and pride.[11] A course of action is not followed because it is right, but because it is 'realistic', 'acceptable' or 'in one's interests'. These are the values of the statesmen and politicians, the actors and artists, the stars of stage, screen and stadium, in the industrialized, media-saturated societies of the Western world. Modern technology places immense power in the hands of government and the business community. One of the most influential creations of modernized, production-oriented societies has been the multi-national company. This is an organization that links capital, technology, materials and labour from many different countries in a single, gigantic productive process. These companies virtually operate in a jurisdiction created by themselves.

It is easy to see how modernization can undermine religious values in general and the values of the Christian Gospel in particular. It is also easy to appreciate how the ancient Christian culture of Europe is threatened by the secularizing tendencies of modernity. Indeed, in the dialogue between the Christian faith and European culture — a culture that is becoming increasingly secularized — Christianity has developed into what Berger calls a 'cognitive minority'.[12] The Church may be enlivened by the challenge, but that does not mean that it has yet discovered how to penetrate and permeate the modernization process. Christianity may be on the way to becoming a sub-culture in the Western culture it helped to create.

In the popular view of it, Scientific Socialism or Marxism is an ideology that claims to be in harmony with the process of modernization, and according to its tenets the process logically excludes religion and belief in God. Although many of its expectations are far from scientific, and although the parallel existence of religion with Marxist régimes appears to contradict its theory, it is an ideology that is militantly anti-religious and anti-Christian. Even though the private practice of religion may be tolerated in certain Communist countries, a systematic discrimination is directed against practising believers in the public sphere because they are an embarrassment to the official theory. When one considers that Marxist ideology justifies the violent expropriation of one class by another, the subversion of non-Marxist régimes, the setting-up of totalitarian governments and the rewriting of history in terms of an evolutionary survival of the fittest or most powerful, it is easy to appreciate the incompatibility of Marxist with Christian values. All of this is coupled with a lamentable record where human rights are concerned. This may be the popular under-standing or misunderstanding of Marxism among Catholics but it does not disprove the presence of truthful insights in Marxist theory.

Marxism's appeal to modernization is one reason why the Church has often tended to resist change in the Western world, since the revolution it proclaims foresees no role for Christian belief and practice, and is vitiated in the eyes of Christians as an explanatory theory and programme for action by its uncompromising atheism. Marxism is even thought by some to pervert science in much the same way that the Fascist ideologies of the mid-twentieth century did so, and it is opposed for the same reason, the fear of

... a new dark age made more sinister, and perhaps more protracted, by the lights of perverted science.[13]

The view that Marxism is a perverse form of modernity does not, however, imply that there are no elements of truth in its system. Marxism offers a critique of capitalism and a critique that is perhaps the most credible assessment available of the unequal relations between rich, capitalist countries and the poor nations of the Third World. The claim that modernization will ultimately benefit the entire population of the world is far from credible. On the contrary, Third World poverty, hunger and indebtedness is increasing. Modern technology is firmly in the hands of the Western powers, and poor countries are forced to submit to the economic and strategic priorities of those who possess the wealth, the power and the weaponry. Even food aid to the starving is used as a form of blackmail and as a means of off-loading uneconomic surpluses. We have already seen how modernization made colonization possible. It also buttresses the op-pressive régimes of racial minorities, like that of South Africa, and the equally oppressive plutocracies of certain Latin American countries.

Although the Church has consistently fought against the perverse effects of modernity in the Western world, there is a 'wry paradox', as Azevedo notes, in the fact that Christian missionaries have accepted to become part of the modernization process in the so-called 'mission countries' of the Third World. Of course, it would have been difficult for them to stand aloof from development work in these countries. In many arid areas the survival of the community is in question. In other cases the population is ravaged by disease or pests affecting crops and livestock. Christian missionaries were obliged to become involved in socio-economic development, in medical services and in education. Such involvement was an essential preliminary to evangelization, and a testimony to their human concern.

Christian missionaries were not, of course, in control of the modernization process, and they were, as Jean-Marc Ela remarks, 'innocent' of all its detrimental implications.[14] They were, perhaps, oblivious of the fact that their work for socio-economic development was making the Third World increasingly dependent on the industrialized countries of the West, but they cannot have been entirely indifferent to the dangers of secularism and materialism which modernization entails.

While it is historically naive to see Christian missionaries as conscious accomplices of colonial exploitation and domination there is certainly a disquieting question concerning the Catholic Church's own power-centre that must be faced. To what extent do the central organs of a World Church, geographically and historically associated — as they are — with the industrialized West, owe their pre-eminence and all-pervasive power to the forces of modernization? This is a question to which we must return at different moments and in different forms during the course of this book. It is a question that is vital to the whole theology of inculturation and to its future.

Christianity and Cultural Change

Evangelization is addressed to human individuals who belong to clearly defined social groupings and who are profoundly linked to a cultural tradition. The Gospel cannot, therefore, be transmitted to or from people independently of their culture. In one way or another the culture is evangelized, along with its adepts. Evangelization involves change and it should not be a matter of embarrassment that the Church is an agent of change. The *metanoia*, or conversion of heart, which is the aim of evangelization involves a change at the deepest levels of cultural identity. Evangelization challenges that basic world-view, the religious root of culture, the final location of meaning. It is, therefore, committed to bringing about the most radical kind of change. The Church, in a word, is an agent of structural change.

In acting as a change-agent, it could be argued that the Church is violating the basic human right to culture, but there are several reasons why this is not the case. In the first place, being an agent of structural change is not the same thing as being guilty of cultural domination. In theory, evangelization should not employ either physical or moral force. Of course, in practice, the Gospel may have arrived in mission countries with an overwhelming paraphernalia of mass-produced liturgical art, printed literature and so forth, and it may be difficult to transpose the message from the evangelizing culture to the culture that is being evangelized. If this is the case, it is because the Church's mission is accidentally linked to the modernization process. The Church in a newly-evangelized culture has to be sufficiently self-critical to reject cultural accidentals, even when bombarded by them on a massive scale. However, they *are* accidentals. Christian evangelization is an invitation to the people of the culture to respond in freedom at the deepest level of religious meaning.

In the evangelization process, therefore, people are presumed to retain their cultural autonomy, to make their own choices and their own selections, and to become the agents of their own structural change. The herald of the gospel makes an offer which the hearer is free to accept or reject. It is also presumed that the message of the Gospel undergoes no loss of continuity in meaning. Since the Gospel is not itself a culture there can be no question of cultural domination, if evangelization is properly conducted. The Gospel offers itself to a culture because it is in need of cultural expression, and it may gain surplus meaning thereby. It is itself enriched. Of course, we are speaking here of the ideal. As a matter of historical fact, we have to remember that the Church has barely emerged from a monocultural view of the world, and that considerable violence has been done to cultures in the evangelization process.

Structural change is an outcome of intercultural activity, but this does not have to be cultural domination. Moreover, it is not necessary to see structural change as all loss and no gain. As we noted above, there are continuities even when there is a change in structures. Nor is all change a change for the worse. The Church as a change-agent believes in change that is not only beneficial but redeeming. The change wrought by evangelization is a renewal, the insertion of a given human culture into the mainstream of salvation history, the transcending of its own limits.

Christianity has another positive role to play in the process of cultural change. Although the Church is unwittingly compromised in its evangelization of the Third World by its association with the perverse effects of modernization, this does not mean either that modernization is wholly perverse, nor that Christianity cannot hold a balance between positive cultural values, on the one hand, and modernity, on the other. Although the struggle may seem increasingly unequal, Christianity is the ally, not the enemy, of culture in the combat with perverse modernization. It is opposed to the ideologies of secularism, to the impoverishment of human sensibility and to all that subverts the truth and goodness of traditional culture. Modern materialism encourages conflict and competition. It aggravates acquisitiveness and favours dishonesty. In the phase of organizational change, when people are operating on a larger scale, but with their traditional loyalties, it is the cause of corruption and nepotism. Many of the social justice problems current in Third World countries are due to the impact of modernization on traditional cultures. In the modern, large-scale, context, for example, the tribute from a client to a patron becomes a bribe. The Church shares with traditional cultures their attachment to personal values and their concern for the preservation and promotion of life in all its aspects. It can certainly help to cushion the impact of modernity and to canalize its forces in ways that respect cultural autonomy and ensure continuity. The traditional cultures of the Third World are certainly undergoing a radical transformation as a result of structural change and modernization, but this radical transformation need not be a disorientation or an alienation. In the course of history the Church has often been a repository of culture, and there are signs that it is playing this role again in the case of the ethnic cultures of the Third World.

We come now once more to the question of acculturation and the fear that it can inspire in the minds of people who wish to remain loyal to their traditional culture and to reaffirm it. Inculturation presupposes acculturation. This is because the Gospel cannot exist without a contingent cultural expression. If the Gospel is to make an impact through evangelization on a non-Christian culture, it must arrive in an alien cultural form. The Gospel always comes from 'outside'. It can even be argued that the Gospel is in origin essentially extraneous, and that Jesus Christ is the 'stranger' *par excellence*, the original and greatest 'outsider'. There are cultures, of course, which, through an inherent conceit, pride themselves on accepting nothing from strangers. Shusaku Endo's novel *Silence* offers an instance from the sixteenth-century mission to Japan.[15] The Japanese of that period were obliged to reject Christianity simply because it was foreign. In their eyes nothing good could possibly originate from an alien culture. This view was echoed by the Church of the time. Such an attitude is born of ignorance. It is a form of xenophobic ethnocentrism or extreme cultural incapsulation.

Acculturation is not cultural alienation. The borrowing of images and conceptions from other cultures is frequently necessary when it is a question of expressing new and unfamiliar experiences and meanings. Such borrowing extails a transformation of the existing configuration of images and conceptions, setting up a new relationship between them, a new symbiosis and a new interpretation, perhaps. However, it does not necessarily mean that the borrower-culture has changed, as it were, into another 'animal' . There are continuities both of symbolism and meaning.

Christianity cannot ignore its past. It is a historical religion and its originating experience was expressed through an interplay of Near Eastern cultures in the first century AD. Since then, that experience has received successive cultural expression in diverse historic cultures. It would therefore be unthinkable that Christian evangelization should not entail the transmission of certain cultural elements from one culture to another, and vice versa. That is simply history being made. However, this is a far cry from imposing an entire cultural system upon people of another culture.

In the next chapter we shall examine the Christian term of the inculturation 'equation', and we shall look in greater detail at the cultural implications of evangelization.

References

1 Pelikan 1985.

2 Berger 1980.

3 Cf. Shorter 1983, pp. 28–29 for the application of Berger's deductive option to the Catholic Church.

4 Cohen and Middleton 1970.

5 Beattie 1964 p. 247 (quoting Raymond Firth); Wilson 1971, pp. 6–17.

6 Beattie *op. cit.*, p. 247.

7 Soyinka 1976, *passim*: Ngugi and Mugo 1976, p. 49.

8 Soyinka *op. cit.*, p. 122.

9 Cf. Kuhn 1970 (1962).

10 Azevedo 1982.

11 Kavanaugh 1985.

12 Berger *op. cit., passim.*

13 Churchill 1957 (1940), p. 33.

14 Ela 1985.

15 Endo 1971.

5

The Christian term
of inculturation

The Subject-Matter of Inculturation

In common with all religions the Christian faith can only be expressed and lived through a human culture. Like other world religions it is accessible to more than one culture. Indeed, its mark of Catholicity implies a will to make itself accessible to all cultures, without exception, and this in turn entails a multiple process of inculturation. In Chapter 1 inculturation was defined as 'the ongoing dialogue between faith and culture or cultures'. Up to this point we have been discussing the cultural implications and contexts of this dialogue, and we have analysed it in the light of social science and the science of culture. Now we must examine the other term of inculturation, its subject-matter, so to speak. We must also look at some of the theological presuppositions of a multicultural Church. A Church composed of many cultures requires institutional links, and there arises the crucial question of the cultural form these links should take.

Hitherto we have spoken about the inculturation of the Christian 'faith' or the dialogue between this 'faith' and culture or cultures. Faith, in the sense of a religious tradition or affiliation — as opposed to a theological virtue — is a broad and undefined concept, and the word was deliberately chosen, pending a fuller discussion of the subject-matter of inculturation. A term that is frequently used in this connection is 'message'. Thus, inculturation is said to be a dialogue between the Christian message and a human culture. We have already seen that this message does not exist independently of culture. Furthermore, the word 'message' carries the danger of thinking exclusively of a set of doctrinal propositions or dogmas. Edward Schillebeeckx has written the 'Christianity is not the religion of a book but of a person',[1] and there is a real sense in which it can be said that the message of Christianity is Christ himself, that he is the subject of his own message. Of course, conceptual propositions can and should be deduced from the Christ-event, but Christianity cannot be limited to theological formulation or catechesis alone. Such concepts are a necessary part of religious education, but Christian faith and life cannot be reduced to the mere rational assent given to propositional truths. Our relationship with God does not even have to wait for us to form concepts of him. We affirm his existence as a being in whose life we participate by being ourselves and by using our talents. The act of faith has to do with wonderment and awe, with personal risk and commitment, not with rational proof. The gift of God's love in Jesus Christ reveals who he is and what he asks of us. Faith is not simply believing a message to be true, but a dwelling in the Truth. The knowledge that comes of faith is the 'eye of love'. It is part of our loving response to God in Christ revealing himself to us in our experience.

Another tendency is to speak of the 'Gospel' as the Christian term of inculturation — the dialogue between Gospel and culture. The limits of this way of speaking must also be recognized. The Gospel or 'Good News' is good news about Christ. Furthermore, Christ can even be described as *being* himself the Good News. The word 'Gospel' is also used to refer to the whole Christian way of life, the doing of Christ's word, living according to his Gospel values. This again, cannot take place except in cultural forms. Although the Church is the chosen instrument of the Good News, we do not usually speak about the Church being inculturated. 'Church' refers to those individuals who come into existence as a people through the preaching of the Gospel and who witness to the Gospel. They are the evangelized turned evangelizers. To speak of the Gospel or Good News is to speak of a transforming confrontation with the person of Christ.

Another phrase that has been used in official statements about inculturation is to speak about the 'essence of the Gospel'. According to this usage, the essence of the Gospel is transposed into a new cultural form through inculturation. If, by 'essence', is understood a series of conceptual propositions, this would hardly describe what is essential in the Gospel. It is Christ alone who is ultimately essential. In any case, the Gospel does not exist 'in essence'. As de Gasperis rightly points out, in inculturation we do not move mysteriously from a world of essences into the real world of history and culture.[2]

This is the error of classicism. The gospel is 'caught', rather than 'taught', through the witness of human beings who live its values culturally.

The phrase 'essence of the Gospel' may, on the other hand, refer to its authentic and recognizable character wherever it is observed at work. Love, self-sacrifice, forgiveness, abnegation, spiritual poverty and so on are recognizable Gospel values which have to be practised in a cultural context in order to be observed and assessed. They are necessarily personal or interpersonal values, learned from the example of Jesus Christ. As such, they are secondary to the person of Christ himself with whom the believer experiences a mutual indwelling in faith, hope and love.

The end result of evangelization — the proclamation of the Gospel of Jesus Christ — is to enable the one who is evangelized to recognize the presence of Jesus Christ in his or her own life, both individual and communal. Through evangelization, and thus through an entry into the tradition of faith that goes back to the original, historical experience of the Gospel and the first Christian communities, the one who is evangelized is enabled to have a transforming encounter with the crucified and risen Lord. This encounter is what gives birth to the imaginative and creative act that we call the act of faith.

The person of Christ — the Christ of faith — is apprehended imaginatively. That is to say that conceptions concerning Christ which are clothed in the primary symbols of the Gospel become imaginatively credible to the believer. Since these conceptions radically affect the profoundest level of culture — that of meaning, they initiate a chain-reaction, a kind of cultural 'nuclear fission', which disturbs the patterns of meaning that are already there and creates new patterns out of the symbolic 'particles' old and new.

It can be truthfully said that what is inculturated is Jesus Christ himself. He is the subject-matter of inculturation, the Christian term of the inculturation-equation. It is he who enters into dialogue with human culture. Inculturation is a further and definitive step by which Jesus Christ enters into a living relationship with a cultural tradition. Before evangelization-inculturation this relationship was hidden and, from the human point of view, limited in scope. Afterwards it becomes an explicit relationship and acquires a new and conscious scope in the personal lives of believers. Pope John Paul II has shown a preference for this personal approach to inculturation. He told an African audience in Nairobi in 1980: 'In you, Christ has himself become African.'[3] And the Pope has repeated this sentiment on his pastoral journeys to other countries and continents, adapting it to other audiences and cultures.

This approach brings out the interpersonal and intersubjective character of inculturation. It is an interpersonal encounter with personal and interpersonal consequences. It is a transforming encounter, one that transforms the thought and behaviour of a society. The image of Christ, who is experienced as present in the social life of the believer, stands at the centre of a configuration of Christian images which represent a constellation of meanings. Through evangelization, these images are brought into contact with an existing framework of meaning in the culture being evangelized. The latter thus acquires new or surplus meanings. In this renewed cultural system the image of Christ is dominant.

The possibility of Christian inculturation is proved by actual experience. The normal consequence of successful evangelization is that Christianity becomes 'at home' in the evangelized culture. It becomes 'customary' — part of a people's custom. Meanings and motivations are transformed from a Christianized culture to a culture in course of being Christianized and vice versa. Each undergoes a reinterpretation without losing its identity. As we have stressed in earlier chapters, it is not a wholly conscious process, nor is it the work of individual 'experts' in isolation from their communities. It is very much a community process. The individual theologian, priest or expert must play a prophetical role in the community, with regard to inculturation. In a diocese the bishop, as E. J. Pénoukou remarks, is a privileged instrument of inculturation.[4] He and other church leaders must listen to their people, interpret and refine their understanding of Christ, and help them to be more and more creative in expressing and living their faith.

Through inculturation Jesus Christ adopts new forms and new approaches in carrying out his saving mission to the world, the Gospel acquires a new cultural language and the Church is thereby enriched. Every sector of Christian life is affected. Theology is reformulated. Religious education renders explicit the dialogue between Christ and the local culture. The liturgy gives cultural expression to the people's faith, and local structures of community and ministry are created at the secondary or particular level. The universal, hierarchical structures of the Church are not replaced, but, since they operate in the service of the Christian community, their functions acquire new tasks in the dialogue with culture.[5] These tasks serve to render explicit the presence and the activity of the Holy Spirit in the community, who co-ordinates its creative gifts and guides it in its understanding and its living of the mystery of Christ.

Christ is the Truth, as well as the Way and the Life.[6] This Truth is absolute and universal and these qualities demand inculturation. If this Christ-Truth who possesses us is everywhere and at all times the image of the unseen and unchanging God, he must be susceptible of cultural representation. He cannot impose a cultural uniformity, for this is to invite superficiality and syncretism which is the failure to communicate meaning. Evangelization is not a mere lip-service or verbal code learned by rote. It invites a real response of faith and conviction to the Truth in Christ and this demands inculturation.

Culture and the Christian Patrimony

Inculturation, which is nothing other than the profound evangelization of a people in their culture, comes about, as we have seen, through an initial process of acculturation, the interaction of a culture in dialogue with Christ and a culture not yet in dialogue. This interaction has consequences for both the cultures involved (interculturation), and these include an exchange of cultural elements. This importation of cultural elements should never be so overwhelming as to alienate people from their own original culture. Furthermore, it should not normally result in the emergence of a Christian sub-culture. It is obvious that in the first phase of evangelization alien cultural elements should flow predominantly in one direction, from the culture of the missionaries to that of their followers, but this phase should not be unduly prolonged. As the missionaries become culturally educated, and strive to present the person of Christ and his teaching in terms of the new culture, they should begin to perceive new insights into their Christian faith. Gradually the clumsy translations and approximations of their first efforts will be replaced by new images and new connections of ideas. Some of the imported cultural elements will fall away to be replaced by indigenous ones. When evangelization begins to be placed in the hands of the indigenous Christians themselves, then the process is speeded up, and the whole cultural system should start to be enlivened from within. This is the beginning of inculturation properly so-called, but everything depends on the decision as to which of the imported cultural elements are essential and which are non-essential.

At the end of this book we shall have the final task of trying to assess the present extent and future prospects of inculturation in the Church. Without anticipating that assessment it should be noted here that by and large the Church has become immobilized in the acculturation phase. There are even many Church leaders and members of the faithful who are complacent about the situation. At the present time of writing it is not yet half a century since the official Church abandoned the dream of a world Christian culture. A world culture is an illusion, but a world Christian sub-culture is very far from illusory. The reality of the Roman Catholic Church today may well be that of a universal sub-culture ubiquitously present as a sub-system in the various cultures of humanity. Such a predicament does not seem to square either with the human right to cultural self-determination, or with the demands of effective evangelization. Just what should the cultural contribution of Christianity amount to?

It is not easy to answer this question. Christianity is a historical religion and it must needs have a cultural patrimony of its own. The originating experience of Christianity was culturally conditioned, and from the very beginning of the Church's history the dialogue between the Christ of faith and human cultures began to take place. Inculturation is essentially a historical phenomenon and the Church's history is a history of inculturation. Modern instances of inculturation cannot fail to be affected by previous cultural transformations of the Gospel. As a consequence of this process a cultural patrimony has been built up.

This patrimony contains two important sources. The first source is Jesus Christ himself, and the second is the Church expounding and living his word and example. In the case of Christianity history must be strongly affirmed as the basis and foundation of faith. Christianity is a historical religion with a historical tradition. This means not only that the terrestrial Jesus is the foundation for the Christ of faith, but that, with the events, he and his disciples bequeathed a trajectory of meaning within which subsequent interpretation by the Christian community was to take place and which would be augmented in succeeding generations and cultures.[7] Arising from this point of departure are certain behaviour patterns in the spheres of morality, ritual and organization. Although there may be a discussion among theologians as to their precise irreducibility, Christians are agreed that there are certain irreducible elements in this tradition, elements which are conditioned by biblical and subsequent cultures. The discussion about the sacramental 'matter' of the Eucharist, for example, is one of irreducibility. Bread and wine, as the common food and drink of first-century Palestinians, have cultural connotations. If they are to be replaced in cultures where such forms of food and drink are unknown by less unfamiliar and more available materials, it can be asked how far one can go before symbolism and reality are invalidated and the link with the historical Christ severed. For eight years the bishops of two dioceses in northern Cameroun and Chad allowed millet bread and millet beer to replace unleavened wheat bread and wine from the grape. The experiment came to an end with the publication in 1980 of the Vatican's Instruction *Inaestimabile Donum* (not necessarily a final decision).[8] Whatever the merits of the arguments in favour of such an experiment, exponents of the change would surely admit the necessity of a symbolic link with the rite instituted by Christ. The Eucharist cannot be reduced to the cultural circumstances of an everyday meal.

The word and example of Christ are mediated by the Church. Reflecting upon them and applying them to the realities of succeeding ages, new insights, understandings and surplus meanings have been acquired. These are expressed in faith-statements, in the imagery of spirituality and ritual and in the externals of behaviour and organization. It is in this manner that the doctrine and praxis of the Church develop. All such expressions conform to a given cultural context and must be understood within that context. They possess cultural dimensions. We have said that the history of the Church is a history of inculturation. Intercultural borrowing is therefore a facet of this history. It was inevitable that a certain cultural patrimony should build up in the Church's life, that there should be an accumulation of meanings and images which derive from a variety of cultural sources and which are still useful to us in their original form. Some of them, on the other hand, may have been neglected or suppressed. Others may be in need of reformulation. At all events, at any one moment in the history of the Church there is a currency of such ideas, images and behaviour.

This currency or patrimony, call it what you will, is not to be confused with Sacred Tradition itself. Sacred Tradition concerns the truth about Jesus. It is the testimony to that truth which is preserved in unwritten form and in the inspired writings of Scripture, and which is the subject matter of the dialogue with culture, as we have already seen. This Sacred Tradition makes progress in the Church and there is 'a growth in insight into the realities' that are being passed on.[9] The patrimony we are speaking about concerns the cultural forms taken by such moments of insight. The meaning of authoritative faith-statements cannot be contradicted or whittled down, but it can only be understood in a cultural context and it may need subsequent reformulation in order to be grasped by people of another culture.

The Church's cultural patrimony is a changing and varied phenomenon. Not only does it include culturally conditioned dogmatic formulation, it also comprises forms of devotion, traditions of spirituality, schools of liturgical art and even such trivia as styles of ecclesiastical dress. The priest's biretta vanished with the appearance of the new Roman Missal. The General instruction of 1969 does not list it among the various vestments to be worn, and its passing has not been generally lamented. While priests gladly consigned their birettas to the dustbin, bishops and cardinals clung tenaciously to their more exotically coloured specimens. That a purple biretta still forms part of episcopal choir-dress possibly means that this piece of European sixteenth-century academic headgear is an external symbol of Catholic hierarchy. If such a justification were outweighed by local cultural considerations, the thing should be jettisoned without regret. Analogies could be drawn with other trivia of acculturation such as judges' wigs in former British colonies or academic gowns in universities of the Anglo-Saxon tradition.

Other elements in the Church's cultural patrimony are more important, but not all are irreducible in the sense of providing a necessary symbolic and conceptional link with Christ. In the field of popular piety such things as devotion to the Sacred Heart, the local cult of saints, the Rosary or the Way of the Cross are all marked by historical epochs and cultural contexts. They have been officially recommended by the highest authority, in some cases to the entire Church. But they are ultimately only of use when they become part of a contemporary and living culture. The popularity of the thirteenth-century Franciscan devotion, the Way of the Cross, in tropical Africa today may well be because it is assimilated to African cultural traditions concerning mourning and funeral ritual.

The same can be said of doctrinal formulations, although this aspect of the cultural patrimony is of immediate concern only to the minority of Christians who are professional theologians or catechetical specialists. If an African theologian prefers to build his Christology on the concept of Christ as ancestor or healer, rather than on that of Christ the King, this does not change the truth about Jesus, but it may bring about a further human understanding of that truth.

The history of the Church is accidentally weighted towards the culture of Europe. This means that the Church's patrimony is culturally top-heavy. If the intercultural process is really allowed to get under way in the Church, then there should be a more balanced exchange of cultural elements. We can perhaps already begin to observe some signs of this exchange. It is not only Africa or India that must venerate Our Lady of Lourdes or Our Lady of Czestochowa. Europe and America must begin to take an interest in the exuberance of liturgical dancing or the asceticism of Christian Yoga. Perhaps we shall witness the break-up of the Catholic sub-culture and its replacement by a much more fluid cultural *ensemble*. In such a patrimony, certain cultural elements would be retained. At one end of the spectrum would be elements that are deemed irreducible. At the other end would be found elements that are deemed to be merely useful.

A universal sub-culture is clearly an obstacle to genuine inculturation, because it means that Catholics are somehow distanced from their own cultures. It also means that there is no genuine complementarity among particular churches. The universal sub-culture of the Church is heavily coloured by its Western origins. However, Catholicity demands a real communion of faith, teaching and worship that unites the particular churches of diverse cultures, and this communion has to be visibly structured. In the next section of this chapter we shall consider the cultural implications of universal communion and the demands of ecclesial complementarity.

Culture and Communion in a World Church

Much of what we have called the cultural patrimony of the Church is not essential and should be sloughed off as soon as it outlasts its usefulness. Otherwise, as we have seen, it constitutes a danger to true inculturation. Nevertheless, Catholic unity depends on the existence of a real bond of communion, and this communion takes a visible form which is not unaffected by cultural conditions. It should be noted that here we are going beyond the mere sharing of cultural elements in a common patrimony. We are considering something essential to the life of the Church and its *modus operandi* in the world. We are not speaking about a particular historic phase of evangelization, but about enduring structures that determine the interaction between the various inculturated forms taken by the Christian faith. The discussion therefore enters the realm of ecclesiology.

One of the most important insights of the Second Vatican Council was to locate the primary reality of the Church in the particular church. Speaking of the particular churches, the Council Fathers declared: 'It is in these and formed out of them that the one and unique Catholic Church exists.'[10] The Catholic Church is not a kind of multi-national corporation with local branches or subsidiaries. It is a communion of particular churches. These particular churches are Church in so far as they are open towards, and in communion with, one another. They are the Catholic Church in a particular place. This openness and communion are essential to their ecclesial identity, because, as Leonardo Boff explains, although the whole mystery of salvation is contained in the particular church and it is 'wholly Church', it does not exhaust by itself the whole wealth of the mystery. It is not 'the whole Church'.[11] Within this communion of churches the particular church of Rome and its bishop, the Pope, exercise a ministry of unity. This does not mean that the particular church of Rome should be universalized and a cultural uniformity imposed upon other churches by Rome. But it does mean that the successor of Peter enjoys an effective primacy over all the churches, effective because it is a primacy of jurisdiction, as well as of honour.

The Second Vatican Council has other important ecclesiological insights. One of these is that of co-responsibility among particular churches for the good of the whole Church, a co-responsibility that is exercised chiefly in episcopal conferences and regional associations, but also at the higher and lower levels of the Synod of Bishops and of priests' associations and pastoral councils within the dioceses.[12] There is also the emphasis placed on what are called 'the great socio-cultural regions' and on human groupings in general.[13] Finally, a lesson we draw both from *Lumen Gentium* and from *Gaudium et Spes* is that the Church's mission must not be centred on its own structures, on its own self-implantation in human cultures, but upon the world of which the Church is the sacrament and upon integral human development.

The old ideas of the Church as a 'perfect but unequal society' are no longer dominant in the Council texts. Although it is described as hierarchically structured, it is also called a 'mystery' and a 'communion', the latter being one of Vatican II's key concepts.[14] This opens up the possibility of progress towards a more egalitarian Church, with a greater complementarity of functions and charisms.[15]

Such a type of Church corresponds to the needs of newly emancipated countries in the Third World.

Pride of place among other structures of communion must be given to religious and missionary institutes. These share, not only in the life of the Church, but also in its mission to the world. Religious and missionary institutes are in many ways a microscosm of the Church as a whole, and their interculturality reproduces and reinforces the problems and opportunities of the whole Church.

Not everyone, at one or other level in the Church, has wholeheartedly accepted the new insights of Vatican II. Apart from the few who admit to rejecting the Council *en bloc*, there are those who interpret it selectively and those who would whittle away its new insights.[16] There is also the problem of translating these insights into pastoral practice, and this raises the question of universal norms and, in particular, the 1983 Code of Canon Law. It should be obvious that the pastoral insights of the Council cannot be exhaustively translated into judicial terms, and that, however pastoral in character the new code may be, it is bound to constitute a restriction on the conciliar texts. A clear example is provided by Canon 449 on the erection of episcopal conferences.[17]

There is, however, a much more fundamental objection to the operation of a universal law in the communion of particular churches that constitutes the Catholic Church. This is the objection that Canon Law is culturally Western, that its whole spirit reflects its origins in the ancient culture of Rome and that it is intrinsically incapable of expressing the concerns of non-Western cultures. Although the Second Vatican Council itself was not yet sufficiently open to these concerns, it did encourage the prospect of further research in the matter.[18]

Criticisms from Third World countries soon followed in the wake of the 1983 Code. Setting aside for the present the imposition of a uniform Roman liturgy, a measure that has its roots in the inadequate approach to inculturation of the conciliar constitution on the liturgy (and that will be discussed more fully in Part Four of this book), there has been a general feeling that the Code is not in harmony with non-Western cultures. This is particularly the case with the law governing marriage. Steven Bwana argues that the new Code ignores important African realities like the communitarian character of marriage and the parallelism of Church and customary rites.[19] The Code emphasizes the Western, nuclear concept of the family. Bwana further argues that the Code is irredeemable as it stands, and he takes up an idea of the Symposium of Bishops of Africa and Madagascar that there should be an African Canon Law.[20] This should flow from African theology, just as the new Code emanates from Western theology.

Law has many positive uses, not least among them being the protection of individuals and communities and the guaranteeing of their rights. Although the new Code cannot probably be expected to last as long as the Code of 1917, and any new code is likely to be shortlived, there is probably a need for a general law. However, unless such a law is complemented by particular laws, it is difficult to see how a truly multicultural Church can come into being. Inculturation in the field of liturgy is a comparatively simple prospect, even if it has not been fully implemented, compared to inculturation in such fields as that of marriage, family life or the practice of healing and medicine. A universal Church Law cannot ever hope to do justice to the diverse cultural realities of the entire world.

Canon Law is possibly the most serious instance of cultural bias among the structures of communion in the Universal Church. It is necessarily a juridical expression of uniformity and of Western cultural superiority. However, there are other structures of communion that are affected by cultural bias. One of these is the Vatican Diplomatic Corps, which was criticized by the Bishops of Africa in 1974 as nationalistic and lacking a universal character.[21] Another area that has been criticized is the exercise of the Petrine ministry itself.[22] Where the priorities of the particular church in question are taken into account, the Pope's pastoral journeys may possibly favour inculturation. However, in Third World countries there is always the danger of introducing an unfamiliar agenda from outside. J. B. Metz has written:

> Despite, perhaps because of, the pope's world travels the intentions, inspirations and promises represented by the poor churches of the Third World are being increasingly removed from the agenda of the Universal Church.[23]

In Rome, no doubt, the journeys are seen as a means of strengthening the unity of faith that binds the particular churches, but is it certain that they always have this result? The Pope is greatly esteemed and warmly welcomed as a personal symbol of Catholic unity, but even Pope John Paul II's charisma and extraordinary linguistic versatility cannot do justice to the cultural diversity that he encounters. There is always a danger that, from the point of view of inculturation, papal journeys will be counter-productive.

It can be seen, therefore, that the cultural bias of the Church's structures of communion reinforce the phenomenon of a universal sub-culture and encourage cultural parallelism in the particular churches. When it is recalled that this cultural bias is buttressed by all the resources of a dominant technology and all the forces of the modernization process originating in the West, then it appears as a formidable obstacle to inculturation.

Putting one's finger on the problem is easier than finding a solution,. It is easy to say, for example, that the Church's structures of unity should reflect its cultural diversity, or that its power-centres should be multicultural in their appearance, their methods and their concerns. To translate such an ideal into practice must inevitably take time. It also depends on the will to make a radical break with the old monocultural Church of the past. What signs are there that such a break is feasible or likely? That is a question that we shall attempt to answer in the final part of this book. In the programme of inculturation the Church is confronted by formidable obstacles, and in an ecclesial climate of 'restorationism' or of 'stabilization in a backward direction', pessimism is understandable.[24]

Having opened up the question of the Christian subject-matter of inculturation, it is necessary to go more deeply into its theological implications. Part Two therefore studies its underlying Christology and soteriology, and judges them in the light of the biblical evidence.

References

1 Schillebeeckx 1980, p. 33.

2 de Gasperis 1983, p. 60.

3 John Paul II, Nairobi 1980; cf. *AFER* Vol. 22, No. 4, p. 198.

4 Pénoukou 1984, chap. 3.

5 Boff 1986, p. 24.

6 Jn 14:6.

7 I employ the word 'trajectory': cf Brown 1985 p. 28: ' . . a doctrinal trajectory should be traceable from the NT outlook to later dogma, even if the connection between the two goes beyond pure logic.'

8 de Dinechin and Tabart 1986, pp. 156–8.

9 *Dei Verbum*, 8.

10 *Lumen Gentium*, 23.

11 Boff 1986, p. 18.

12 Cf. *Lumen Gentium*, 23; *Christus Dominus* 5, 38.

13 *Ad Gentes*, 22.

14 Congar 1986, pp. 135–6.

15 Sobrino 1986, p. 38.

16 *Ibid.* p. 39.

17 *Christus Dominus*, 38 left the decision to erect an episcopal conference in the hands of the participating bishops. Canon 449 reserves the decision to the Holy See.

18 *Ad Gentes*, 22.

19 Bwana 1986, pp. 133–140.

20 *Acts of the Fifth Assembly of SECAM*, Accra, 1978, p. 225.

21 'Report on the Church in Africa', 1974, in Hickey 1982, p. 241.

22 Metz 1981, p. 93.

23 *Ibid.*

24 *Ibid.*; and Stacpoole 1986, p. 88.

PART TWO

THE THEOLOGY
OF
INCULTURATION

6

Christology
and inculturation

The subject-matter of inculturation is Jesus Christ himself, that is why we begin the strictly theological part of this book with a perspective on Christology and inculturation and then go on, in Chapter 7, to speak of the salvation brought by Christ and how it affects our understanding of inculturation. After this, we shall go back to look at the data of the Old and New Testaments. Another possibility would have been to go at once to the Bible and trace current theological ideas deductively from the biblical evidence. The more inductive method is preferable for our present purpose, and it has the merit of allowing Part Three, which deals with the history of Christian evangelization, to follow on from the picture of the early Christian communities that we derive from the New Testament.

The Eternal Logos at the Heart of Culture

In Chapter 1 mention was made of the *Epistle to Diognetus* as a curtain-raiser to the Apologists in the latter part of the second century. The most famous of the Apologists, properly so-called, was St Justin Martyr, who died about 165 AD. Justin was a diffuse and rambling writer who was born in Samaria and who had dabbled in Stoic, Pythagorean and Platonic philosophy before becoming converted to Christianity. It is even said that, as a Christian in Rome, he still wore the academic cloak of a teacher of philosophy. Justin's one original contribution to Christian thought was the idea of the 'Spermatic Logos'.

Later in Part Two, in the examination of biblical data, we shall deal with the biblical antecedents of the concept of Logos. It had, however, its counterpart in Greek philosophy, particularly among the Stoics, where it was presented as the creative word or reason of God, the principle of rationality in the Cosmos. Justin taught that the whole Logos took shape in Christ and became man in the Incarnation. Before that definitive event, people of every culture had been able to glean elements of the truth because they possessed 'seeds' of the Logos of Divine Reason. Justin's phrase 'seeds of the Word' has enjoyed a new lease of life in the Church, since the Second Vatican Council used it in connection with the concept of inculturation.[1]

Justin taught that the Spermatic Logos or seed-bearing Word had been implanted in the heart of every human culture, since all things were created through him and with him. Plato had described how the Demiurge split the 'soul-stuff' of the universe and placed the two halves together in the form of a cross or Greek letter *chi*. For Justin this was another indication of the identity of the Logos, 'the power next to the first God, [that] was placed crosswise in the Universe'.[2] In Part Three we shall see how the Apologists ransacked pagan philosophy for 'seeds of the Word'. For the moment we shall remain with Justin and his conception of the Spermatic Logos itself. It will be seen that there was no question of culturalism in Justin, no desire to baptize the whole of pagan philosophy. Christ was the criterion of Truth in its fullness.

> We are taught that Christ is the First-born of God, and we have explained above that he is the Word [reason] of whom all mankind have a share, and those who lived according to reason are Christians, even though they were classed as atheists. For example; among Greeks, Socrates and Heraclitus; among non-Greeks, Abraham, Ananias, Azarias, and Misael, and Elias and many others.[3]

> I confess that I prayed and strove with all my might that I might prove a Christian: not because Plato's teachings are contrary to Christ's, but because they are not in all respects identical with them: as is the case with the doctrines of the others, the Stoics, the poets, and the prose authors. For each, through his share in the divine generative Logos, spoke well, seeing what was akin to it; while those who contradict them on the more important matters clearly have not obtained the hidden wisdom and the irrefutable knowledge. Thus, whatever has been spoken aright by any men belongs to us Christians; for we worship and love, next to God, the Logos which is from the unbegotten and ineffable God; since it was on our behalf that he has been made

man, that becoming partaker of our sufferings, he may also bring us healing. For all those writers were able, through the seed of the Logos implanted in them, to see reality darkly. For it is one thing to have the seed of a thing and to imitate it up to one's capacity; far different is the thing itself, shared and imitated in virtue of its own grace.[4]

Justin tended to see himself as a philosopher and to concentrate on the rational truth of Christianity. Nevertheless, his conception of the implanted, seed-bearing Logos is profoundly theological. The Logos is God's agent in creation, existing also in disseminated form. Its seeds in human thought enable non-Christians to 'see reality darkly'. Divine Truth is already implanted in their traditions, but it is not yet fully known.

Justin's conception of the Logos was eagerly remembered by mid-twentieth-century theologians, confronted after sixteen centuries by the reality of cultural pluralism. It offered a convenient image of the relationship between non-Christians and Christianity, an optimistic image that envisaged a positive outcome from the dynamic encounter between faiths. Seeds betoken growth, development, creative evolution. The historical interaction of religious traditions as lived realities is the basis of on-going revelation and of growth in the Truth.[5]

Observing the world-seeding Logos at work and identifying the 'seeds of the Word' is not an easy task. Justin, in particular, was adept at unearthing superficial similarities between paganism and Christianity. As we have seen in Chapter 3, every religious system has a symbolic matrix. Charles Davis has further suggested that there is a 'centre' of this symbolic structure.[6] Divine Truth inhabits this centre and reaches out to the fullness of Truth in the incarnate Word proclaimed by Christians. The Word does not become fully known through a process of purely verbal dialogue. The seeds grow to maturity through the experience of intercultural penetration and ultimately of inculturation. Although the process of inculturation can be stimulated by theologians and by experts in other fields of Christian life, the seeds of the Word can only be clearly identified *post factum*. Most theologians who consciously undertake an 'inculturated' theology are articulating the patterns of thought and behaviour of the community they represent.

Although inculturation is one of the theological catchwords of Third World countries, and particularly of Africa, and although most African theologians are actually engaged in a conscious process of inculturation, very few have elaborated a theology of inculturation itself. This is surprising in view of the current emphasis on Christology among African theologians. One exception is Efoé-Julien Pénoukou of Benin, who postulates a strong link between Christology and inculturation, a link inspired by St Justin's conception of the seed-bearing Logos.[7]

For Pénoukou, inculturation is the only serious problem of the African Church. It is not a compromise with paganism, as some devout, culturally alienated Catholics wrongly suppose. Still less is it a form of 'theological *apartheid*', Pénoukou's colourful term for culturalism. Racism is the refusal to love others in their difference, and that is not Christianity. Universal love must recognize, and reckon with, cultural differences. A lived faith demands inculturation and the acknowledgement of other people's right to an inculturated faith. Pénoukou sees inculturation as a direct consequence of the great commandment:

> You must love the Lord your God with all your heart, with all your soul, and with all your mind . . . You must love your neighbour as yourself.[8]

The Christ who took human flesh is the Word in whom all has been created. This means that he is at the heart of all human cultures, that he is responsible for whatever is true and good in them and that he makes them vehicles of salvation. Christ is already present in non-Christian religious traditions before the Gospel is explicitly proclaimed. The Incarnation of Christ is merely a further and final step in Christ's solidarity with human culture. Although, therefore, Pénoukou clearly indentifies inculturation as a question of faith in Christ, the Christ who was born, who died and was raised to life for us, the foundation for the dialogue between Gospel and culture is rooted in created human nature itself.

It follows that the non-Christian cultures of Africa are not irrelevant to Christianity. They are not outmoded by the Incarnation or by the proclamation of the good News about Christ. The cultures must be opened to the Gospel and the Gospel must be opened to African cultures. The incarnate Christ gives them a fuller meaning through his birth, life, death and resurrection as a human being and a member of a human culture. Africa remains African, not in spite of, but because of, being evangelized. However darkly or obscurely, the dialogue between the eternal Logos of God and human cultures has been going on since the creation of the world.

In spite of Pénoukou's stress on the pre-existent Logos, he gives full weight to the conversion that must follow upon the proclamation of the Gospel. Human cultural traditions must be converted to Christ. They are not an absolute, but God-in-Christ is. The reason that cultural facts must be interrogated in the light of God's call of love and of Christ's cross is precisely because the implicit dialogue of Logos and culture is continued explicitly after the Incarnation. It is one and the same process, intensified by the Christ-event, the Word becoming flesh. The Logos was always challenging human cultural traditions. After the Incarnation the challenge became a definitive and crucial challenge. It was now clearer than ever before that God does not side with death or with evil in any cultural tradition. The Christ-event issues a clarion-call to culture to be true to itself and to evolve creatively towards the *pleroma*.

Pénoukou admits that there must always be room for discussion about the actual content of the core of the Christian message, because inculturation is concerned with a concrete and actual way of life. There are three questions that must be asked: How are we to discern what is Christian or not Christian in African tradition? Is a European conception of the world necessary as a motive or model for Africa? How, as Christians, do we promote traditional African values? These are all questions which this book is attempting to answer in one form or another. The particular interest to us of this theologian is the way in which St Justin's concept of the Spermatic Logos has been revived and applied to the evangelization process in Africa and to the prospect of a Christian rehabilitation of African culture.

The Logic of the Incarnation

If current theology has revived the conception of a world-seeding Logos, and has thereby pushed the dialogue between Word and culture back to the creation itself, it has also used the economy of the Incarnation as a model for inculturation. In the previous example, we saw how the incarnation was fitted into a model centred on the pre-existent Logos. In the theology of the Second Vatican Council we also find the Incarnation taken as a starting-point for an understanding of inculturation.[9] This was, in fact, one of the Council's most creative insights. In the conciliar documents the incarnation model coexists not only with the idea of 'seeds of the Word', but also with a concept of 'adaptation' which does not rise above the level of acculturation or even of an idea of the Church as a monolithic cultural hybrid. We shall examine the Council documents in detail in Part Four. For the moment it may be noted that the incarnation model played an important role in the development of the notion of inculturation and in the — at least theoretical — rejection of adaptation. The words of the Bishops of Africa and Madagascar at the 1974 Synod will be remembered in this connection:

> The Bishops of Africa and Madagascar consider as being completely out of date the so-called theology of adaptation. Instead they adopt the theology of incarnation.[10]

The way in which the analogy of the Incarnation was first used suggests that it served what is called a 'Christology from above'. The purpose of inculturation was compared to the Son of God taking human flesh and adopting a human culture as a necessary concomitant of his human nature. In other words, the model was one of Christ's own enculturation, his cultural education as a first-century Jew from Galilee. There are several positive values in such a comparison. In the first place, as we have already seen, the subject-matter of inculturation is Jesus himself, the Christ to whom the Gospels testify. Through his dialogue with culture, Jesus is inculturated in successive traditions. As Pope John Paul II put it, Christ in his members is (for example) 'himself African'. He accepts human cultures and expresses himself through them. He lives their way of life.

In the second place, the analogy indicates Christ's need of cultures in order to spread his Good News of the Kingdom and to share his life with humanity. There could have been no earthly ministry for Jesus if he had not adopted the cultural concepts, symbols and behaviour of his hearers. His cultural solidarity with the Palestinian communities of his day was a necessary condition for communication with them. The same is true of the Church in every age and place. Inculturation is a necessity for the continuation of Christ's mission.

Thirdly, the cultural education of the earthly Jesus, his adoption of a specific human culture, inserted him into the whole historical process of communication between cultures. This is evident from the New Testament itself, as we shall see in Chapter 9. In any case, as we have noted already, cultures do not stand alone. They interact as a matter of course. By adopting a given cultural identity, Jesus accepted the ways in which that culture influenced, and was influenced by, other cultures. His own personal attitude towards other cultures in general, and towards the minority Samaritan sub-culture and the culturally dominant Romans in particular, will be discussed later. Enough to say here that Jesus accepted the intercultural process as a consequence of his own enculturation, and that this should be a sufficient precedent for the Church that continues his mission.

The Incarnation possesses a logic of its own. Once the mystery of the Word made flesh is grasped, the implications are seemingly endless. Every cultural reality is graced and transformed. A new value is set on everything that is true and good in human traditions. The celebration of the Incarnation in Third World countries tends, in my experience, to have overtones of inculturation — to be, in fact, a feast of inculturation. The Maasai pastoralists of Kenya and Tanzania tell the story of how they found their first prophet-leader or Laibon. Formerly they were leaderless. Then one day some of their warriors found a strange child alone in the bush. They asked him what he wanted and he replied that he wished to be adopted into one of the Maasai clans. The warriors took the child back to their camp and one of them adopted him. The child began to prophesy and to work miracles and in the course of time became the first leader of the Maasai. This charming story is reproduced in other forms by different East African peoples, and it may yield a clue to the African understanding of Christmas. In Christ, Africa has adopted a mysterious, divinely-sent child and made him a member of the family. As a result, miracles of grace occur and a new leader is found.

In spite of its stimulating character, the analogy of the Incarnation has serious inadequacies if it is limited to the human enculturation of Jesus, and these inadequacies may account for the fact that incarnation terminology has been largely superseded by the more sociological vocabulary of inculturation. Ugly and unromantic though the word sounds, 'inculturation', rather then 'incarnation', is now the term preferred by theologians.

In the first place, if the concept of Incarnation is limited to the cultural education of the earthly Jesus, when the analogy is applied to the evangelization process the impression is created that this is equated with the first insertion of the Gospel into a culture. The understanding of inculturation as an on-going dialogue between Gospel and culture is more or less overlooked. This is a serious defect which can only be overcome if the notion of Incarnation is enlarged to include the whole Christian mystery, the life, death and resurrection of Jesus Christ, and their consequences for humanity. In fairness to some theologians, it must be noted that the word 'incarnation' is sometimes used as shorthand for the whole mystery of Christ which the Incarnation inaugurated.

Secondly, and in spite of what has been said above about the intercultural implications of the Incarnation, the analogy encourages in practice a one-way view of inculturation. This is because it is a Christology 'from above'. The model is essentially that of the Eternal Logos, a pre-existent divine being, taking human flesh. It is, of course, impossible for the human mind to comprehend what such a pre-existent being is like, since we encounter the Son of God already enfleshed, as it were. One is immediately tempted by the analogy to think of inculturation in terms of a disembodied essence being injected into a concrete human culture. As we have been at pains to point out in previous chapters, there is no world of essences. The Christian message — Christ himself — is transmitted from culture to culture, from history to history. To use an electrical image, it is the spark that passes through the contact made when the acculturation switch is thrown. To that extent, therefore, Christ's own enculturation was a unique and unrepeatable event. Today, in the process of inculturation, there is no virginal conception, no coming down 'to earth from heaven'. Once inaugurated, the Incarnation continues upon earth to recruit culture after culture through the ordinary processes of history and human communication.

In the third place, the incarnation-model may encourage people to succumb to the temptation of culturalism. In concentrating upon the enculturation of Jesus, upon how he accepted and identified with a specific culture, we may forget to ask how he himself challenged the culture of his adoption. We are so absorbed by the notion of the Son of God learning a human way of life, that we overlook the fact that he clashed with that human tradition and that he proposed a radical revision of the way his contemporaries understood it. It is not enough to look for concordance between Christ and culture. His challenge as a 'stranger' must also be considered.

All of these defects in the incarnation-model are remedied when a more inclusive approach is taken to the mystery of the Word made flesh. This is, in fact, the main theological criticism that has to be made of the analogy between Incarnation and inculturation. One cannot use only one aspect of the Christ-event to illuminate the dialogue between Gospel and culture. The whole mystery of Christ, passion, death and resurrection, has to be applied analogically to the process of inculturation. It is only when this is done that a Christological understanding of inculturation becomes possible. The emphasis must be shifted from Incarnation to Paschal Mystery. This is what will be attempted in the next section of this chapter.

The Challenge of the Paschal Mystery

A clearer and more accurate picture of the inculturation process emerges when the Paschal Mystery is used as the analogy, rather than the Incarnation alone. The Paschal Mystery is inseparable from the Incarnation, as its goal and purpose. The Incarnation took place so that humanity could be saved and come to the knowledge of the Truth.[11] The work of human salvation was accomplished principally through the Paschal Mystery, the redeeming death of Christ and his resurrection-ascension to glory as Lord. Jesus died, as all human beings are obliged to die, but his resurrection gave him an entirely new form of existence. The disciples experienced the Risen Christ as radically different and yet infinitely familiar and close to them in faith.

The Resurrection enabled Christ to transcend the physical limitations of an earthly life bounded by time, space and, of course, culture. The intercultural contacts of the earthly Jesus were necessarily limited. After the Resurrection, Christ belonged to every culture at once. The Resurrection made it possible for him to identify explicitly with the cultures of every time and place, through the proclamation of the Gospel to every nation. The Resurrection made possible the release of the Spirit to people of every culture, and this was effectively symbolized by what happened at Pentecost, when people of diverse languages heard and understood the one language of faith. The Paschal Mystery, then, is intimately linked to the inculturation process itself. It is precisely because of the Resurrection that we can become members of Christ and that Christ, in his members, can become African, Indian, American and so on.

Apart from the causal link between the Paschal Mystery and inculturation there is the further question of the use of the Paschal Mystery as an analogy for inculturation. Christ died and rose again. Can it be said that a culture dies and rises again when it is confronted by the Risen Christ? The proclamation of the Gospel, of the Risen Christ as Lord of the universe, is necessarily a challenge to a human tradition. We have already noted that cultures are not always faithful to their best and truest insights. The Gospel invites people to reappraise their cultures in the light of radically new values — values that turn human thinking upside-down. Cultures are to be evangelized and to undergo *metanoia* or conversion at their profoundest level. They must 'die' to all that is not worthy of humanity in their traditions, all that is a consequence of accumulated guilt and social sin. If human structures can be vitiated by sin, then human cultures can be similarly vitiated. Cultures can be sinful and destructive. They can be 'cultures of death', rather than of life.[12]

It is clear, then, that cultures are called upon by Christ to 'die' to everything that is opposed to the ultimate good of humanity. They are to be purified and made to submit to the test of the Cross, for the Cross, as Newman reminds us, places a new value on every action, every event, every word or thought.[13] It is only in the light of the 'doctrine of the cross' that the real worth of human culture can be seen. Faced by the challenge of the One who died and rose again, cultures are called upon to die in order to rise to a greater splendour.

The Risen Christ was experienced by his followers as a radically new reality, a new creation, yet the apparition stories constantly stress continuity with the earthly Jesus, his corporeality, his wounds, his characteristic 'breaking of bread'. He is the same Jesus radically transformed. The disciples are even able to bear physical separation from him with joy and to recognize his continued presence in their communities through the Spirit. Finally, they are encouraged to transcend the limits of their own communities and cultures and to announce the *kerygma* of the Risen Christ as Lord.

Pursuing the Paschal Mystery analogy, the culture that engages in constructive dialogue with Christ is also radically transformed. Through the Holy Spirit the Risen Christ is perceived as personally present in the socio-cultural sphere. The universal message of the Risen Christ accentuates the shared element in human experience and facilitates exchange between cultures. Obedience to the *kerygma* is an invitation to a culture to transcend its own limits.

On the other hand, there is a real continuity with the pre-Christian culture. After evangelization a culture is identifiably the same culture that it always was. If anything, it should be more recognizable, more authentic. Its positive values and insights become clearer and more attractive, as a result of an access of meaning. The Paschal Mystery, therefore, appears to be a more satisfactory analogy for inculturation from every point of view. It takes care of continuity and renewal and also, to some extent, of aspects of interculturality.

However, the analogous use of the Paschal Mystery in this way must not encourage a static view of inculturation. The Risen Christ 'now lives no more to die'. In himself, the conflict has been resolved and his glory is unchanging and eternal. This is not the case for the evangelized culture. After the proclamation and explicit acceptance of Christ as Lord, the struggle to be faithful to this revelation continues. A culture that has been once Christianized may still be lost to the Church, and history is full of sad examples. The death and resurrection of a culture under the influence of the Spirit of Christ cannot be definitive until the end of history. The dialogue between culture and the Risen Christ is an on-going process. Even where a culture is continuously faithful to the mind of Christ, it can only achieve this through constant renewal. This is because culture itself, as we have already indicated in earlier chapters, is not a static phenomenon. It undergoes continual development and change, as it acts and reacts in the communication which takes place between cultures. The risen Christ adopts a multiplicity of cultural identities when members of these cultures become his members through faith and Baptism. This is the cultural extension of the Risen Christ through time and space, but it is contingent upon the co-operation of these members. It stands or falls by their faith and loyalty. It depends, for its greater historical and geographical extension, on the creative efforts of Christians to transcend the limits of privatized religion and to bring their conviction and their commitment to bear upon their social and cultural life. Finally, it depends upon the continuance of the mission and the bringing of the *kerygma* of the Risen Christ from culture to culture and from history to history.

So far in this chapter we have considered the idea of St Justin that the world-seeding Logos, from the moment of creation, planted in the various human traditions germs of a Truth that would be fully revealed at the Incarnation. We have also considered inculturation from the standpoint of the Incarnation itself: the fact that Christ, because of the Incarnation, submits to a learning process in every culture, taking over the riches of that tradition and further ennobling them. What can be said of the Paschal Mystery in relation to the positive values that are already present in cultures before the proclamation of the *kerygma*?

In answering this question we are helped by a remarkable passage from the Second Vatican Council's Pastoral Constitution on the Church in the Modern World. The Council Fathers were speaking of our vocation to be partners in the Paschal Mystery and they had this to say:

THE THEOLOGY OF INCULTURATION

The Christian is certainly bound both by need and by duty to struggle with evil through many afflictions and to suffer death; but as one who has been made a partner in the paschal mystery, and as one who has been configured to the death of Christ, he will go forward, strengthened by hope, to the resurrection.

All this holds true not for Christians only but also for all men of good will in whose hearts grace is active invisibly. For since Christ died for all, and since all men are in fact called to one and the same destiny, which is divine, we must hold that the Holy Spirit offers to all the possibility of being made partners, in a way known to God, in the paschal mystery.[14]

We are thus confronted by the Council's conviction that even those who have not explicitly accepted Christ are partners in the Paschal Mystery, called to die and to rise again, and this, presumably, at the cultural, as well as the individual, level. The next chapter will be devoted to the whole question of salvation, but it needs to be said here that God does not save people in opposition to their culture. Culture is a part of them and it is therefore through culture, not in spite of it, that they are saved. This means that the Risen Christ is already active in non-Christian cultures, albeit in a hidden way.

This raises the question of how this comes about. J. B. Metz has voiced the objection that such a view dispenses non-Christians from being a part of Christian salvation history and ecclesial praxis.[15] They are somehow exempted from the historical memory of Christ, and Metz cogently asks how non-Christians can be affected by the Paschal Mystery as a historical event before the event took place or before they became aware of its relevance. Karl Rahner's reply to this criticism was to visualize the effective memory of the Paschal Mystery as working forwards, as well as backwards.[16] This memory is already active among non-Christians as an *a priori* possibility of historical experience. Such anticipations of the Paschal Mystery presumably take a historical form and are part of an unfolding historical praxis or revelation. As such, they are part of the 'prehistory' of the Risen Christ.

This perspective raises the further question of the providentiality of such historical anticipations in relation to the growth and development of the Church. Such non-Christian anticipations of Christ may be limited and implicit, but they are paradoxically Christian, in so far as they conform to the truth about Christ, and in so far as the power of the Risen Christ operates salvifically through them. They are not, therefore, to be rejected when the process of evangelization takes place. On the contrary, they are to be diligently sought out as important 'allies' of the Risen Christ in his dialogue with their culture. Furthermore, they are likely to bring new insights and applications to bear upon the Christian message and to promote a growth and a progress in the Christian understanding of the word.

In this chapter we have examined inculturation Christologically, from the standpoints of the Creation, the Incarnation and the Paschal Mystery. All of these approaches have their advantages and their drawbacks, and it is not enough to concentrate upon one to the exclusion of the others. Nor should it be thought that these different theological entries into the problem are contradictory or mutually exclusive in themselves. This is not the case, since they are, of their nature, partial approaches to the same problem, that of the dialogue of Christ with diverse cultures. As such, they are complementary, rather than contradictory.

The reality of inculturation raises the further question of how far the non-Christian cultures of the world are salvific as well as bearers of Christian revelation. Just as, in Chapter 2, we charted the Church's evolving understanding of culture as a plural phenomenon, so now in Chapter 7 we must trace the steps by which the Church developed its present theology of salvation. As we shall see, an important leap forward was made at the Second Vatican Council, at the very moment when the reality of culture as a plural phenomenon was recognized.

References

1 *Ad Gentes*, 11, 22.

2 Justin cited by Pelikan 1985, p. 42.

3 Justin, *Apologia* I, 44, tr. Bettenson 1956, p. 83.

4 Justin, *Apologia* II, 13, tr. Bettenson 1956, pp. 87–8.

5 Cf. Shorter 1983, p. 238.

6 Davis 1970, p. 103.

7 Pénoukou 1984.

8 Mt 22:37, 39.

9 *Ad Gentes*, 22.

10 *AFER*, Vol. 17, No. 1, 1975, p. 58.

11 1 Tim 2:4.

12 John Paul II's Address to the Jubilee of Youth, 1984, *L'Osservatore Romano* (Engl.) 17.

13 Newman 1868, Vol. 6, pp. 84–5.

14 *Gaudium et Spes*, 22.

15 Metz 1980, p. 158ff.

16 Rahner 1981, pp. 47–9.

7

Inculturation
and salvation

The Necessity of Baptism

In 1542 St Francis Xavier visited the coast of what is now Kenya and
spent several weeks at Malindi. While he was staying there a Muslim
sheikh asked to see him. Their conversation dwelt upon the neglect
of religion in Malindi. The sheikh complained to St Francis that, out
of seventeen mosques in the town, only five were in actual use, and
he asked the saint's opinion as to the reason. The saint replied
uncompromisingly that God finds no pleasure in infidels and hates
their prayers. In the opinion of St Francis the mosques were deserted
because God wanted Muslim prayers to cease, since he is not served
by them.[1]

We revere St Francis Xavier as a missionary of unparalleled zeal,
yet his intolerance comes as a shock to us. This is because we have
seen an extraordinary development in the theology of salvation in
our own lifetime — in the last twenty-five years to be exact. St
Francis Xavier was merely echoing the sentiments of St Augustine's
disciple St Fulgentius of Ruspe, who had lived one thousand years
earlier:

> There is no doubt that not only all heathens, but also all Jews
> and all heretics and schismatics who die outside the Church will
> go into that everlasting fire which was prepared for the devil and
> his angels.[2]

Doubtless St Fulgentius would have included Muslims in his list of
damned souls, had Islam existed at the time. A prayer attributed to
St Francis Xavier begins:

> O eternal God, creator of all things, remember that the souls of
> the heathen are the work of thy hands . . . behold, O Lord, how
> hell is being daily filled with them.[3]

This prayer became the model for others, such as the prayer to Our Lady of Africa, composed by Cardinal Lavigerie in the nineteenth century, which spoke of the 'Muslims and other infidels of Africa' who 'fall daily into hell'. Thus, for virtually the whole of the Church's history this intolerant view of other religions was held by Christians.

Now, in our own time, there has been a dramatic change of attitude. The late Karl Rahner considered this change to be of fundamental importance, and he linked it with an altogether new approach on the part of the Church towards other religious and cultural traditions.

> Doctrinally, the Church did two things [at the Second Vatican Council] which are of fundamental importance for a world-wide missionary effort. In the Declaration on the Relation of the Church to Non-Christian Religions (*Nostra Aetate*), a truly positive evaluation of the great world religions is initiated for the first time in the doctrinal history of the Church. Furthermore . . . the documents on the Church (*Lumen Gentium*), on the Missions (*Ad Gentes*) and on the Church in the Modern World (*Gaudium et Spes*), proclaim a universal and salvific will of God which is limited by the evil decision of the human conscience and nothing else. This implies the possibility of a properly salvific revelation-faith even beyond the Christian revelatory word.[4]

Let us trace some of the steps in this revolution in the Church's thinking about other faiths. Doctrinal changes do not just fall from the sky. They are the outcome of a long process of maturation as the Church reflects on the deeper implications of the tradition of Faith. In this case, thinking centred on baptism and membership of the Church. As we shall see, doctrinal developments were stimulated by the intercultural process.

The starting-point of this discussion was the universal salvific will of God, and the knowledge of, and commitment to, the means of salvation that God desires. There was no doubt in the minds of the members of the first Christian communities that when the truth about Jesus Christ was made known, it demanded assent and commitment. To refuse was to invite condemnation:

> No one who believes in him will be judged; but whoever does not believe is judged already, because that person does not believe in the name of God's only Son.[5]

90

Whoever believes and is baptized will be saved; whoever does not believe will be condemned.[6]

These texts occur in contexts which concern the proclamation of the Good News, and they make it clear, at the very least, that condemnation is the lot of those who resist the known truth about Jesus Christ. However, they assume the prior proclamation of that truth. The question remains: What is the lot of those to whom the Gospel is not proclaimed? This question is rendered even more acute by the insistence on Jesus Christ as the unique means of salvation. One example of this insistence is provided by the speech of Peter and John before the Sanhedrin:

Only in him is there salvation; for of all the names in the world given to men, this is the only one by which we can be saved.[7]

Another example, the oft-quoted passage from the Pastoral Epistles, places the unique mediation of salvation by Christ in the context of God's universal salvific will:

He [God, our Saviour] wants everyone to be saved and reach full knowledge of the truth. For there is only one God, and there is only one mediator between God and humanity, himself a human being, Christ Jesus, who offered himself as a ransom for all.[8]

Full knowledge of the truth is more than a merely cognitive knowledge. It implies an experiential, or lived understanding of the truth, in other words, a commitment of faith.

How does one achieve salvation through Christ? The answer that has always been given is: by being baptized into the community of the Church. Baptism is the foundation sacrament of faith. By it, the believer enters into the community of faith and becomes a member of the Body of Christ. Peter compared salvation through Baptism with the saving of 'eight souls' in Noah's ark:

Christ himself died once and for all for sins, the upright for the sake of the guilty, to lead us to God. In the body he was put to death, in the spirit he was raised to life, and, in the spirit, he went to preach to the spirits in prison. They refused to believe long ago, while God patiently waited to receive them, in Noah's time when the ark was being built. In it only a few, that is eight souls, were saved through water. It is the baptism corresponding to this water which saves you now — not the washing off of physical dirt but the pledge of a good conscience given to God through the resurrection of Jesus Christ, who has entered heaven and is at God's right hand, with angels, ruling forces and powers subject to him.[9]

The image of the Church as ark was taken up by numerous Fathers, notably Ignatius of Antioch, Irenaeus and Clement of Alexandria, who taught that a person could only be saved by Baptism and membership of the Church. It was Origen who gave the formula its negative form: *extra ecclesiam nulla salus*, 'outside the Church there is no salvation', and the Jansenists who made the formula even more intransigent. Their proposition: *extra ecclesiam nulla conceditur gratia*, 'outside the Church there is no grace', was condemned by Pope Alexander VII. Finally, in 1949 Pope Pius XII declared against Leonard Feeney's opinion that explicit membership of the Church was necessary for salvation, and the stage was set for more positive statements about the possibility of salvation outside the visible Church by the Fathers of the Second Vatican Council.

As long as the world known to Christianity was restricted to the countries surrounding the Mediterranean, the sea that, according to the ancient geographers, was at the centre of the earth, it was more or less reasonable to expect the fairly rapid evangelization of all the world's inhabitants. Moreover, the claim that the *kerygma* had been everywhere effectively proclaimed appeared fairly credible, and precluded any discussion about the possibility of invincible ignorance on the part of the unbaptized.

The discovery of the Americas and the East Indies, and the voyages of Portuguese and other explorers from the end of the fifteenth century onwards, suddenly multiplied the ranks of the unevangelized. As time went on, and more and more unexplored areas of the globe were revealed, the imminent conversion of the entire population of the world became less and less credible. As explorers, traders and missionaries came to know the peoples and cultures of these new worlds, and found that many of them appeared to be morally good, the doctrine that the unbaptized were damned became less and less tenable. There were further awkward theological questions to be confronted concerning the efficacity, in these circumstances, of God's universal salvific will, and the fate of the untold numbers of unbaptized individuals who had died before encountering a Christian missionary. Origen's formula was ripe for reinterpretation.

The principal way out of the dilemma was through the notion of Baptism by desire, or Baptism *in voto*, as opposed to Baptism *in re*.

This distinction was taught by Bellarmine and Suarez and was adopted by the Council of Trent itself. At the beginning it was applied to those who ardently desired Baptism but who had died without receiving the sacrament. Later it was applied to other categories of the unbaptized, including those whose ignorance of Christ was invincible. Pius IX refused to lay down the limits of such ignorance in the case of the unbaptized and even in the case of the baptized who had separated themselves from the visible, Catholic Church.[10] This could only mean that the salvific activity of Christ was not limited by the visible frontiers of the Church, and that it was a question of 'no salvation without Christ', rather than of 'no salvation outside the Church'.

Minimum Explicit Faith and Implicit Faith

By the end of the nineteenth century, Catholics were beginning to believe that salvation was possible outside the visible Church. Discussion among theologians then began to be centred on the means of such salvation. Salvation, it was argued, depended on supernatural love, and supernatural love depended on supernatural or revealed faith. Some theologians demanded a minimum repertoire of such faith, which included such items as belief in God the Creator of all things and Rewarder of good and evil, as well as faith in Christ as Revealer and Saviour. Such a requirement was based on a dualism of natural and supernatural, which, while it may be useful in theory, is not verifiable in concrete reality, since nature is already graced. There is no such thing as *natura pura*, because nature is entirely ordained to supernatural salvation. The requirement was, of course, unrealistic from a missiological point of view as well, since it begged the question of invincible ignorance among the unbaptized. It was no solution at all to the problem of how the vast majority of the human race are saved.

The Suarezian solution which posited a purely natural life for the unbaptized, a life destined towards a goal of purely natural happiness, was open to the same objections of dualism already mentioned. It also undermined the efficacity of God's universal, salvific will, since it settled for something considerably less than a universal call by God to share in his divine life.

If Christ is the one and only mediator of salvation, and if it is through faith in him that human beings are saved, it follows that, when they are ignorant of this fact, their faith can be nothing else than implicit. This is the clear idea conveyed by the relevant passages in the documents of the Second Vatican Council:

> Those who through no fault of their own, do not know the Gospel of Christ, but who nevertheless seek God with a sincere heart, and moved by grace try in their actions to do his will as they know it through the dictates of their conscience — those too may achieve eternal salvation. Nor shall Divine Providence deny the assistance necessary for salvation to those who, without fault of theirs, have not yet arrived at an explicit knowledge of God, and who, not without grace, strive to lead a good life.[11]

> . . . in ways known to himself God can lead those who, through no fault of their own, are ignorant of the Gospel to that faith without which it is impossible to please him . . .[12]

> Since Christ died for all, and since all men are in fact called to one and the same destiny, which is divine, we must hold that the Holy Spirit offers to all the possibility of being made partners, in a way known to God, in the paschal mystery.[13]

Various modern theologians have explored the connotations of implicit faith. In general, they reverse the order of a supernatural love that follows and depends on supernatural faith. On the contrary, the virtue and habit of faith are born of love. God speaks an inner word of love which, according to Lonergan, becomes an 'outer word'.[14] Faith is to be compared to the judgements of value and the commitments of a person in love. The gift of God's love reveals to us who he is and what he asks of us. All the purely cognitive aspects of faith are the 'questions of a lover', seeking a more complete knowledge of the loved one.[15]

This is a very different point of view, both from the early Fathers of the Church whom we cited above and from conservative, Evangelical Christians today. The latter distinguish between a knowledge of God that saves and a knowledge of God that is incapable of saving. This is based, in turn, upon a further distinction between the revelation of God's holiness and power, on the one hand, and the revelation of his love for sinners on the other. John Stott, in a commentary on the Lausanne Covenant of 1974, states:

> What, then, about those ignorant of the Gospel? Are we to say that they are ignorant of God altogether, including those who

adhere to non-Christian religions? No. 'We recognize that all men have some knowledge of God.' This universal (though partial) knowledge is due to his self-revelation, what theologians call 'his general revelation' because it is made to all men, or his 'natural' revelation because it is made 'in nature', both externally in the universe and internally in the human conscience. Such knowledge of God is not saving knowledge, however. 'We deny that this can save', partly because it is a revelation of God's power, deity and holiness but not of his love for sinners or of his plan of salvation, and partly because men do not live up to the knowledge they have. On the contrary, they 'suppress the truth by their unrighteousness', and the rejection of the truth which they know leads to idolatry, immorality and to the judgement of God. So, far from saving them, their knowledge actually condemns them. And they are without excuse. Therefore, it is false to suppose that sinners can be saved through other systems, or that 'Christ speaks equally through all religions and ideologies'. We firmly repudiate 'every kind of syncretism and dialogue' which suggests this as derogatory to Christ and the Gospel. For these are unique, and non-Christian religions know nothing of them.[16]

This opinion is open to the objection of dualism between nature and grace, already mentioned. Not only does it assume the unrighteousness of those ignorant of the Gospel, but it attributes their condemnation in part to God's failure to reveal his saving love to them. Such a division in God's self-revelation is derogatory to God, at variance with Catholic tradition, and in contradiction to God's universal, salvific will.

St Thomas Aquinas taught that it was impossible for venial sin to be present in anyone with original sin and without mortal sin. If, before the age of reason, a child cannot commit a mortal sin, then equally he cannot commit a deliberate venial sin. If, on attaining the use of reason, he directs himself to his due end, he will by means of grace receive remission of original sin, and this is an implicit act of supernatural love.[17]

Taking this opinion of St Thomas Aquinas as his starting point, Piet Fransen has popularized the notion of the 'fundamental option for God', which can be expressed in any form of authentic conversion of heart, and this is an implicit act of love for God.[18] Every human being is confronted by two mutually exclusive forms of love which St

Augustine of Hippo characterized as *amor sui usque ad contemptum Dei*, 'the love of self that leads to the contempt of God', and *amor Dei usque ad contemptum sui*, 'the love of God that leads to the contempt of self'. There is no other option that a human being can make, and salvation is thus available to all who do not freely make self-love the goal of their whole existence.

The concept of the fundamental option of love is now a commonplace of contemporary Catholic theology. However, it raises several further questions which are relevant to the process of inculturation. One question concerns the relationship of salvation through implicit faith to the explicit faith in Christ that is found in the Church. Another asks how an implicitly Christian faith is expressed culturally. In other words, how it relates to a non-Christian religion which is necessarily a cultural system. Finally, the question of the relationship of non-Christian faiths to the visible Church must be considered. This is especially important for evangelization, for it supposes that inculturation includes a process of inter-faith dialogue and that this dialogue is probably at the very heart of inculturation, if, as we argued in Chapter 3, religion constitutes the core of human culture.

The Church and Other Religious Cultural Systems

The late Karl Rahner developed a well-known thesis in which he called unbaptized people who were nevertheless at rights with God 'Christians' in an anonymous sense.[19] According to this thesis, Christianity is the one absolute and universal religion to which all members of the human race are called. However, until the Christian Gospel actually enters a historical situation and thence into the consciousness of the individual, the latter can adhere lawfully to a non-Christian religion, fulfilling the obligation to worship God socially and culturally. The lawfulness of this religious or cultural system depends on whether it offers its adepts positive means towards a right relationship with God or not. This it can do, despite errors and deficiencies in the system.

According to Rahner, human beings live, as a matter of fact, in a supernatural order of grace. They enjoy an openness to God and to his self-revelation which is gratuitously bestowed by God. Rahner calls this general self-communication of God through human experience 'transcendental revelation'. The human being's radical capacity to respond to God's self-gift he calls the 'supernatural existential', a permanent modification of the human spirit which orientates it towards God.[20]

Although these unbaptized people are recipients of a Christic revelation and salvation, they are unconscious of Christ. However, their religious systems contain many supernatural or grace-filled elements. Those who profess them, even though they are not in contact with the history and tradition of Jesus Christ, still receive the Spirit and the effect of Christ's mystery in their lives and consciousness. There is thus no other revelation or salvation outside of Christ, and it is the duty of the missionary in the process of evangelization to bring the 'anonymous Christian' to explicit consciousness of the 'latent Christ' in his own religious system.

In the previous chapter we discussed the theological problem of how the Paschal Mystery as a historical event can influence those who are not explicitly related to that history. The important idea to retain is that all histories meet in Christ and have a future in him. It follows that the 'grace-filled elements' which Karl Rahner discerns in non-Christian religions are not simply ignored in the evangelization process. They are important components of the new cultural form adopted by the Christian faith after evangelization, and they may also offer insights to the Universal Church in the exchange which takes place between the particular churches. Although Rahner leaves the identification of the 'grace-filled elements' (which we may also call 'seeds of the Word') to the historians of religion, it is abundantly clear that the individual non-Christian is saved with and through his own religious cultural system, and not apart from it, or in spite of it.[21] We may also deduce from Rahner's thesis that elements of the religious cultural system of the non-Christian have a future within explicit Christianity, and that there are cognitive aspects of what — from a Christian point of view — is an implicit faith which may already parallel the affirmations of Christianity before the Risen Christ is explicitly proclaimed.

Piet Fransen has also carried his concept of the fundamental option of love further, and has considered its social and cultural implications. The non-Christian does not make his fundamental life-option in a vacuum. It has to be expressed in a socio-cultural form, and this further implies a dialogue by the individual with the existing religious cultural system.

While Rahner approached the problem from the side of God's self-manifestation and saw 'transcendental revelation' becoming explicit in cultural and historical categories, Fransen approaches the question from the point of view of the individual believer. According to him, the latter gives expression to his fundamental life-option through a personal creed. This personal creed is nothing other than the appropriation by the individual believer of a collective creed emanating from his own cultural tradition. His own cultural system provides him with the categories and symbols in which to express his orientation and commitment. There is, if you like, a dialogue between the individual and a religious cultural system.[22]

The late Bernard Lonergan developed his ideas in a similar way. Taking Friedrich Heiler's seven common features of the so-called world religions, he demonstrates that they are implicit in a fundamental and unrestricted option of love. The seven features are: that there is a transcendent reality; that he is immanent in human hearts; that he is supreme beauty, truth, righteousness, goodness; that he is love, mercy, compassion; that the way to him is repentance, self-denial, prayer; that the way is love of one's neighbour, even of one's enemies; that the way is love of God, so that bliss is conceived as knowledge of God, union with him, or dissolution into him.[23]

Lonergan then goes on to show how the fundamental love-option relates to common cultural factors and finds expression through them.

> For however personal and intimate is religious experience, still it is not solitary. The same gift can be given to many, and the many can recognize in one another a common orientation in their living and feeling, in their criteria and their goals. From a common communion with God, there springs a religious community.
>
> Community invites expression, and the expression may vary. It may be imperative, commanding the love of God above all things and the love of one's neighbour as oneself. It may be narrative, the story of the community's origins and development. It may be ascetic and mystical, teaching the way to total other-worldly love and warning against pitfalls on the journey. It may be theoretical, teaching the wisdom, the goodness, the power of God, and manifesting his intentions and his purposes. It may be a compound of all four, or of any two or three of these. The compound may fuse the components into a single balanced synthesis, or it may take some one as basic and use it to interpret and manifest the others. It may remain unchanged for ages, and it may periodically develop and adapt to different social and cultural conditions.[24]

At this point Lonergan shows how a religious tradition becomes historical and how it provides basic components for the personal development of its adepts, as well as for on-going social organization and the elaboration of cultural meanings and values. He then turns to the theological question of God's personal entrance into human history and the belief in salvation-revelation as a historical initiative from God. It is this type of belief which Davis ascribes to the 'prophetical' religions in a greater or lesser degree. It is, of course, the central characteristic of Judaism and Christianity, and it means that faith is essentially a response to a divine initiative. Such a belief enables Christians to elaborate a theology of universal salvation, but it places salvation firmly in a historical perspective, and it demands that inter-faith dialogue as a historical phenomenon be given due importance in this theology.

Pietro Rossano, in his capacity as Secretary of the Vatican Secretariat for Non-Christian Religions, addressed himself many times to this problem.[25] For him, the diversity among religions is due to differences of history and culture, since the human response to God's initiative is historically and culturally conditioned.

> If it is true, historically speaking, that the variety of religions depends on the particular genius and character of each people, their history and existential situation, it may also be asserted, theologically speaking, that each religion represents the traditional manner of response of a given people to the gift and enlightenment of God. It is a response given within a particular frame of culture and language, which often makes the relation and communication of religions among themselves extremely difficult.[26]

Rossano sees the duty of evangelization as twofold: proclamation and dialogue. Our first duty as evangelists is to proclaim Christ. Our second duty consists in a long and thorough hermeneutical effort to enter into the 'horizon of meaning' of other religious traditions, and this for two reasons: firstly, in order to point out the significance of the Christian message for the adepts of these religions, and secondly, in order to acquire a fuller understanding of the very message proclaimed by the Church.

It can be seen, therefore, that inter-faith dialogue is part and parcel of inculturation and/or interculturation. By inviting people to believe in the Good News of Jesus Christ that we proclaim, we are not intending to detach them from their culture or from the truths contained in the religion to which they adhered before and which are expressed in terms of their own culture. Moreover, by inviting them to believe in the Gospel we are also asking them to contribute to Christianity from the riches of their own religious and cultural traditions. In other words, evangelization and conversion presuppose the continuance of an inter-faith dialogue as part of the inculturation process.

This is the basis of the Church's new and profound respect for other religions which Karl Rahner believed to be doctrinally so important. It is well summed up by the Fathers of Vatican II:

> The Catholic Church rejects nothing of what is true and holy in these religions. She has a high regard for their manner of life and conduct, the precepts and doctrines which, although differing in many ways from her own teaching, nevertheless often reflect a ray of that truth which enlightens all men. Yet she proclaims and is in duty bound to proclaim without fail, Christ who is the way, the truth and the life (Jn 14:6). In him, in whom God reconciled all things to himself (2 Cor 5:18–19), men find the fullness of their religious life.
>
> The Church therefore urges her sons to enter with prudence and charity into discussion and collaboration with members of other religions. Let Christians, while witnessing to their own faith and way of life, acknowledge, preserve and encourage the spiritual and moral truths found among non-Christians, also their social life and culture.[27]

Bishop Rossano notes that no general theory emerges from the documents of the Second Vatican Council as to how this dialogue is to be carried out.[28] Islam and Judaism are mentioned specifically in two of the Council's documents, while Buddhism and Hinduism are mentioned by name in one place.[29] The Fathers of the Council seem to assume that the actual diversity of religions in the world imposes a variety of approaches. Dialogue takes different shapes and forms because the human responses to God's self-manifestation and to the Gospel proclamation are varied and culturally conditioned. The interlocutors also differ. In many of the so-called world religions there are religious *virtuosi* — monks, teachers, scholars and holy men or women. In the smaller-scale ethnic religions, such as those of Africa and Oceania, for example, it is much harder to find representative spokesmen for non-Christian religions. Often the dialogue takes place in the minds and consciences of Christian or Muslim converts. This is particularly the case in Africa. An advantage of such 'internal' dialogue is that it is truly experiential and not a purely notional process. A disadvantage is that there is a danger of imbalance. The individual is tempted to incline to one side or the other — to cultural alienation, on the one hand, or to culturalism, on the other.

There are also numerous obstacles to inter-faith dialogue in the modern world. The confrontation between religious faiths at the present time imposes either a negative or a positive stance, or else an attitude of *laissez-faire*, the attitudes that Peter Berger has dubbed 'deduction', 'indication' and 'reduction'.[30] The positive stance envisages a dialogue that is faithful to the traditions of the interlocutors. The negative stance consists in hostile reaction and/or incapsulation.

Many negative examples come to mind, most of them due to the temptation of fundamentalism which affects Islam, Buddhism and other religions besides Christianity. It is a vast oversimplification which allows the followers of a particular religion or sect to 'write off' the rest of the world from a religious point of view and even actively to oppose outsiders as a threat to religious and cultural purity. But the negative stance takes other, more subtle forms as well. The Hindu, for example, belongs to a diffuse and pluralistic religion, and may be tempted to absorb other faiths on his own terms, forcing them against their will into his own syncretic mould. Even more insidious may be the results of an uncritical attitude on the part of African Christians towards their pre-Christian traditions. African traditional religions were eminently permeable, welcoming conceptions and images from many sources and bestowing on them their own characteristic interpretations. An uncritical approach to African religious tradition on the part of the African Christian may result in an undeclared absorption of Christianity by a non-Christian tradition — a form of religious culturalism with a vengeance.

Inter-faith dialogue is not a simple process, but, complex though it may be, it is a necessary concomitant of a multicultural Church. It means living optimistically and constructively with religious pluralism, and it means applying the Christian world-vision of salvation to a historical process that cannot be avoided, but which must be hopefully embraced.

In this chapter we have traced the history of a doctrinal *volte face* where the salvation of the unbaptized is concerned. At first sight, it looks as if there is nothing in common between the teaching of St Fulgentius of Ruspe or St Francis Xavier, on the one hand, and that of the Second Vatican Council or of Karl Rahner, on the other. Yet,

101

different though these attitudes undoubtedly are, they all stem from the struggle to understand the workings of God's salvific will and to reconcile this understanding with contemporary knowledge of the world, its religions and its cultural systems. The revolution in salvation theology, to which the Second Vatican Council gave expression, has coincided with the empirical approach to human cultures and to the expansion of the Catholic Church throughout the world. It has therefore given added point to the 'inculturation explosion', the Church's simultaneous grappling with a multiplicity of human traditions. And we have seen what is the particular, soteriological contribution to the theology of inculturation.

All of this has prepared us for a cultural and a universalist reading of the Bible. The contemporary experience of religious and cultural pluralism stimulates Christians to reread the Bible and to try to discern the divine plan in human history. The Bible is far from being as ethnocentric or intolerant as may be supposed. When it meets with forms of pure religion it welcomes them and takes them up.[31] A re-examination of the Old Testament in the light of the contemporary experience of inculturation shows us how humanity was providentially prepared to receive a universal Saviour and how the ground was made ready for a people of God, composed of many nations and cultures. Above all, it convinces us of the essentially intercultural character of God's self-revelation.

References

1 Schurhammer 1977, Vol. 2, pp. 111–112.

2 *De Fide ad Petrum*, 38, 79; quoted in Küng 1967, p. 32.

3 Quoted in Ball 1986, p. 54.

4 Rahner 1980, p. 327.

5 Jn 3:18.

6 Mk 16:16.

7 Ac 4:11, 12.

8 1 Tim 2:4–6.

9 1 Pe 3:18–22.

10 Cf. Küng 1967. pp. 32–3.

11 *Lumen Gentium*, 16.

12 *Ad Genies*, 7.

13 *Gaudium et Spes*, 22.

14 Lonergan 1973, p. 119.

15 *Ibid.*, p. 116.

16 Stott 1975, p. 15.

17 *Summa Theologiae*, Ia IIae, 89, 6 in c.

18 Fransen 1967, pp. 67–122.

19 Rahner 1976; Rahner 1981.

20 Rahner 1978, pp. 138ff.

21 Fransen 1967.

22 *Ibid.*, pp. 92ff.

23 Cf. Lonergan 1973, pp. 109–110.

24 *Ibid.*, p. 118.

25 Rossano 1978; Rossano 1980. These are two examples (in English) among many.

26 Rossano 1980, p. 23.

27 *Nostra Aetate*, 2.

28 *Lumen Gentium*, 16; *Nostra Aetate*, 3.

29 *Nostra Aetate*, 2.

30 Berger 1980, *passim*.

31 Cf. Rossano 1980, pp. 26–7.

8

Inculturation in
the Old Testament

God's Acculturation

We reread the Bible today with many new interests that emanate
from our contemporary situations and contemporary philosophies.
Thus there are structuralist and psycho-analytical readings of the
Bible, feminist and ecological readings and even a Marxist reading of
the Bible. Scholars and theologians today are interested in a cultural
reading of the Bible, a reading that reflects the reality of cultural
pluralism and which also emphasizes universal perspectives. This is
understandable as our Church becomes more truly a multicultural
and a world Church.

The purpose of this and the following chapter, therefore, is to take
note of the intercultural process as discerned by Bible scholars in the
world of the Bible and to discover how far God's plan of salvation was
accomplished through this interaction of cultures. These chapters
have two further purposes: to look for scriptural evidence for the
currents of contemporary theology which concern inculturation
— the Christological and soteriological perspectives just outlined in
the two preceding chapters — and also to offer a ground-base for the
history of the Church's approach to cultures in Part Three of this
book.

'The Book of the Consolation of Israel' in Isaiah contains the
following words in its conclusion:

> Seek out Yahweh while he is still to be found,
> call to him while he is still near.
> Let the wicked abandon his way
> and the evil one his thoughts.
> Let him turn back to Yahweh who will take pity on him,

to our God, for he is rich in forgiveness;
for my thoughts are not your thoughts
and your ways are not my ways,
declares Yahweh.
For the heavens are as high above earth
as my ways are above your ways
my thoughts above your thoughts.
For, as the rain and snow come down from the sky
and do not return before having watered the earth,
fertilizing it and making it germinate
to provide seed for the sower and food to eat,
so it is with the word that goes from my mouth:
it will not return to me unfulfilled
or before having carried out my good pleasure
and having achieved what it was sent to do.[1]

Donald Senior and Carroll Stuhmueller see in this text an expression of what they call God's 'acculturation'.[2] It is an analogous use of the term, but it contains an idea that is fundamental to an understanding of salvation history. Creation is in need of salvation and this is a progressive process throughout human history. The good values of human cultures have been deformed by sin, by weakness and prejudice, but God takes the initiative to purify and redirect them. This is God's 'acculturation'. It is a plan that exists from all eternity, but it is not known until, like rain, it has penetrated the earth and caused new forms of life to spring up. God's Word is pictured as a powerful, regenerating force, a messenger that necessarily accomplishes what he is sent out to do.

Let us note, in passing, that we already have here an Old Testament antecedent of the world-seeding Logos, the concept that underlies the Christological approach to inculturation. We shall look more closely at this antecendent later in the chapter.

Senior and Stuhmueller's analogous use of the word 'acculturation' may appear confusing. They are not referring exactly to either of the sociological and theological categories defined in Chapter 1 as acculturation and inculturation. Rather, they are speaking about God's self-revelation within the culture of Israel at any one moment of its history, as Israelites reflected on the meaning of historical events. It is a concept that is very close to inculturation, but it prescinds from the reality of the intercultural process, without, however, excluding acculturation in the sociological sense. It is God's voice speaking within the history of a culture.

105

God's 'acculturation' is an on-going dialogue between biblical faith and the culture of Israel, this faith having been arrived at independently through reflection on Israel's history and its encounter with other cultures (acculturation in our sociological sense), without the need for a first insertion of that faith from a previous, non-Israelite cultural form. The concept differs, therefore, from the insertion of biblical faith into, say, the culture of Canaan and its subsequent dialogue with that culture (inculturation in our theological sense). It is, if you like, an 'auto-inculturation'.

Although the Old Testament data are presented here under different headings, we are dealing with interrelated ideas and facts which cannot be clearly separated out. Moreover, as we have said, the idea of God's 'acculturation' is basic, since it is the process of God's revelation-salvation in human history, God inserting his thoughts and his ways into the culture of Israel.

It is a common opinion that the Bible is culturally ethnocentric because its dominant theme is that of God's action towards a particular people, the Jews. Although the Jews were not free from the temptations of ethnocentrism, particularly in later Old Testament times, such a generalization is, in fact, very far from the truth. Jewish culture was but one component in a historical process of interaction between many cultures. The 'fertile crescent' of the Middle East was a veritable crossroads of cultures from the earliest times. The Jewish people and their traditions were, humanly speaking, the product of this remarkably varied cultural interaction, and were themselves contributors to the on-going intercultural process.

Ugarit was a northern Phoenician town, situated now in modern Syria, and it seems to have been an extraordinary melting-pot of foreign cultural influences. Its archives, consisting of more than 4,000 clay tablets, were brought to light between the years 1929 and 1973, and they constitute a remarkably varied documentation. There are myths, legends, psalms, lists of offerings, letters, bills and treaties, for example. Although the local language of Ugarit was ancient Canaanite, its documents are written in no fewer than eight languages. The records to which we are referring belong to the last of three Late Bronze Age strata and date from between the second to the last quarter of the second millennium BC. There are as many as 250 names of gods in the texts, from many different religious traditions. Among them we find the 'Supreme God', Baal-Hadad, and the god of the sea, Yam, the monster driven out by Baal-Hadad.[3] These are names and themes which reappear in the books of the Old Testament. Ugarit already provides us with clues for understanding the extent to which Israel carried out a dialogue with the culture of Canaan.

Some five hundred and seventy years before the period represented by the Ugarit texts, Abraham would have entered Canaan from Mesopotamia. More than four hundred years before the beginning of the Ugarit series, the Patriarchs were in Egypt. Undoubtedly, these ancestors of the Jews were a part of the cultural ebb and flow which characterized the region. The stories that were handed down about them were often the common patrimony of several ancient cultures. As Beauchamp has expressed it, there was a 'listening to each other's stories', and these narratives had a way of crossing over a whole set of Near Eastern cultures. Sometimes, a narrative even outlasted its culture of origin. At other times, it played an important role in the foundation of a cultural tradition.[4]

Rossano notes that the priestly code already recognized a plurality of covenants, distinguishing, for example, between the covenant of Moses and the covenant of Noah, a covenant that embraced all the peoples of the earth.[5] This universalist strain pervades the earliest biblical traditions, and especially the Yahwist interpretation of them, and is an eloquent testimony to the fact that the history of salvation relates to a diversity of cultures and to an interaction between them. It also suggests the truth noticed earlier in this book, that God calls each culture to cross its own frontiers. Speaking of biblical attitudes towards the non-Jewish religions, Rossano writes:

> The Bible only appears to be hostile towards the religions when they represent a threat to the (Mosaic) covenant, or assume forms of a cosmic and vitalistic monism, or draw men to the worship of idols and thus substitute the creature for the Creator. When it meets with forms of pure religion or with forms that are reconcilable with faith in the God of the Covenant, it welcomes them and takes them up: it is enough to refer to the cases of Melchisedek, of Jethro, of Job, non-Jewish religious personalities, who were nevertheless recognized and praised for their faith.[6]

The book of Genesis is not comprehensible without reference to the ancient creation myths and epic legends of Mesopotamia. Equally, the laws of the covenant are to be placed in the tradition of the Mesopotamian codes, particularly that of Hammurabi, c. 1700 BC, and the structure of the prophetic oracles of Israel bears a strong resemblance to that of the oracles discovered at Mari, a centre destroyed by the same Hammurabi.[7]

The book of Genesis also bears witness, in the story of Joseph and his brethen, to influences from ancient Egypt. These influences persisted in the tradition of Israel. A celebrated example is that of Psalm 104, which bears strong resemblances to the hymn of Akhenaton, the 'heretic' pharoah who worshipped the sun-disc Aton. Akhenaton's hymn dates from about 1350 BC, a century or so before the Exodus. The similarities between the Egyptian hymn and the Jewish psalm are strong enough to suggest a direct borrowing. Nevertheless, there are also important differences which show that a dialogue has taken place with original Jewish ideas. One of these is the emphasis on rain as God's gift, and another is the fact that Yahweh is equally at work during the night as well as during the day, whereas the sun-disc Aton is completely absent during the night in the Egyptian original.[8]

Such examples illustrate the conviction that God revealed, and still reveals, himself through the dynamic of acculturation. Throughout the whole Bible story, the cultural fortunes of God's people wax and wane. At one time, they are subject to a particular, alien cultural influence, at another time, they are subject to another. Mesopotamian, Egyptian, Canaanite, Persian, and Hellenistic forms succeed one another. God's relationship with his people is influenced in each epoch by the prevailing cultural form or milieu. Israel's response, too, is similarly conditioned by the successive cultural influences. Whether it responds positively or negatively to the covenant, it does so in harmony with the religious psychology of the contemporary cultural framework.[9]

God's own challenge from within Israel's culture, which Senior and Stuhmueller call God's 'acculturation', takes on a cyclical pattern. In the first phase Israel experiences God's 'violent intrusion', his upsetting of established ideas and relationships. Then follows a period of indigenization, during which God's 'violence' is tamed, as it were, and the people experience stability, success and a feeling of control over their own destiny. Indigenization proves to be all too human and to stand in need again of redemption. Thus the cycle of divine 'acculturation' repeats itself, and the dialogue between faith and culture within Israel itself is continued.[10]

The Canaanite Inculturation

Between the Exodus and the Exile, Israel had to contend with the various forms of Canaanite culture encountered in the promised land. It was a culture of varied origins, as we saw in the previous section. By and large Israel reinterpreted this culture in the light of its own experience of revelation-salvation. This was the Canaanite inculturation, perhaps the most outstanding instance of inculturation in the Old Testament.

Israel's understanding of life after death differs little from the opinions reflected in the archives of Ugarit. However, unlike the people of Ugarit who practised a cult of the dead, Israel strongly opposed such rites.[11] Nevertheless, Canaanite mourning ceremonies continued in Israel without attracting a prophetic condemnation. The Canaanite theme of the struggle between the Creator-God and the sea-monster reappears again and again in the Psalms and in Isaiah,[12] while Ezekiel seems to have made use of a Canaanite myth in his satirical poem against the King of Tyre.[13]

The Psalms generally borrow themes, style and rhythm from Canaanite hymns. Psalm 29 is a striking example. It celebrates the royalty of God who reveals himself in his powerful voice of thunder. The whole of the earth, the hills and the plains, tremble with terror at the sound of this voice, because it announces the coming of God himself. However, the sound is ultimately a sign of salvation for God's people, a sign of their strength which brings peace. Seven times in the course of the psalm the phrase 'Yahweh's voice' occurs:

> Yahweh's voice over the waters, the God of glory thunders;
> Yahweh over countless waters,
> Yahweh's voice in power, Yahweh's voice in splendour;
> Yahweh's voice shatters cedars,
> Yahweh shatters cedars of Lebanon,
> he makes Lebanon skip like a calf,
> Sirion like a young wild ox.
> Yahweh's voice carves out lightning-shafts,
> Yahweh's voice convulses the desert,
> Yahweh convulses the desert of Kadesh,
> Yahweh's voice convulses terebinths,
> strips forests bare.[14]

Although this psalm has authentic Israelite features which, among other things, ensure that Yahweh is presented as the King 'enthroned forever', its structure is too artistic for it not to have been patterned on an earlier Canaanite hymn which strongly resembles it. This hymn was discovered among the Ugarit texts and was composed in honour of Baal-Hadad, god of the tempest. 'Baal makes his voice resound . . . his voice resounds and the earth trembles . . . the hills and the earth leap. Baal's enemies hide in the forests.'[15]

Perhaps the most extensive inculturation took place in the field of worship. The architecture of the Temple itself strongly resembles the temples of Syro-Phoenicia, especially that of Tell Tainat in Syria. We should remember, too, that Solomon obtained Phoenician artists from Hiram of Tyre in order to embellish the Temple in Jerusalem. The decorations, palm trees and cherubim; the utensils, such as the bronze serpent attributed to Moses; the sacrificial animals and even the various types of sacrifice themselves; all these things have almost exact parallels in the religious culture of Canaan.[16]

Then there are the various feasts in the Israelite calendar. These were originally 'nature feasts' or agrarian rituals which were reinterpreted by Israel as celebrations of salvation wrought by Yahweh. In spite of inculturation, they never entirely lost their original meaning. Among such rituals was the Feast of Unleavened Bread which celebrated the holiness of the grain, as it came from God's hand. This feast was later subordinated to the memorial of the Exodus and became the Passover. Another nature ritual was the harvest festival of the First Fruits, which became the Feast of Weeks that recalled the enjoyment of the land of promise. There was also the Feast of Ingathering when the harvest was completed. This became the Feast of Booths or Tabernacles, a commemoration of the way the Israelites had dwelt in such shelters during their journey from Egypt. Other feasts, and even the Sabbath itself, also derived from Canaanite traditions.[17]

Hosea is the best example among the prophets of the Canaanite inculturation. It appears that, in his time, people did not distinguish very clearly between the religion of Baal and the Yahwistic religion. In his polemic Hosea tried to wean the people from the rituals of Baal and the agrarian emphasis of the Canaanite religion, and to bring them back to the God of the Exodus. Through a sacred marriage, which Hosea presents as the heavenly counterpart of sacred prostitution in the religion of Canaan, Yahweh is presented as a God who is personally concerned with the fortunes of his people in all the vicissitudes of their history. Hosea unites opposite sets of symbols from Israel and from Canaan, challenging them both and enriching them in the process. Senior and Stuhmueller see Hosea's prophecies as an exact model of the missionary's work of inculturation, an adaptation of, and a polemic against, the indigenous culture.

> Hosea so challenged Canaanite culture that its finest perceptions are salvaged and purified, and then they are given a new life within the Mosaic, covenantal tradition. The sensuous laxity of the Canaanite was fiercely counteracted by Israel's remembrance of the Sinai desert and its strong, homespun morality. At the same time Canaanite culture had its own impact upon the covenantal theology by enabling Israel to speak of God's love in terms of marital union and its mystical depths.[18]

The Canaanite inculturation gave the Yahwistic faith better expression, and helped a nomadic, clan-structured people to adapt to an agrarian economy and to become a nation.

The Tension Between Israel's Election and Universal Mission

Israel was a chosen people, but other nations have also been conscious of a divine election at various times and in various places. Among the Near Eastern nations of biblical times both Egypt and Mesopotamia felt called for a special role, and saw the riches and the power that they enjoyed as proof of divine election. Israel's was the choice of a helpless people in the midst of powerful nations. Moreover, Yahweh had rescued his people from the bondage of Egypt by a mighty demonstration of power that owed nothing to their riches or military strength. Israel was first of all 'a stranger' in patriarchal times. Then the people were in bondage in Egypt. After their entry into the land of promise, they were repeatedly punished by God through the instrumentality of foreign nations. Eventually they were exiled, and when the captivity was over, Jerusalem became a virtual ghetto, while the rest of Jewry was scattered throughout the Mediterranean world. If Israel was conscious of a divine election, it was an election in poverty, in suffering and in destitution.

However, a people is not chosen merely for the sake of being chosen. There is a purpose implied in the choice, a vocation or a call to carry out God's plan and to further the salvation of the world.

Israel's consciousness of divine election was in tension with this world mission, and the history of Israel is a history of this tension — of the problem of uniting the election of one people with the salvation of all peoples.

At first the scenario of world salvation was visualized in terms of subjection to Israel. There was a crude ethnocentrism which saw Israel as the centre of the universe and all the nations of the earth as its slaves, flocking to Jerusalem with riches and tribute. The restoration of Israel was to be a new golden age, comparable with that of King Solomon. Later, a more religious, and a more universal, view is taken of Israel's role as 'light of the nations'. Moreover, God's gift of salvation and his covenant are not solely or primarily for Israel.

> He said, 'It is not enough for you to be my servant.
> > to restore the tribes of Jacob and bring back the survivors of Israel;
> I shall make you a light to the nations
> > so that my salvation may reach the remotest parts of earth'.[19]

At length, this election which began in suffering and destitution is extended to the whole world through the suffering 'servant of Yahweh'. However, the tension was still present at the end of the Old Testament period when Israel was challenged by the Hellenistic culture, and cultural purists could still hope for a political and cultural restoration, which savoured of ethnocentrism.

Israel, as we have seen, was not the only nation that was conscious of a divine election. It was also not the only nation which reflected the universality of God's plan. There have been many religious and cultural traditions in world history with a universal dimension. What was unique in the case of Israel, writes Beauchamp, was the combination of election and universal mission.[20] Israel's election was a constant call to a universality that remained unfulfilled in the Old Testament. It was a continual challenge that the chosen people failed to take up fully. In fact, Israel was continually tempted to resist the obligations of universality and often the sins of the chosen people were caused by a too exclusive understanding of their election.

Israel's experience of God's revelation-salvation was undoubtedly unique. The historical experience of every people is unique and unrepeatable, and Israel's religion was historical. God's interventions were apprehended in and through historical events, and even the world of nature was subordinated to history. This unique character of Israel's historical experience did not, in theory, undermine the universality of its mission. Strangers from other cultures were invited to share Israel's story, to enter into Israel's history, as it were. True universality is the universalizing of the particular, rather than the particularizing of the universal. It is the sharing of what is unique. That, in essence, is what intercultural communication is all about — the process according to which the unique is shared. Once again, we are affirming that God reveals himself through the interaction of cultures, but, just as God, in the Incarnation, identified with an original cultural situation, so in Christ's 'pre-history', the Old Testament, God also identified with a particular culture. The basic theme of Chapter 9 will be that Jesus spoke from one cultural situation to all others. So, throughout the centuries of Old Testament history, God spoke through the cultural situation of the ancient Jews to peoples of other cultures.

Israel was not taken out of the intercultural process as a result of its election. There are, as we have seen, many elections and many covenants, and the intercultural process is nothing other than the interaction of peoples, each of which has its own vocation or divinely bestowed purpose. Israel's election was to be, in a particular way, a paradigm for all elections, just as the life, death and resurrection of Jesus became a paradigm for all his subsequent 'incarnations'.

Israel did not only teach other cultures in a positive fashion. They were also expected to learn from Israel's faults and infidelities. Even the ethnocentric tendency, which has already been mentioned, had a didactic value. Cultures can be stagnant or complacent. They can solve their problems through violence and warfare, through incapsulation or through domination. God used the culture of Israel for both praise and blame. Whether the Israelites co-operated or not, whether they were faithful or not, he could still use Israel as his chosen instrument for the instruction and salvation of others. However, Israel was chosen for a constructive dialogue with God's Word, for an inculturation of that Word, in fact. As we have seen, when speaking of God's 'acculturation', Israel was obliged to come to terms again and again with its faith in Yahweh and to let that faith reinterpret its contemporary culture.

Israel's election was a pointer to the universal element that is to be found in all cultures, to the core of religious truth at the heart of every human tradition. God's self-revelation to Israel was therefore an interrogation of all cultures. This fact is especially evident in what

Rossano calls the sapiential or Wisdom economy,[21] of which the most important and long-lasting instance was the encounter between Israel and Hellenism.

The Cultural Implications of the Wisdom Economy

The sapiential or Wisdom economy refers to the common element discerned by the biblical writers in cultures. It is the supposition that all cultures are ethically linked, and that God speaks to all of humanity irrespective of cultural particularities. Rossano describes it thus:

> By 'sapiential' economy I refer to the action of God through Wisdom which is described in the great collection of the so-called Wisdom literature, but also in the first chapters of Genesis and in parts of Deuteronomy, of the prophets and of the New Testament writings . . . (the) link between Wisdom and the ethical-religious life of mankind.[22]

Wisdom is with God and proceeds from him. It is present throughout the whole of creation and rejoices to dwell among people of every culture. Wisdom is given to every human being as an internal illumination, and passes into holy souls, making them 'God's friends and prophets'.[23] Wisdom is the source of right conduct and of salvation, teaching the fear of God and justice towards others. Wisdom is life and gives an assurance of immortality, being incarnated in a special way in the Torah of Israel.

Wisdom is ultimately God's own self-revelation, and as such is personified as a kind of female companion of God. One gets the impression from the Wisdom literature that Wisdom is a personified divine attribute with an independent personal existence. However, Wisdom is clearly a creature of God, created with the world itself, but it is no mere principle of rationality in the cosmos. Rather it is the fact that God makes creation bear witness to himself for those who have faith.

In the New Testament John draws a parallel between the Wisdom of God who invites all to her table and Jesus who sates the hunger and quenches the thirst of those who come to him.[24] Paul speaks openly of 'Christ Jesus, who for us was made wisdom from God'.[25] John seems to have drawn upon Semitic sources for his use of the term Logos as a name for Christ as a pre-existing divine being.

Scholars today are more doubtful about the possibility of a Hellenistic philosophical source for the Johannine term. They are considering more favourably a link with the use of the term *memra* in the Targums, designating God's command or creative word. This term is used especially in contexts where there is question of God's relationship with the world. The creative *memra* shines like a light in the darkness that is spread over the face of the abyss.[26]

The sapiential literature of the Old Testament and the Targums thus provided the Semitic background for the Johannine Logos. Philo of Alexandria, who lived from 20 BC to AD 54, seems to have made the first link between the Jewish sapiential tradition and the Logos of Greek philosophy. However, his concept is not that of John. His Logos occupies an intermediary position between God and creatures and is not divine in the strict sense of the term. It can be seen, however, that the stage was clearly set for St Justin, in the second century, to marry the sapiential and Greek philosophical traditions in his conception of the Spermatic Logos.

The sapiential literature of the Old Testament draws upon many non-Jewish cultural sources, Egyptian, Mesopotamian, Assyrian and Greek. The latter is represented principally by the Book of Wisdom, which Maurice Gilbert proposes as a good example of inculturation in the Old Testament.[27] The author of the Book of Wisdom wrote primarily for his fellow Jews who had adopted the language and culture of the Greeks. In Alexandria, Jews were strongly attracted by Hellenistic philosophy, science and mystery cults. The author hoped to safeguard their orthodoxy through his writing.

The Book of Wisdom is a Jewish work of the first century BC that has been transmitted to posterity by Christianity. Its literary form and structure, however, are entirely Greek and have no obvious affinity with Old Testament literary forms. It is, in fact, a Greek eulogy or encomium, or to be precise, an exordium followed by a eulogy. Its discourse is borrowed from Hellenism, but its originality lies in its Jewish ideas and purpose. The book has a religious character and dwells on the events of the Exodus, contrasting Jews with Egyptians and attacking the pagan animal-worship and pantheism. It is a meditation on the religion of the Jewish people. However, not a single biblical person is named in the work, and it is not only the language, style and vocabulary that is Greek. There are many allusions to Hellenistic culture, thought and values. The fruits of wisdom are typically the Greek virtues of self-control, prudence, justice and courage.[28] However, the author's fundamental commitment is to Israel, and we find that Greek categories are often transformed by his biblical faith. A good example is his reinterpretation of the Hellenistic concept of immortality, as a gift of God which the just already possess in this life. The book is, as Gilbert claims, a successful example of inculturation, the dialogue between Jewish faith and Greek culture. As such, it helped to steer the Jewish community in Alexandria away from the dangers of syncretism.

The Jewish Encounter with Hellenism

In Palestine itself the Jews were divided in their reaction to the inroads of Hellenistic culture. They were not agreed as to whether they should accept or refuse this culture, with its language, its theatres, its sports and its religious values, beliefs and practices. In pious circles Hellenism provoked the reaction of the Hassidim and the heroic revolt of the Maccabees. However, the Hasmonean princes finally adopted the Greek customs and had High Priests appointed in defiance of the Law. This, in turn, provoked the reaction of the Essenes, a group of Jewish purists, who sought refuge in the Judean desert at Qumran.

For the Jews dispersed beyond the borders of Palestine, as we have seen in the case of the intended readership of the Book of Wisdom, there was little chance of holding their own against a dominant Hellenistic world of the Mediterranean: Egypt and north Africa, Syria and Asia Minor, Greece, Sicily and southern Italy and the islands of Cyprus and Crete. In the cities and towns of this Mediterranean world, they adopted the Greek language and urban culture. They absorbed Greek philosophical ideas and something of the Greek religious psychology.

Revolt against, or flight from, Hellenistic culture was impossible for them. However, they managed to retain their identity and their biblical faith. For them, inculturation was a strict necessity, not a luxury. It was, in fact, the only safeguard possible against syncretism. The Jews of the Diaspora were greatly assisted in their fidelity to the faith of their ancestors by their possession of a Greek Bible. The Septuagint constituted a wider collection of books than the exclusively Hebrew selection used by Jews in Palestine and some of them had no Semitic original. The Book of Wisdom was the last of the books that made up this Bible. The Septuagint, therefore, did not merely represent a translation from the Hebrew. It was part of a process of profound inculturation brought about by the Diaspora.

In this chapter we have considered a few of the ways in which the Old Testament underpins our theological thinking in the matter of inculturation. We have seen how God's self-revelation challenged and purified culture in the Bible and we have also seen how that saving revelation occurred typically in cross-cultural situations. We have noticed how the biblical faith in Yahweh entered into dialogue with diverse cultures that came to dominate the Jews at different periods of their history, and we have noted how their religious response was expressed in these cultural forms.[29]

It was particularly the culture of Canaan, itself subjected to diverse cultural influences, that the biblical faith had to contend with, and which was to give that faith perhaps its finest expression. We have seen also that Israel was conscious of a divine election which placed it at the very centre of the intercultural process. Much of what Israel itself received from this experience is contained in the sapiential literature of the so-called Wisdom economy. It is here we encounter the biblical antecendents of the Johannine Logos and ultimately of the Spermatic Logos of the Apologist Fathers which is the basis of much of the Christology of inculturation we considered in Chapter 6.

Finally, we considered the impact on the Jews of the Hellenistic culture at the end of the Old Testament period. This was an intercultural experience of immeasurable importance for Christianity. Jesus Christ himself was to be brought up in the culturally heterogeneous corner of Palestine that was Galilee, while his followers were to spread the Gospel throughout the Hellenized world of the Mediterranean after his death and resurrection. It was to the Hellenistically formed Jewish communities of the Diaspora and their Gentile sympathizers that the apostles first addressed themselves on their missionary journeys, and it was from the communities they formed in this Mediterranean world that the Greek writings of the New Testament emerged. It is true to say that the Christian inculturation was founded on an earlier stage, that of the Hellenistic inculturation of Judaism. We now turn, in Chapter 9, to the evidence of the New Testament.

References

1 Is 55:6–11.

2 Senior and Stuhmueller 1983, p. 37.

3 Notes supplied by the Rev. Dr H. Hauser; cf. also Dahood 1978; Fisher 1980.

4 Beauchamp 1983, p. 12.

5 Rossano 1980, p. 25.

6 *Ibid.*, pp. 25–6.

7 Hauser *loc. cit.*

8 *Ibid.*, citing Barucq.

9 Rossano 1980, p. 26.

10 Senior and Stuhmueller 1983, p. 40.

11 Hauser *loc. cit.*

12 *Ibid.*

13 Ezk 28:11–17.

14 Ps 29:3–9.

15 Hauser *loc. cit.*

16 *Ibid.*

17 Rossano 1980, p. 26.

18 Senior and Stuhmueller 1983, p. 68.

19 Is 49:6.

20 Beauchamp, *op. cit.*, p. 7.

21 Rossano 1980, p. 25.

22 *Ibid.*, pp. 25–6.

23 Wis 7:27.

24 Jn 6:34, 35.

25 1 Cor 1:30.

26 McNamara 1983, pp. 235–9.

27 Gilbert 1984, p. 1.

28 Rossano 1980, p. 25.

29 A further point of interest, not dealt with in this chapter, concerns angelology. Much of the later angelology of the Old Testament and of the New Testament may be attributed to the infiltration of Iranian ideas.

9

Jesus
and cultures

Jesus: Promise to the Nations

Although the enculturation of Jesus has been used as an image for
the theological concept of inculturation, it is not his cultural education as a Jew, so much as his contestation of that culture, which
interests us. Jesus posed a very strong challenge from within his own
culture, which was a prolongation of what we called (in Chapter 8)
God's 'acculturation'. It was, in fact, the final and most devastating
of God's intrusions into Jewish culture, the glory of God shining
forever in the human and Jewish flesh of Jesus.[1]

The earthly Jesus was enculturated in the culturally heterogeneous corner of Palestine known as Galilee. Galilee was particularly
influenced by Graeco-Roman culture. The new city of Tiberias stood
on the shore of the lake that had been given the same foreign name.
However, Jesus was 'born a subject of the Law' and 'lived under the
authority' of artisan parents.[2] Through his education at Nazareth he
belonged to a popular level of Jewish culture and found himself
excluded from the culture of the establishment, a fact that should be
noted when we ask the question later in this book: 'Whose culture
are we considering?' It could even be said that Jesus was enculturated against the Jewish establishment.

As an adult, Jesus strongly challenged certain aspects of the
culture he had inherited, the culture lived by his contemporaries.
Like one of the classic prophets of the Old Testament, he inveighed
against the established order so as to prepare the new order willed by
God. He defied the law on innumerable occasions. He called for the
abolition of rules for ritual purity. He questioned the regulations of
the Sabbath Day rest. He opposed the severe punishment which was
legally due to the woman taken in adultery. He foretold the destruc-

tion of the Temple, the principal monument of contemporary religious culture. He 'purified' it in a dramatic and controversial way, by driving out the merchants and money-lenders. And he consorted daily with tax-collectors and public sinners. In a word, Jesus taught love, in opposition to the legalism and formalism of the establishment 'ghetto'.[3] The opposition of Jesus to these aspects of Jewish religious culture earned him the hatred and hostility of the religious authorities and led inevitably to his passion and death. It was the climax of God's 'acculturation'.

Galilee and Jerusalem were sufficiently cosmopolitan for Jesus to encounter representatives of non-Jewish cultures: Syro-Phoenicians, Romans, convert Greeks and the heterodox Samaritans. He gave a personal example of particular attention to, and predilection for, such people, but these encounters were comparatively rare. His mission was to 'the lost sheep of the house of Israel', and he concentrated on the Jews first of all and on his principal interlocutors, the Pharisees. That is the picture presented by the Gospels. It is noticeable, in fact, that the non-Jews sought out Jesus, rather than the reverse. What then of the universal mission of Jesus?

All the texts concerning a mission to the nations and cultures of the world are post-Resurrection texts. That is to say, they are not attributable to the earthly Jesus, but to the risen Christ. Senior and Stuhmueller enumerate four general opinions concerning the universal mission of Jesus to the Gentiles.[4] Firstly, there is the opinion that the earthly Jesus called the apostles in his lifetime to the Gentile mission. As we have already indicated, this is difficult to reconcile with the evidence of the Gospels themselves. Secondly, there is the opinion that the earthly Jesus did not inaugurate the Gentile mission in his lifetime, but that he had such a mission in mind and instructed his apostles accordingly after the Resurrection. It is, of course, equally impossible to demonstrate from the Gospel accounts what the earthly Jesus 'had in mind' on this matter.

An opinion at the other end of the spectrum, as it were, is that the Gentile mission was a product of the early Church, reflecting on the implications of Jesus' life and message. However, this opinion does not take account sufficiently of eschatological expectations about the 'end of time'. Finally, there is the opinion of Joachim Jeremias that the Gentile mission did not come directly from the earthly Jesus, nor from deductions drawn by the apostles after the Resurrection, but from the impact of the Resurrection itself which convinced the followers of Jesus that the final age had come. This final age included the pilgrimage of the nations to Zion, hence the universal mission. Even this opinion has several drawbacks. It fails to explain the dynamism of the mission and it does not explain the relationship of the message of the earthly Jesus to the missionary proclamation of the apostles.[5]

Senior and Stuhmueller propose a more acceptable theory. It is centred on the Kingdom preached by Jesus, the universal reign of God which is a saving and an eschatological event.[6] In the teaching and example of the earthly Jesus, we see something of the universal scope of the Kingdom he preached. We witness his intimacy with the Father and how the Father's indiscriminate love shone through him. The ministry of Jesus was essentially a ministry of compassion to poor and peripheral people. Both in his words and in his actions, we encounter God's availability to all.

Jesus held an inclusive, not an exclusive, view of God's people. The symbolism of 'the Twelve', together with the 'Seventy' or 'Seventy-Two', already implies a universal perspective — the tribes of Israel and the traditional number of the Gentile nations — although, in the case of the 'Seventy' or 'Seventy-Two', we probably have an instance of Luke reading a universalist intention back into Jesus' earthly ministry. Jesus declares that people from east and west will sit down at the messianic banquet, and that, while the Galilean towns reject him, the Gentiles — and even the town of Sodom — will accept him.[7] There are many other instances of such 'inclusive' statements.

In his teaching and his actions, Jesus communicated a positive view of salvation. God's victory was assured and the triumph of goodness and life over evil and death was equally certain. These two victories converged in his eschatological vision. Moreover, the victory was already inaugurated. The Resurrection vindicated Jesus and revealed to the apostles his true identity. In the light of this revelation they were able to reinterpret the Jesus tradition authentically. The risen Christ is Lord of all the world; his Kingship is universal. It follows that the mission of the Apostles should be to the 'uttermost ends of the earth'.

In Chapter 8 mention was already made of the hypostasized Wisdom and of the personified use of the creative *memra* of God as antecedents for the Johannine use of the term Logos. McNamara considers that if the term *memra* was in use, together with other concepts known to the Targums, such as the Glory and the Shekinah (the Lord's presence or dwelling), when the Johannine Prologue came to be written, then it is likely that they influenced the choice of words used.[8]

The Prologue of John is the expression of a profound theological reflection on the identity of Jesus. The term Logos is used to affirm the previous divine existence of Jesus and his intimate association with the creative work of God. He is not only the Lord and Redeemer of the universe, but is also its creative principle.

> Through him all things came into being,
> not one thing came into being except through him.[9]

St Justin's concept of the world-seeding Logos, which has proved so fruitful for theologians of inculturation and which was taken up in the texts of the Second Vatican Council, would have been impossible without the insight of John's Prologue, whatever else it owes to Greek philosophy.

The ministry of the earthly Jesus was a promise which the Resurrection abundantly fulfilled, a promise to the nations and to all the excluded ones within and outside Israel. The Johannine Christology of the 'word of life' located this promise in the act of creation itself, and its first fulfilment in the Incarnation.

Paul, the Apostle of the Nations

Saul, the Pharisee, who became Paul, apostle of the Gentiles, is a striking instance of how the Resurrection of Christ revealed the universal dimension of his mission. Paul's conversion radically changed his whole way of life. He suddenly realized that the Jesus whose followers he was persecuting was the Messiah, and had been raised from the dead. It was also a revelation to him of the final age, the moment when God was offering salvation to Jew and Gentile alike. Left to himself, Saul the Pharisee could not have come to this realization. It had to come from outside.

This realization, and the fact that Jesus exercises his Messiahship through his death and resurrection, lie at the heart of Paul's message. God is not a God of the Jews only, and all who respond to Christ in faith experience the universal gift of salvation which God offers in Christ.

> So for anyone who is in Christ, there is a new creation: the old order is gone and a new being is there to see. It is all God's work: he reconciled us to himself through Christ and he gave us the ministry of reconciliation. I mean, God was in Christ reconciling the world to himself, not holding anyone's faults against them, but entrusting to us the message of reconciliation.

So we are ambassadors for Christ; it is as though God were urging you through us, and in the name of Christ we appeal to you to be reconciled to God. For our sake he made the sinless one a victim for sin, so that in him we might become the uprightness of God.[10]

In the later Pauline letters, the authenticity of which is debated, we find a cosmic Christology developed which parallels that of the Johannine Prologue, although it is less explicit. Christ is the fulfilment of God's intention for his creation. In Christ, God is now recognizable, and through Christ, creation becomes intelligible. Christ was pre-existent in the creation, at least intentionally, and it is now renewed by his work of redemption. The exaltation of Christ has now fulfilled God's plan for the world, and Christ himself is one with the divine Wisdom which gives order and meaning to the cosmos.[11]

Much of the New Testament is, as Senior and Stuhmueller remark, 'mission literature'. Jesus' final commission to the apostles in Matthew is an echo of the longer instruction in Mt 10.[12] Luke also has a final commission in which the disciples are commanded to teach 'all nations, beginning from Jerusalem'.[13] In the Johannine communities we see the process of evangelization extending from Aramaic-speaking Jews to Hellenized Jews and thence to Samaritans and Gentiles. But it is in Acts that we see the final commission of Jesus most accurately fulfilled, with Paul at the centre of the stage. The story takes us from Jerusalem and Judea to Samaria and Asia Minor, thence to Greece and Macedonia and finally to Rome itself. Throughout the book, we see the Holy Spirit constantly opening new doors and widening the horizon of mission.

The geographical scope of Paul's missionary activities is impressive, but it must be asked how far he journeyed culturally, how far he travelled in his encounter with non-Jewish ideas and modes of behaviour. The answer is not easy, because Paul's attitude towards the cultures he encounters appears paradoxical. Herman Hauser notes the astonishing liberty with which Paul questions any and every set of ideas and behaviour in the light of his faith in Christ Jesus. On the other hand, according to Hauser, Paul envisages no radical changes in the social sphere.[14]

While the Jews demand miracles and the Greeks look for wisdom, we are preaching a crucified Christ: to the Jews an obstacle they cannot get over, to the gentiles foolishness, but to those who have been called, whether they are Jews or Greeks, a Christ who is both the power of God and the wisdom of God.[15]

Paul seems to say here that the Christian Gospel transcends the cultural categories and expectations of both Jews and Greeks. It does not espouse the tastes and manners of human cultures. Paul is anxious to stress that he did not come among the Corinthians with oratorical skills or arguments from philosophy, but only with the 'knowledge of Jesus'.[16] Paul was a master of rhetoric and there is considerable evidence of the influence of Hellenistic ideas and styles in his writings. We shall examine the special case of the church of Corinth later in this chapter. For the time being let us consider Paul's attitude towards culture in general.

In a famous passage to the Galatians, he asserts not only that cultural differences are abolished by Christianity, but even social and sexual boundaries as well.

> There can be neither Jew nor Greek, there can be neither slave nor freeman, there can be neither male nor female — for you are all one in Christ.[17]

Paul himself feels free to identify with any culture or social category, relativizing them all beside the Gospel.

> So though I was not a slave to any human being, I put myself in slavery to all people, to win as many as I could. To the Jews I made myself as a Jew, to win the Jews; to those under the Law as one under the Law (though I am not), in order to win those under the Law; to those outside the Law as one outside the Law . . . to win those outside the Law. To the weak, I made myself weak, to win the weak. I accommodated myself to people in all kinds of different situations, so that by all possible means I might bring some to salvation. All this I do for the sake of the gospel, that I may share its benefits with others.[18]

But what does all of this mean in practice? Does it mean that Paul himself adopted successive cultures as part of his missionary strategy? Or does it mean simply that he referred to the cultural situation of his hearers in order to win their attention for the first step in evangelization? Or could it mean that Paul took other cultures seriously and initiated a dialogue between them and the Gospel in order to bring about a new cultural creation?

Let us look at another set of Paul's attitudes. In spite of his relativization of cultures, Paul seems to want the cultural distinctions to continue.

We were baptized into one body in a single Spirit, Jews as well as Greeks, slaves as well as free men, and we were all given the same Spirit to drink. And indeed the body consists not of one member but of many.[19]

As the human body possesses a plurality of parts, so Christ, who is the principle of unity in the Church, brings Jews and Greeks, slaves and free men into the unity of his body. Is this an image of the multicultural Church? Not exactly, since Paul seems to regard such differences as supremely unimportant. It should be noted in passing that the social metaphor of the body was already popular in Graeco-Roman circles.

With the prospect of an imminent *Parousia*, cultural differences mattered little. What was important in Paul's eyes was obedience to God's commandments.

Anyway let everyone continue in the part which the Lord has allotted to him, as he was when God called him. This is the rule that I give to all the churches. If a man who is called has already been circumcised, then he must stay circumcised; when an uncircumcised man is called, he may not be circumcised. To be circumcised is of no importance, and to be uncircumcised is of no importance; what is important is the keeping of God's commandments. Everyone should stay in whatever state he was in when he was called. So, if when you were called, you were a slave, do not think it matters — even if you have a chance of freedom, you should prefer to make full use of your condition as a slave.[20]

Paul carries his principle of socio-cultural passivity even so far as to advise a slave not to seek freedom when the chance is given to him. At least, this is the more common reading of the passage. Equally, in Paul's view, the Jews are entitled to keep their God-given privileges.

They are Israelites; it was they who were adopted as children, the glory was theirs and the covenants; to them were given the Law and the worship of God and the promises. To them belong the fathers and out of them, so far as physical descent is concerned, came Christ who is above all, God, blessed for ever. Amen.[21]

Probably, Paul did not reflect very deeply about cultural matters. In the circumstances, he was not obliged to do so. He was confronted by a cultural *fait accompli*, by Gentiles and Hellenized Jews who shared a common Hellenistic culture. Paul employed the Greek language and the Greek Septuagint, cited by all the New Testament writers. His approach to audiences outside of Palestine was that of a Hellenized Jew and his message was couched in Hellenistic-Jewish terms. He used the vocabulary of popular Hellenistic philosophy. It may well be that such slogans as 'for me everything is permissible', which recurs in 1 Corinthians, were part of that vocabulary. The use of the word 'mystery', especially in its later application to the Christian initiation of Baptism, may also have been influenced by the Hellenistic mysteries. In other words, Paul was himself part of the movement of acculturation in the Mediterranean which predated Christianity. The question remains, however, whether Paul carried the process further and carried out a true inculturation, enlivening the Gentile cultures from within by the power of the Gospel.

If it were applied to the dialogue between faith and culture, Paul's advice to the Philippians would, as Hauser notes, be excellent counsel for missionaries engaged in inculturation.

> Finally, brothers, let your minds be filled with everything that is true, everything that is honourable, everything that is upright and pure, everything that we love and admire — with whatever is good and praiseworthy.[22]

This advice is even couched in the language of the Greek moralists, but it is followed by the precept to do what the Corinthians have learnt from Paul 'and have heard and seen me doing'. It is therefore unlikely that the context was cultural.

Paul's speech before the Council of the Areopagus is sometimes cited as evidence of inculturation in the New Testament. It is, in fact, the only recorded attempt by Paul to combat paganism through the use of secular wisdom. However, it must be admitted from the start that the speeches which Luke puts into the mouths of people in the Acts of the Apostles are probably not their own words. This fact considerably reduces the value of the Areopagus speech as evidence for Paul's approach to culture. It does not, however, lessen the importance of Athens for Luke. Athens was the intellectual centre of Hellenism and it was, therefore, an important milestone in Paul's second missionary journey. As Luke records it, it was not a success.[23]

The account begins unfavourably for the Athenians by noting Paul's revulsion 'at the sight of a city given over to idolatry'. He argued with some Epicurean and Stoic philosophers who called him *spermologos*, 'seed-picker', a garrulous man who speaks in clichés.[24] It was they who got him to accompany them to the Areopagus.

Paul's speech is a proclamation of the true God in opposition to the idolatrous ideas of the Athenians. The argument is that, since God created the universe, he does not need temples built for him. He created human beings and surrounds them with favours, so it is absurd to identify him with material objects and statues. The speech ends with a call to repentance and a proclamation of the Resurrection.

Paul begins his speech with a reference to the Greek practice of dedicating altars to the 'unknown gods' and uses this device to dwell on the Athenians' heathen ignorance. The key-words of the speech are, in fact, 'unknown' and 'ignorance', and, in the monotheistic apologetics of Hellenistic Judaism, they carry connotations of culpability. Paul uses an expression suggested by Epimenides of Cnossos and also quotes the words of a Cilician poet, the *Phainomena* of Aratus.[25] These are possibly stock references used by Hellenistic Jews in their critique of idolatry. They are not a very serious dialogue with religious themes in Greek literature. In general, however, Paul seems to side with the Epicurean philosophers in their critique of idolatry.

Paul concluded his speech with a call to repentance in view of the divine judgement by the Risen Christ, and was mocked by his hearers. A few Athenians, two of whom are named, attached themselves to him, but otherwise his failure at Athens was complete. The experience of the Areopagus may indeed have discouraged Paul from further references to Greek literature and philosophy, and may account, in part, for his apparent hostility to Hellenistic thought in the first letter to the Corinthians.

The speech to the Athenians of the Areopagus was very far from being an essay in inculturation, and Paul showed no inclination to invite a response to the Gospel from Greek culture. He was certainly not looking for 'seeds of the word' in the writings of Greek philosophers and poets. The most that can be said about the speech, and about Paul's missionary activity in general, is that it was an instance of acculturation, a preliminary missionary encounter leading to a later and more profound intercultural dialogue.

Paul's ministry to the Gentiles was largely exercised within the cultural framework of Hellenistic Judaism. He did not accept the intransigent Judeo-Christian form of the Gospel, and strenuously opposed the imposition of circumcision and other prescriptions of the Mosaic Law upon his Gentile converts. It was this issue that resulted in the compromise of the so-called Council of Jerusalem that exempted Gentiles from the obligations of the Law, except for the

127

prohibition of idol-meats that signified a sharing in sacrilegious worship, the prohibition of blood and of the legal impurity incurred through irregular marriages. There were certain prohibitions in the Mosaic Law which had a fundamental religious meaning and which, in the eyes of some Judeo-Christians, could not be abandoned. They remained as the condition for social intercourse between Jewish and Gentile Christians. Paul, in any case, seems to have ignored the decree in practice.

Raymond Brown distinguishes three forms of Judeo-Christianity. First, there was a group which originated in Jerusalem, and which had some success in Galatia and Philippi, which wanted to impose circumcision and the whole of the Mosaic Law on Christian converts. Secondly, there was the group, associated with James and Peter, which did not insist on circumcision, but which wished to impose the Jewish purity laws on Christians. This movement originated in Jerusalem and was the dominant Christianity of Antioch, Rome and elsewhere. Finally, there was the more tolerant attitude of Jews like Paul himself who did not force their converts to abandon circumcision and the Law, but who did not insist on either. However, they still remained attached to the cultic practices of Judaism, the celebration of its feasts and its Temple worship.[26]

It can be seen, therefore, that early Christianity had the anterior problem of extricating the Gospel from the religious culture of Judaism, before it could begin to take seriously the religious culture of non-Jews. This is illustrated in the following section by the very different examples of the Church of Jerusalem and the Church of Corinth.

The Church of Jerusalem and the Church of Corinth

The antithesis of Jerusalem and Corinth is instructive for a reflection on inculturation in the early Church. The claim that inculturation began with the Church of Jerusalem, or that the Church of Corinth represents an example of an inculturation that failed, are exaggerations.

De Gasperis makes the claim that the Church of the Jews, the Mother Church of Jerusalem, was the first and unsurpassed example of inculturation.[27] The claim is based on the fact that Jerusalem was the original point of departure for the Christian mission to the Hellenistic world, and was also the constant point of reference —

witness the council that was held there and presided over by James. The Church of Jerusalem was the leading Christian minority that ultimately presided over the redaction of the New Testament.[28] Its Christian rereading of the Old Testament also became standard. The Aramaic-speaking Judeo-Christian Church of Jerusalem outlived the community of Hellenistic Christians which existed alongside it and which bore the brunt of the first persecution. It shared the same culture as Jesus himself, and this culture was the starting-point for Christian evangelization everywhere. Its position was a privileged one, since, through the Jerusalem Church, Christians of other cultures entered into the history of Israel, old and new. The Jerusalem Church was the 'Mother of all the churches' and closest to the contingent, historical events through which God revealed himself in Christ and from which the others' faith in Christ was born.

The importance of the Jerusalem Church as the starting-point of the Christian tradition is undeniable, but that it was the first and unsurpassed example of inculturation is, to say the least, arguable. One should be wary of seeing Aramaic-speaking Judeo-Christianity as a straightforward extension of Christ's enculturation, and of his interior challenge to Judaism. Faith in the Resurrection implied a radically new perspective in which Judaism was transcended, and it may be that the Christians of Jerusalem were unable to relativize their culture sufficiently. To the extent that the Judaizers wished to impose the burden of the Mosaic Law on Gentile Christians, this seems to have been the case. At any rate, Jewish religious culture had been relativized by the Hellenists from the very beginning of Christianity.

It can be argued, on the contrary, that the Aramaic-speaking Judeo-Christian Church of Jerusalem was actually an obstacle to inculturation. It was, for example, very slow to develop a Christology, in comparison with other early Christian communities. It did not accept the implications of the universalism of Christ. Its cultural self-criticism did not go far enough. It remained marginal to the whole process of Christian evangelization. The fact is that Christianity's new creation of human cultures only started when the Jewish religious culture was destroyed and the Jerusalem community had ceased to exist.

This happened in the second war of Hadrian, in AD 135 when Jerusalem was captured, rebuilt and colonized. The Judeo-Christians of Jerusalem were dispersed in Transjordan and Syria and became, in the main, the sect of the Ebionites. These did not believe in the divinity of Christ, nor would they accept the epistles of St Paul. It is said that they relied upon only one Gospel, either that of St Matthew or the apocryphal Gospel of the Hebrews. They placed, however, a very strong emphasis on the need for fidelity to the Mosaic Law. This was the inglorious end of Judeo-Christianity in Jerusalem.

The other case we have to consider is that of Corinth. Was it a question of inculturation that failed? Having already seen something of St Paul's approach to Hellenistic culture, we can safely reply 'No'. Inculturation was not even attempted at Corinth, so there was no question of its success or failure. That is not to say, however, that culture was not a factor in the Corinthian situation. It was a very important factor indeed.

Corinth was a Roman colony and port, strategically placed on the isthmus connecting Achaia to the Greek mainland. No doubt, Paul saw it as a springboard for the Christian faith in the whole of that area. Corinth was a great and populous city and a centre of Hellenistic culture. However, this is not to say by any means that it was culturally homogeneous. Gerd Theissen's study of the social setting of Paul's essay on Corinth emphasizes the heterogeneity of this characteristic urban culture.[29] It was a cosmopolitan place, subject to extremely diverse influences, and a centre of attraction for every kind of religion and philosophy. The Roman colony itself had not had time to put down cultural roots. In such a social climate it is understandable that Corinth should have been notorious as a centre of immorality.

The Christian community which Paul established was composed of a cross-section of the population. As a group, they were far from having a definite influence on the city's cultural life and institutions. It was natural that life at Corinth should present a great many obstacles to the integration of the Gospel preached there by Paul. In fact, everything depended on the self-understanding of the Corinthian Christians and their own cultural development. The culturalism of Corinth was very different from that of Judeo-Christianity. It was born of external forces, hostile to the Gospel. The Christians of Corinth were victims of a situation they were powerless to control, and Paul did not completely succeed in transposing the Christian message into terms that they could understand and live.

The letters of Paul to the Corinthians show the extent of the crisis. There were questions of moral conduct and of the order of liturgical and Eucharistic meetings. There were problems of recourse to the civil courts for disputes between Christians, and there was the vexed question of eating meat sacrificed to pagan gods. Finally, and to some extent as a result of the disputes which these problems aroused, the Christian community split up into factions led by different leaders. Christ had been 'divided up'.

As Paul's experience at Athens demonstrated, the folly of the Cross and the doctrine of the Resurrection were uncongenial to the Greek mind and, indeed, to sinful humanity as a whole. Paul was forced to make a strong contrast between Greek culture and wisdom, on the one hand, and the wisdom of the Cross, on the other. There is no hint of a dialogue between the two. On the contrary, it seems to be assumed that Hellenistic culture is impervious to Christianity. However, out of the trauma of the Corinthian crisis Paul's greatest and most profound theological teachings emerged — on Christian liberty, on the supremacy of love, on union with Christ and communion among the churches. This fruit of Paul's coming to grips with the confused urban culture of Corinth was an important contribution to his inculturated ecclesiology and ethics.

Whatever else he achieved, Paul did not solve the problems of the Corinthian community in either the short or the long term. The letter of Clement of Rome to the Corinthians c. AD 94 shows that in spite of Paul's magnificent teachings, the situation was unchanged, and that factions were still plaguing the Christian community there.

As we might reasonably expect, the New Testament demonstrates how evangelization and acculturation went hand in hand in the first stage of realizing the universalist implications of the Resurrection and the Kingdom. The time depth is altogether too shallow for a profound dialogue to have taken place with pagan cultures, envisaging their transformation. However, there is no doubt that the different Christologies, ecclesiologies and ethics of the various New Testament communities were a product of the incipient dialogue with real cultural situations and of a first striving to transcend Judaistic acculturation. The struggle for cultural liberation from Judaism also shows this.

Little has been said about Rome and its culture, which was very often parasitic towards Hellenism. The Book of Revelation is the only New Testament book which contains a severe criticism of the Roman Empire and the yoke of alien rule which it imposed on other nations. The whole of pagan culture is seemingly condemned as an instrument of the 'Beast'.[30]

There are a number of conclusions to be drawn from a cultural reading of the New Testament. Firstly, the fact that it does not describe a process of explicit inculturation does not mean that the New Testament itself is not a product of inculturation implicitly begun, nor does it invalidate the universalist implications of faith in the resurrection and exaltation of Jesus.[31] Secondly, we are able to appreciate the fact that Old and New Testaments are inseparable and that the Old Testament legacy of Hellenistic Judaism was a crucial breeding-ground for Christianity in the Mediterranean world. Thirdly, the fact that the Jewish Christian Church of Jerusalem proved to be a dead-end does not lessen its historical and symbolical importance as the Mother Church, sharing the native culture of Jesus Christ himself. Indeed, the ultimate failure of the Jerusalem Church seems to have stimulated the Christian dialogue with Judaism in other cultural forms. Hengel suggests that the Christian community of 'Hellenists' at Jerusalem may even date from the Feast of Weeks following the Passover during which Jesus was crucified, and that dialogue between Christianity and Hellenistic Jews dates from that time.[32]

As de Gasperis points out, Christianity owes a great deal to the strictly Jewish characteristics of the first Christian communities.[33] Jewish forms of worship in the synagogue, for example, are at the origin of Christian liturgical development. We can regret the disappearance of the Aramaic-speaking church of Jerusalem, while at the same time noting that it was especially the Church of the Hellenistic Jews, dispersed after the persecution in which Stephen gave his life, that carried the Resurrection faith to the Greek-speaking communities of the Mediterranean. Hengel notes that insufficient attention has been paid hitherto by scholars to the language difference between Christians in Jerusalem, a difference that would have quickly led to separate arrangements for worship.[34] It may even be that we have underestimated the extent of Hellenistic influence on the Aramaic culture of Jesus himself.

The cultures of the Bible are remote from us in time and form, yet they are the authentic source of our faith. As such, they are indispensable to the Christian tradition, and contribute to the irreducible content of the Christian patrimony. In Part Three of this book we examine the historical continuation of the Church's mission, the origins of which we have observed in the New Testament. We shall note how the cultural confrontations of the apostolic age bore fruit in the development of a conscious inculturation.

References

1 De Gasperis 1983, p. 61.

2 Gal 4:4; Lk 2:51.

3 Notes supplied by Dr H. Hauser.

4 Senior and Stuhmueller 1983, p. 143.

5 *Ibid.*; cf. Jeremias 1958.

6 Senior and Stuhmueller 1983, pp. 145–58.

7 Mt 10:15; 11:20–24.

8 McNamara 1983, pp. 234–9.

9 Jn 1:3.

10 2 Cor 5:17–21.

11 1 Cor 1:30.

12 Mt 10; 28:16–20.

13 Lk 24:47; Ac 1:7–8.

14 Hauser, *op. cit.*

15 1 Cor 1:22–4.

16 1 Cor 2:1, 2. In fact, Paul actually uses the Greek literary form of the diatribe in 1 Cor.

17 Gal 3:27–8.

18 1 Cor 9:19–23.

19 1 Cor 12:13–14.

20 1 Cor 7:17–20.

21 Rm 9:1 – 11:36.

22 Phil 4:8.

23 Ac 17:16–34.

24 Ac 17:18.

25 Ac 17:28.

26 Brown 1985, pp. 133–4.

27 De Gasperis 1983.

28 *Ibid.*, p. 53.

29 Theissen 1982.

30 Rv 13:17.

31 Cf. Niebuhr 1952, p. 129: 'The New Testament contains no document that clearly expresses the synthetic view, but there are many statements in gospels and epistles which sound the *motif*, or which can be interpreted, without violence to the text, as containing (the) solution to the Christ and culture problem.'

32 Hengel 1983, p. 11.

33 De Gasperis 1983.

34 Hengel, *op. cit.*, p. 14.

PART THREE

MISSION
AND
INCULTURATION

10

Inculturation and the early missions

In Parts One and Two of this book the concept of inculturation has been analysed sociologically and its theological and biblical foundations have been examined. Before we study the official teaching of the contemporary Church in Part Four, it is necessary to give some account of inculturation in the history of the Church's missionary activity. Historians are beginning to rewrite the history of the Church in terms of cultural pluralism, just as biblical scholars are undertaking a cultural rereading of the Bible. From the historical point of view, the New Testament is obviously an unfinished story, however complete it may be as an apostolic testimony to the originating Christ-event. As we have seen in Chapter 9, the New Testament provides evidence for the first insertion of Christian Resurrection faith into the cultures of the Mediterranean area and for the beginning of a dialogue between that Faith and those cultures. We do not, however, see the Christian faith becoming a principle that animates, directs and unifies those cultures, transforming them and turning them into a new creation. In other words, although the New Testament is itself a product of the first strivings for inculturation, it does not fully achieve the conscious process.

The dialogue begins with the culture of Hellenistic Judaism. From this form of Judaism the step was made towards the non-Jewish or 'pagan' cultures of Greece, Rome and the Near East. It is in the second half of the second century, with the Apologist Fathers, that the dialogue with these cultures explicitly begins. In this chapter we shall try to illustrate the dialogue between Christianity and diverse cultures that took place up to the period of the Reformation. It is not intended to be a complete historical outline.

The Rise of the Eastern Churches

As Gentile converts increased and begun to outnumber those of Hellenistic Jewish origin, it became necessary to evangelize the Gentile cultures, and in particular the dominant Graeco-Roman culture of the Mediterranean world. Christian apologists came to believe that every cultural tradition expected the Messiah, and they sought to identify the questions in those traditions to which Jesus Christ provided the answer. As they scrutinized the philosophy and literature of the Gentile world, they developed methods which Jaroslav Pelikan has grouped under three headings: (a) non-Jewish prophecies of a Christ; (b) Gentile anticipations of the doctrine about Christ; (c) pagan foreshadowings or 'types' of the redemption achieved by his death.[1]

(a) Among the pagan anticipations of Christ identified by the Apologists, the most dramatic was the *Fourth Eclogue* of the Roman poet Vergil. It was a poem composed in honour of the Emperor Augustus, but, as Pelikan remarks, for Christians it was reminiscent of the Book of Isaiah, with its references to a new order, a virgin, the birth of a child that would inaugurate a golden age and even a transformation of the human race itself. The first Christian Emperor, Constantine, claimed *c*. AD 313 that this poem was a prophecy of Christ. As a consequence, Vergil was held in honour as a pagan saint throughout the Middle Ages of Europe and found a place in Dante's *Divine Comedy*.

Vergil's reference to the Graeco-Roman Sibylline oracles, and especially to the Cumaean Sibyl, in his *Fourth Eclogue* and in the *Aeneid*, was cited by Christian apologists as further evidence of non-Christian prophecy concerning the birth of Jesus Christ and concerning his second coming. Throughout the Middle Ages the oracles of the Sibyls were esteemed as prophecies of the Last Judgement. The *Dies Irae* sequence in the Mass for the Dead referred to the Sibyl, and Michelangelo contrasted pagan Sibyls with Old Testament prophets in his painting on the Sistine Chapel's ceiling.[2]

(b) Clement of Alexandria, at the end of the second century, is one of the most notable early Fathers to recognize anticipations of Christian doctrine in pagan traditions. Philosophy, he taught, not only prepared the Greeks for Christ, it also contributes to the development of true religion.

> Philosophy was necessary to the Greeks for righteousness, until the coming of the Lord: and even now it is useful for the

138

development of true religion, as a kind of preparatory discipline for those who arrive at faith by way of demonstration. For 'your foot will not stumble', as the Scripture says, if you attribute to Providence all good things, whether belonging to the Greeks or to us. For God is the source of all good; either directly, or indirectly, as in the case of philosophy. But it may even be that philosophy was given to the Greeks directly; for it was a 'schoolmaster', to bring Hellenism to Christ, as the Law was for the Hebrews. Thus philosophy was a preparation, paving the way for the man who is brought to perfection by Christ.[3]

(c) St Justin, whom we already encountered in Chapter 6, was expert in discovering types of figures of Christianity in the works of pagan authors. He produced a veritable catalogue of pagan types for the cross of Christ, chief among them being the mast to which Odysseus was bound as he sailed past the sirens. St Clement of Alexandria developed this image and later Christian commentators on the *Iliad* and the *Odyssey* continued to hail Jesus as the Christian Odysseus. Another type was Socrates, compared sometimes to Moses and sometimes to Christ himself, put to death by the enemies of reason and the Logos.[4]

Throughout the first two centuries Christian allegiance to Jesus Christ clashed with the kingship and lordship of Caesar. Christians refused to accept Caesar as 'Lord' and to pay divine honours to him, always preferring martyrdom to compromise. When, in the early fourth century, the Caesar himself became a Christian and attributed his ascendancy to the special favour of Jesus Christ, the stage was set for the marriage of Christ's kingship with that of imperial Rome. Constantine claimed to enjoy the specific assistance and guidance of Christ, thus laying the foundation for the concept of a Holy Roman Empire. The rituals of kingship celebrated at Constantinople, the former Byzantium and now the 'New Rome', coloured the Christian liturgy and shaped the Church's hierarchical tradition. When the Western Empire finally collapsed, the imperial mantle descended upon the shoulders of the Pope at the 'Old Rome' and the papal monarchy began to evolve. These developments held far-reaching implications for the subsequent relationship of Eastern and Western Christianity and for the rivalry between political and ecclesiastical power after the revival of the Holy Roman Empire in the West in AD 800.

During the first three centuries the evangelization of the Middle East was completed: Greece, Asia Minor, Syria, Persia, Armenia,

Rumania and Southern Russia. In the fourth century, Egypt and Ethiopia entered the history of the Church. It was a time of controversy and confusion, when Arianism held sway in the official circles of the Empire. By AD 431, when the Council of Ephesus was convened, local churches had developed their own distinctive cultural forms. Pope Paul VI described the rise of the Eastern Churches in the following sympathetic manner.

'It was in Palestine, first of all, that the apostles established faith in Jesus Christ and founded churches. Then they set out across the whole world and announced throughout the world the same doctrine and the same faith.' (Tertullian) Each nation received the good seed of their preaching according to their own mentality and their own culture. Each local church grew with its own personality, its own customs and its own personal way of celebrating the same mysteries, without this harming the unity of faith and the communion of them all in charity and respect for the order established by Christ. That is the origin of our diversity in unity and of our catholicity, always an essential property of the Church of Christ, and of which the Holy Spirit has given us a new experience in our time and in the Council.[5]

Theological controversy and eventual schism consolidated these differences still further. No doubt important differences of theological interpretation were at stake, but cultural and political factors also exerted an influence, which is why whole churches broke away from communion with Greek and Latin Christendom. At the Council of Ephesus the Nestorians of present-day Iraq, Iran and India (Malabar) went their own way, and twenty years later, at Chalcedon, the Monophysites of Egypt, Ethiopia, Syria and Armenia became separated from Rome and Constantinople. After the schism between East and West in 1054, Rome was left with Latin Christendom, to be joined eventually by the Syriac Maronites, the Greek Melkites and the ex-Nestorian Chaldeans. Eventually, also, Uniate forms of the otherwise Monophysite Syrians, Copts, Ethiopians and Armenians came into being within the Roman communion. The non-Roman forms of Christianity in the East served relatively small populations and were, for the most part, prevented from expanding after they had been engulfed by Islam. This fact also helped to preserve and even to incapsulate their cultural traditions.

Gregory I and the Anglo-Saxon Mission

The Gospel was carried early to Italy, Spain, southern France and north Africa. By the middle of the fourth century we hear of Christianity in Hungary, Austria and Bavaria, and in the fifth century of Christians in Britain and Ireland. There had been a shift from Greek to Latin culture in the Western Empire, and when the Western line of emperors died out and barbarian hordes overran the Roman dominions, the Roman Church and Papacy replaced the Empire as the chief agent of Latin cultural domination. The Church remained the only stable organization in an otherwise confused situation.

The new, pagan rulers of Europe were eager to appropriate the remnants of Roman civilization and to make use of its bureaucracy and Latin literacy. It was thus that St Gregory the Great found himself at the head of an 'imperial' Church structure that enjoyed considerable moral prestige and practical utility in the eyes of pagan rulers. This ensured a welcome for the missionaries he sent out from Rome. When St Augustine of Canterbury and his companions were sent by Gregory in AD 597 to pagan Anglo-Saxon England, they rode out upon the wave of a superior culture and their Roman ethnocentrism precluded any serious dialogue with the culture of the Anglo-Saxons.

The letter which St Gregory sent to St Mellitus on his departure to join St Augustine in Britain in AD 601 is an interesting statement of his cultural policy. There is no explicit desire to evangelize the Anglo-Saxon culture from within. Nor is there any consciousness of the need for dialogue. What is proposed is a forcible appropriation of Anglo-Saxon religious institutions, a substitution of religious meaning, with the barest physical or seasonal continuity.

> To our well loved son Abbot Mellitus: Gregory, servant to the servants of God.
>
> Since the departure of yourself and your companions, we have been somewhat anxious, because we have received no news of the success of your journey. Therefore, when by God's help you reach our most reverend brother, Bishop Augustine, we wish you to inform him that we have been giving careful thought to the affairs of the English, and have come to the conclusion that

the temples of the idols in that country should on no account be destroyed. He is to destroy the idols, but the temples themselves are to be aspersed with holy water, altars set up, and relics enclosed in them. For if these temples are well built, they are to be purified from devil-worship, and dedicated to the service of the true God. In this way, we hope that the people, seing that its temples are not destroyed, may abandon idolatry and resort to these places as before, and may come to know and adore the true God. And since they have a custom of sacrificing many oxen to devils, let some other solemnity be substituted in its place, such as a day of Dedication or the Festivals of the holy martyrs whose relics are enshrined there. On such occasions they might well construct shelters of boughs for themselves around the churches that were once temples, and celebrate the solemnity with devout feasting. They are no longer to sacrifice beasts to the Devil, but they may kill them for food to the praise of God, and give thanks to the Giver of all gifts for his bounty. If the people are allowed some worldly pleasures in this way, they will more readily come to desire the joys of the spirit. For it is certainly impossible to eradicate all errors from obstinate minds at one stroke, and whoever wishes to climb to a mountain top climbs gradually step by step and not in one leap. It was in this way that God revealed himself to the Israelite people in Egypt, permitting the sacrifices formerly offered to the Devil to be offered thenceforward to Himself instead. So He bade them sacrifice beasts to Him, so that, once enlightened, they might abandon a wrong conception of sacrifice, and adopt the right. For, while they were to continue to offer beasts as before, they were to offer them to God instead of to idols, thus transforming the idea of sacrifice. Of your kindness, you are to inform our brother Augustine of this policy, so that he may consider how he may best implement it on the spot. God keep you safe, my very dear son.

Dated the seventeenth of June, in the nineteenth year of the reign of our most devout Lord and Emperor Maurice Tiberius Augustus, and the eighteenth after his Consulship. The fourth indiction.[6]

St Gregory's missionaries were not only confronted by the pagan culture of the Anglo-Saxons. They also found in the country the remnants of British Christianity, with its own hierarchy and its own customs which were at variance with the Roman usage. These customs concerned, among other things, the date of Easter and the shape of the clerical tonsure. The Roman missionaries also accused the British bishops of a reluctance to join with them in evangelizing the Anglo-Saxon newcomers to their island. Bede in his *History of the English Church and People* describes how the controversy came to a head at the Synod of Whitby in AD 664.[7] The arguments on the Roman side, which was the side that prevailed, included an appeal to uniformity throughout the Christian world, as well as to the Petrine authority of the Pope.

It is clear, therefore, that while missionary strategy may have demanded the appropriation of native religious institutions, it was always intended that the Latin language and culture be taught along with the Christian faith, and that Celtic and Anglo-Saxon Christians be obliged to worship in Latin. Thus, in western Europe, the dominance of Latin culture prevented a repetition of Eastern ecclesial pluriformity. From the seventh century onwards, helped in several cases by missionaries from England, the pagan areas of Germany and Holland, and eventually Scandinavia, Pomerania and Poland, were evangelized in the same manner. This made the contrasting example of Saints Cyril and Methodius in the ninth century all the more remarkable.

Saints Cyril and Methodius

Although the claim that Saints Cyril and Methodius were paragons of inculturation needs qualification, their contribution to the Church's cultural history is noteworthy, to say the least.[8] Missionaries of the Eastern churches tended to be more liberal than their Latin counterparts, since they came from a background of well-established cultural pluralism. While the Western church espoused an aggressive policy of Latinization, Eastern Christians paid lip-service to the three languages of the Cross — Aramaic, Greek and Latin, regarding the use of any other language in church as a dangerous innovation.[9] Cyril and Methodius broke with this tradition to create a Slavonic Christianity.

Cyril and Methodius were brothers, born in Thessalonika in AD 825 and 826, respectively. From a monastery on the Bosporos they were sent by the Emperor Michael to evangelize the Khazars in Russia in 861. Two years later, they were sent to evangelize Moravia, now part of modern Czechoslovakia. Their particular genius was to have created the Glagolitic (predecessor of the Cyrillic) alphabet, on the basis of the Greek alphabet, and to have used this to commit a particular dialect of Slavonic to writing. The written Slavonic of Cyril and Methodius held the same kind of attraction for people of other Slavonic traditions as the literate Latin culture of the Roman missionaries did for the Anglo-Saxons and other peoples of western Europe. What Cyril and Methodius did was to create a unified, literate, Slavonic culture. They translated the Greek and Roman liturgies into Slavonic. They created codes of civil and church law in that language, and, after Cyril's death in AD 869, Methodius went on to translate the whole Bible into Slavonic. The language of Saints Cyril and Methodius is still the liturgical tongue of Russians, Serbs, Ukrainians and Bulgars today.

In the ninth century the final schism of East and West had not yet taken place, but Saints Cyril and Methodius were essentially Greek missionaries. The churches they founded were placed unequivocally under the jurisdiction of the Byzantine emperor at Constantinople. Moreover, their mission strategy among the pagan Slavs was even less tolerant than that of St Gregory the Great in Anglo-Saxon England. St Cyril, for example, went out of his way to destroy pagan shrines and sacred trees among the Khazars, and the saintly missionaries required a total abjuration of all non-Christian practices from their converts.[10] Their crowning achievement was to have developed and united the culture of the Slavs, in the act of evangelizing it. It is difficult to evade the charge of cultural domination, or at least manipulation, in the case of Saints Cyril and Methodius, even if their forceful methods eventually resulted in a balanced dialogue between faith and culture for the Slavs. It has, however, been a temptation of missionaries at many times and in many places to manipulate an oral culture at the moment of giving it a written form.

The mission strategy of Saints Cyril and Methodius had other important repercussions. In their vigorous pursuit of a vernacular church in Moravia they clashed with the Latin clergy of Bavaria, for whom Latinity was inseparable from evangelization.[11] As we have seen in the case of St Gregory the Great's mission to the Anglo-Saxons, the Latin language was linked to the affirmation of Papal jurisdiction. There was also the debate about the advisability of making the Bible available to the laity in their vernacular.[12] The upshot of this clash was that the holy brothers were delated to Rome on suspicion of heresy. St Nicholas I summoned them to Rome to answer the charge, and his successor, Adrian II, not only exonerated them, but ordained them both bishops. St Cyril died at Rome in AD 869 and was buried in the Basilica of San Clemente, after which St Methodius returned alone to Moravia and Pannonia.

The dispute with the Latin clergy flared up once more, and the Emperor Louis the German imprisoned St Methodius, who was again summoned to Rome to answer the charges against him. Pope John VII at first forbade the use of Slavonic in the Roman liturgy, but then rescinded the prohibition on condition that the readings at Mass were read in Latin as well as in Slavonic. Methodius returned to the field once more and to his task of creating a whole Slavonic sacred literature. He died in AD 884.

The value of the example of Saints Cyril and Methodius consists in demonstrating that even in the heyday of the Church's monoculturalism, concessions were made — with papal backing — to non-Latin cultures. After the final schism between East and West in AD 1054, the interaction between Eastern and Western traditions, exemplified by Saints Cyril and Methodius, became impossible.

The Christian Kingdom of the Kongo

The Kingdom of Kongo, situated in modern Angola, was evangelized by Portuguese secular priests in 1491. It has long been argued that Kongo Christianity was syncretist and superficial, that it remained essentially a foreign religion — a façade which enhanced Kongo's diplomatic relations with Europe. Of this Christianity, it is said, nothing substantial survived which could be recognized, let alone used, by later nineteenth-century missionaries. There were nothing but a few religious carvings used as fetishes, crucifixes, statues, bells and confession sticks.

This pessimistic, though common, evaluation of the Christian Kingdom of Kongo has recently been challenged by John Thornton.[13] The accusations of superficiality and insincerity, levelled against the Kings and other leaders of Kongo, stem from hostile sources, notably the Portuguese, who tried unsuccessfully to use the Church for political ends, and the Jesuits whose mission of 1548–55 had been a failure because the rulers of Kongo preferred local secular priests.

> Since Kongo converted to Christianity of its own free will, the shape and structure of the Church and its doctrines were determined as much by Kongo as by Europeans. Because Kongo

controlled the Church, attempts to use the Church for political leverage by outsiders were not successful, although the Porrtuguese tried regularly to do so. Although modern research has shown that there was considerable syncretism in Christian practice in Kongo, the European clergy who visited Kongo, and their superiors in Rome, both accepted it as orthodox. Because of the way in which Christianity was made a part of indigenous religion, its survival was not in question and the cult can be documented from the early sixteenth century to the present day. Its apparent disappearance in the nineteenth century was not due to a lack on the part of Kongo, a resurgence of suppressed local religion or a failure on the part of the clergy. Instead it was caused by a changing definition among European clergy (including Rome) as to what constituted Christianity, coupled with more chauvinistic attitudes towards non-Western (and especially colonial) peoples that arose after 1850. Christianity in Kongo may have changed little, but the way in which it was perceived by foreigners changed substantially, and what had been considered orthodox before were now no more than interesting and unedifying survivals.[14]

The missionaries who came to Kongo at the end of the fifteenth century came from the unreformed Church of the later Middle Ages. The Council of Trent (1545–63) was to impose a rigid liturgical and theological uniformity on the Catholic Church, but this standardization of Latin Christianity still lay in the future when Kongo was evangelized. The first missionaries to Kongo were prepared to tolerate a large measure of ecclesial diversity. They did not come with a vastly superior technology or with ready-made pictures, statues or other religious artefacts. They proclaimed the Word of God without obliging the Kongo to receive the biblical images in Western form.[15] They had, to use Thornton's term, an 'inclusive' conception of the Faith. Any aspects of Kongo culture which were not fundamentally opposed to Christian teaching were considered to be acceptable. The missionaries waged a campaign against fetishes and against marital irregularities, but, Thornton argues, if they accepted an insertion of Christian doctrine into traditional Kongo cosmology, it was because the latter was compatible with the Church's teaching. The missionaries came as the invited guests of a powerful and unconquered king, and they presented their message in as attractive a form as possible. They even referred to themselves as *nganga*, the term for a traditional diviner-doctor. The Kongo situation was altogether different from

146

that of the Americas where Christianity was introduced as the religion of the Spanish and Portuguese conquerors.

The first bishop of Kongo was Henrique, son of King Afonso I, who was sent to Europe for training and who was probably very largely responsible for creating this unique form of Christianity. When Henrique died in 1531, the Kongo church was placed under the administration of the Bishop of São Tomé. The Kings of Kongo, however, resisted the bishop's attempts to exercise his jurisdiction in their territory. In 1596, at the request of the King of Kongo, the country was made into a separate diocese, but the King of Portugal retained the right of appointment to the see. The Portuguese tried vainly to control the Kongo Church and through it the Kingdom of Kongo itself. When this attempt failed, they resolved to destroy it by starving it of priests. In 1624 the Bishop moved permanently to Luanda and stopped ordaining Kongo priests.

Priests and bishops were, of course, hierarchically appointed and ordained. If the Kongo church was denied a clergy, its chances of recognition were slim. Until the seventeenth century missionaries had come to Kongo in a somewhat haphazard manner and local Kongo priests had been more easily ordained. After the Council of Trent, the training and provision of priests was standardized throughout the Church. At the same time the Church's missionary work was also unified and placed under centralized direction in Rome. The Kings of Kongo, however, made every effort to obtain clergy. The Capuchin mission of 1645–1768 and the so-called 'mixed mission' of 1781–88 were responses to these appeals. To this day, the monument designed by Caporale and erected by Pope Urban VIII to the memory of the Kongo ambassador, António Emmanuel, can be seen in the baptistery of St Mary Major in Rome. The ambassador had been robbed of all his possessions by Dutch pirates and was obliged to spend more than three years in Lisbon and Madrid before he could proceed to Rome. Pope Paul V had planned an impressive reception for him in Rome on his arrival there in 1608, but António died on the very day of his reception in the Baradis apartment next to the Sistine Chapel. The Kongo ambassador's dramatic journey and death, which is also the subject of a fresco in the Vatican library, illustrate the lengths to which the Kongo kings went to maintain contact with Rome.

The seventeenth- and eighteenth-century missionaries, imbued with the Counter-Reformation's zeal for uniformity, did not approve of the Kongo church's specialized vocabulary and religious practices.

However the Kongo themselves remained firmly in control of their church. When the avenue of the priesthood was denied them, educated Kongo became lay assistants to the foreign clergy, interpreters, 'masters' of churches or chapels and catechists. It is usually assumed that Christianity declined in Kongo along with the diminishing number of clergy, but Thornton argues that a viable lay church came into being which preserved the religion and kept Kongo a Catholic country.[16] De Castello da Vide has left a moving account of the Christian devotion of the people of Kongo at the end of the eighteenth century.[17]

Unfortunately, nineteenth-century European visitors to Kongo were not so appreciative of Kongo Christianity. The lack of priests was regarded as the cause of differences in church discipline which were now considered unacceptable. Father António José de Sousa Barroso, the founder of the modern Catholic mission to Angola, condemned what he saw as useless and irredeemable.

> After visiting a village of catechists in 1881, which he described in fair detail, he concluded that while the village was a tribute to the work of the Capuchin mission, the original work of those Italian friars was lost. This Christianity, ready to hand, and perhaps even helpful to permit the Church and Portugal to claim Kongo against Protestant and English, French and Belgian rivals, was not a model to follow, and the Church must remake the country in order to succeed.[18]

If Thornton's thesis is accepted, the story of the Kongo church testifies, not to the decline of a Christianity deprived of clergy, so much as to the evolution of official Catholicism away from the cultural tolerance of the late medieval missionaries. The Church of the Counter-Reformation was not ready for inculturation, or indeed for any measure of cultural pluralism.

The Dialogue of Faith and Culture in Medieval Europe

If the medieval Church's encounter with non-Christian cultures in the mission field did not always result in true dialogue, there nevertheless remained the ever-present internal dialogue of faith and culture within Latin Christendom itself. Much of the evidence for this dialogue has been presented by Jaroslav Pelikan in his recent fascinating study.[19] The Church in Europe had to reckon with ancient pagan beliefs in demonic powers, and it did much, wittingly or unwittingly, to reinforce these unhealthy beliefs and fears. The great medieval antidote to evil magic and demonic power was the sign of the Cross, and cruciform gestures and images were multiplied indefinitely. The veneration of relics of the True Cross were also part of this practical expression of Christianity. These practices were, moreover, reflected in the reigning theology of the Wisdom of the Cross, of the Christ who conquered by means of the Cross, and of the Anselmian doctrine of satisfaction of the demands of divine justice through the Cross. As Pelikan notes, St Anselm's doctrine of satisfaction also derived from medieval penitential practice. Christ was the cosmic 'penitent', making restitution of all that had been lost through the sin of the world.[20]

Another important theme was that of monastic abnegation. The spread of monasticism in western Europe and the successive foundations of monastic orders were closely connected with repeated reform and renewal in the Church as a whole. They were also connected with the Church's missionary impetus. Significantly also for the theme of inculturation, it was the monks who preserved the cultural traditions of Greece and Rome, and who made possible the appeal to these resources in the twelfth-century renaissance. Finally, St Francis of Assisi applied medieval traditions of chivalry to the monastic life and aspired to a literal imitation of Christ in his poverty.[21]

One of the most interesting of Pelikan's insights concerns the cultural implications of medieval mysticism. This derived in part from the neo-Platonic speculations contained in the pseudonymous writings of Dionysius the Areopagite, but it also owed much to the allegorical interpretation of the biblical Song of Songs. In this Christian allegory Christ became 'the bridegroom of the soul', and the mystical interpretation of this love-poem rejoined medieval literary traditions of courtly love. In the songs and ballads of the troubadours the worship of the lady was a kind of profane 'Marian devotion', and lyrics addressed to the Blessed Virgin and to the poet's sweetheart became interchangeable. Often, as Pelikan notes, the devotional verses were used to conceal a profane love.[22] In these traditions, therefore, there was both a mystical transcendence of eroticism and a reversion to the eroticism which the mystics were reinterpreting. There was also the pantheistic danger of obliterating the distinction between Creator and creature, and the danger of an individualistic emphasis in Christian devotion. These characteristics were destined to resurface in Pietistic Protestantism.

149

The Latin Church at the end of the Middle Ages was culturally very different from what it had been in the fifth and sixth centuries AD. The missionary fervour of those early centuries went hand-in-hand with a zeal for the spreading of Latin language and culture, together with the direct intervention of the papacy in the affairs of particular churches. This fervour and this zeal clashed with the more tolerant tradition of the East, in the persons of Saints Cyril and Methodius during the ninth century. After the final schism between East and West, Latin Christendom became more closed in upon itself, and missionary activity virtually ceased until the discovery of new continents and cultures by Portuguese and Spanish navigators. By this time European Christendom itself was dissolving into component nationalities, and the missionaries who accompanied the navigators and traders were sometimes more open to non-Christian cultures than their early medieval counterparts had been. There was, however, a tension between Western ethnocentricity and the dawning consciousness of cultural pluralism. This tension was heightened by the Counter-Reformation and by Europe's colonial aggression. As we shall see in Chapter 11, it was even difficult to observe in practice the uneasy compromise which distinguished religious from secular aspects of culture. In pursuing the story of the Christian Church of the Kongo Kingdom we have already encountered the intransigence that was a consequence of the Counter-Reformation. We shall now examine the post-Reformation period more fully.

References

1 Pelikan 1985, p. 35.

2 *Ibid.*, pp. 35–9.

3 *Stromateis*, I, v (28,1), cf. Bettenson 1956, p. 232.

4 Pelikan 1985, pp. 41–5.

5 Paul VI, *Address in St Anne's Church, Jerusalem*, 4 January 1964; cf. Wenger and Gallay 1964, pp. 31–2 (my tr.).

6 Bede I, 30.

7 Bede III, 25.

8 Cf. John Paul II, *Slavorum Apostoli* (1985), 21.

9 Timiadis 1985, p. 240.

10 Voulgarakis 1985, p. 235.

11 Dorotheos 1985, p. 219–29.

12 Meyendorff 1985, p. 246.

13 Thornton 1984.

14 *Ibid.*, p. 148.

15 Badi-Banga Ne-Mwine 1981, p. 138.

16 Thornton 1984, p. 166.

17 *Ibid.*

18 *Ibid.*

19 Pelikan 1985.

20 *Ibid.*, p. 108.

21 *Ibid.*, pp. 109–21; 133–44.

22 *Ibid.*, pp. 122–33.

11

Inculturation and the post-Reformation missions

Reformation, Counter-Reformation and Culture

In many ways the Reformation in Europe was a form of incipient cultural modernity. By the beginning of the sixteenth century the old, literate, Latin culture of western Christendom had ceased to exist. National vernaculars had developed to the point of becoming written languages with a growing corpus of literature behind them. Clerical Latinists no longer held the monopoly of university education and scholarship. Moreover, Europe had resolved itself into a collection of nation-states, with a growing sense of national identity and self-sufficiency. Even the Papal States were seen as a principality, competing with others at the same level, and papal policies were often determined by national, rather than ecclesiastical, priorities.

The sixteenth-century Renaissance was a return to classical Graeco-Roman sources and models, a revival of classical learning, in fact, but it definitely was not a revival of medieval Latin culture. It aimed at the spread of classical learning and its findings, the rediscovery of the world and of humanity. This entailed the work of translation from original classical sources into modern vernaculars, and the publication of such translations by means of the newly invented process of printing. Translation into vernacular languages was the order of the day. The Bible was translated into numerous languages, and the Reformed Churches insisted also on a vernacular liturgy.

The principle of *cujus regio ejus religio*, the right of the ruler to dictate the form of Christianity in his own dominions, was the axiom according to which the map of Reformation Europe was drawn. In most of the Churches of the Reformation, the ruling prince exercised a special role of guardianship or governance, repudiating the structures of communion that had held Christendom together hitherto,

152

particularly the Petrine ministry of the Pope. Apart from the 'protest' which gave Protestantism its name, what united the Reformed Churches was their common acceptance of the supremacy of the Bible and their belief that God spoke directly to the believer through Scripture.

All of these factors encouraged heterogeneity and ensured the rise of national Churches. These Churches were established Churches, part of the structure of the State. As such, they obeyed the norms of a national culture. Indeed, at times they were indistinguishable from it. Perhaps it is not going too far to say that the Reformation was characterized by a fair measure of culturalism. Certainly, national cultures were preferred to the cultural implications of universal communion. In England, for example, Catholic communion was rejected as essentially 'foreign'. It implied the interference of a foreign potentate, the Pope, and subjection to the foreign power of Spain. The Protestant Reformation was presented as enabling the English to be masters in their own house.

At the Reformation, the cultures or sub-cultures of Europe came into their own. The period of gestation had been long indeed, and it had been lengthened by the imposition of the dominant Latin culture. This yoke had been finally thrown off and Protestant nations were tempted to go to the other extreme of cultural incapsulation, as well as to compromise the unity of faith, the Christian term, as we have called it, of inculturation. In particular, the English language was at a formative stage of development, which accounts for the richness of idiom in Shakespeare and in the Authorized Version of the Bible and the Anglican Prayer Book. The Reformation corresponded with, and even to some extent called forth, a flowering of national culture. This was especially evident in the creation of new, vernacular liturgies.

The Council of Trent began to meet in 1545, and was to complete its work eighteen years later. Trent set in motion the Counter-Reformation which was to reorganize the Catholic Church in the face of the Protestant challenge. The Fathers of Trent rejected the Reformation, and, with it, the national and cultural distinctions of the reformers. Their priority was to safeguard Catholic unity, and they did this by imposing a rigid liturgical and theological uniformity on the Western Church. It was even decided to abolish liturgical variations in the particular churches as far as possible. Local rites and usages which could not be proved to have been in existence for more than two hundred years were forbidden.

The tragedy of the Catholic Counter-Reformation was that this sweeping standardization of the Church coincided with the discovery of new continents and cultures. At the very moment when a rigid uniformity was being imposed on the Church in every department of the Christian life, explorers and navigators were discovering and colonizing the Americas, the West Indies, the coasts of Africa and the East Indies, and missionaries were either accompanying them or following in their wake. Uniformity implied a Western, homogeneous, ethnocentric view of culture, and a bias towards its Latin origins. The practical effect of this standardization was to ally the Church with the colonizers and conquistadors, reinforcing their belief in Western cultural superiority. As a result, the newly discovered indigenous cultures were, at worst, destroyed, at best, ignored.

Trent made no distinction between theology on the one hand, and its historical and cultural form, on the other. Furthermore, in order to train an effective and exemplary clergy, the training of priests was also standardized through the seminary system. Seminary training was to be uniform throughout the world, making no cultural distinctions whatever. Not only did the uniform training of priests in the world widen the gap between clergy and laity; it also prevented the training of priests in many of the mission countries where it was well-nigh impossible to create the necessary educational facilities on the Western model. We already noted the problem in the Kingdom of Kongo, in Chapter 10. The same problem and policy existed in most of Latin America. In the new mission territories the clergy were almost entirely foreign, removed from the culture of the laity in their homeland, and having no point of contact with the indigenous culture whose adepts they were evangelizing. The way was open for a universal, clerical sub-culture. It was also open for a popular stratum of Catholicism which was removed from clerical influence and was highly syncretist. Popular Amerindian Catholicism and the Catholic façade of African religions among the slaves in e.g. Brazil, demonstrated more than anything else the need for a conscious dialogue between faith and culture. That dialogue was postponed indefinitely because the clergy belonged to the foreign culture of the colonizers, and were in any case unable to distinguish between faith and culture.[1]

Another consequence of Tridentine uniformity was the misguided attempt to Latinize the churches of Eastern rite. Nowhere were the attempts so blatant and the consequences so dire as in Ethiopia during the first quarter of the seventeenth century. It was only in the

154

late nineteenth century that a belated attempt was made to repair the damage that had been done. The concept of the Uniate Church, while it was an acknowledgement of the value of non-Latin forms of Christianity, was nevertheless viewed with intense suspicion as a 'Trojan horse' of Latin Christendom.

The Congregation de Propaganda Fide

Pope Urban VIII founded the Sacred Congregation *de Propaganda Fide* in 1622. This centralized organ of Catholic missionary activity was the ancestor of the modern Sacred Congregation for the Evangelization of Peoples. Its establishment was an important step for the Church because it enabled Rome to take over the direction of the whole Catholic missionary effort. Until the appearance of this congregation, Catholic missionary work was under the *padroado* system, or patronage of the Catholic monarchs, particularly of Spain and Portugal. Evangelization was thus compromised by conquest and colonization, not to mention the Atlantic slave trade.

Since the new congregation insisted on evangelization by peaceful, rather than violent, means, it tended to have some respect for the people's way of life or culture. In this way it acted as a counterweight not only to the violence of the colonizing powers, but also to the standardizing policies introduced by the Council of Trent. There was, however, a limit beyond which *Propaganda Fide* could not theoretically go, and there was also the greater problem of putting theory into practice in a climate of ethnocentric intransigence.

The congregation tried valiantly to oppose wholesale cultural domination, but it distinguished between the religious and secular aspects of culture. Secular culture was not to be touched, but whatever did not conform to Catholic faith and morals must be uprooted. This principle is clearly stated in a circular to Vicars Apostolic in the foreign missions, dated 1659.

> Do not make any effort or use any argument in favour of forcing the people to change their customs or traditions, as long as these are not clearly opposed to religion and morality. What could be more absurd than to import France, Spain, Italy, or any other country of Europe into China?[2]

The distinction between aspects of culture that belong to the sphere of religion and morality, and those which do not, is hard to sustain. In practice, non-Christian religions are cultural systems that underlie and permeate whole cultural traditions. The dualism of sacred and secular, which was coming into vogue in Europe after the Wars of Religion, was not applicable to the indigenous cultures encountered by the missionaries. More seriously, however, there was often disagreement in practice as to what did or did not oppose Catholic religion and morality, and this was the case in the celebrated controversy over the 'Chinese rites'.

The Congregation *de Propaganda Fide* inherited the tradition of a few enlightened missionaries in their struggle against European cultural domination. One of these was Bartolomé de Las Casas. Las Casas went to America in 1502, at the age of twenty-eight. He was disgusted by the inhumanity of the Spanish colonial system, and especially of the *encomienda* or system of tributary labour that was linked, under the *padroado*, with Christian evangelization. He was determined to destroy this system, and to replace military conquest by peaceful colonization and a form of Christianization that respected the freedom of conscience of the Amerindians. Having failed, as a colonist, to convince others of these ideas, he entered the Dominican Order in 1523, and returned to evangelize unpacified regions of Nicaragua and Guatemala.

Back in Spain after 1540, he campaigned against the *encomienda* and was largely responsible for the New Laws that brought about its suppression. In 1544 he returned again to Latin America as bishop and founded the mission of Vera Paz. Three years later he went back to Spain, where he died in 1566. His last years were spent in writing and publishing his indictment of Spanish colonial policy. In particular, he lamented the destruction of whole peoples and their cultures in America.

Las Casas opposed the conquest and exploitation of the indigenous people of America. His period of missionary and literary activity coincided almost exactly with the sessions of the Council of Trent and he was, therefore, relatively free of that Council's standardizing outlook. However, he cannot be said to have advocated an equal dialogue between the Catholic Faith and indigenous Amerindian cultures, although such a dialogue was the logical consequence of his respect for freedom of conscience.

Neither Las Casas nor *Propaganda Fide* could ultimately prevent the cultural domination of Latin America by Spain and Portugal, and the driving underground of the Amerindian cultures. As a result of this domination, syncretism or parallelism flourished at the popular level.

Occasionally, a happier, and theologically orthodox, synthesis was achieved in popular cults and devotions, such as the Mexican devotion to Our Lady of Guadalupe which had an Indian origin.[3]

In spite of this considerable cultural heterogeneity, the countries of Latin America remain 'Latin', that is to say, they have an overriding layer of Hispanic culture which is the legacy of conquest and colonial domination, and a consequence of four centuries of close ties with Spain and Portugal. It is an ill wind that blows nobody any good, and it is noticeable that the cultural experience of Latin America gives it a position of influence and importance in the Church today. Latin American countries have problems of poverty and dependence which place them in the sphere of the so-called 'Third World'. However, their Hispanic culture gives them a cultural proximity to Europe and the Western World, and this, in turn, enables them to exercise an influence on a Church which is still culturally 'in bondage' to the West.

Matteo Ricci and the Chinese Rites

Matteo Ricci lived and died before the foundation of the Congregation *de Propaganda Fide*, but his achievements aroused fierce controversy after his death, and the debate has continued up to our own times. Ricci was an Italian Jesuit, born in 1552, who went as a missionary to China. Imperial China possessed an ancient and sophisticated culture, articulated in the Confucian philosophy which had already absorbed and transformed the Buddhist faith. It was a culture that set great store by science and scholarship and which was highly ethnocentric, not to say xenophobic. The Jesuit missionaries, under the impetus of Alessandro Valignano, decided that only one course of action was possible, namely the Christian penetration of Chinese culture from within. The Jesuits, therefore, set themselves to propagate Western science and technology and in this way to make a contribution to Chinese scholarship.

Ricci's first plan was to adopt the dress and style of life of a Buddhist monk. Buddhists tended to be less critical of Christian teaching than Confucianists. However, this policy was soon discovered to be a mistake. Buddhism was not the dominant religious culture of China, and there was a danger of Christianity being rejected as identical with Buddhism.[4]

Ricci therefore decided to adopt the identity of a Confucian scholar and mandarin in order to win over the intellectual masters of a society dominated by Confucian ideas. From 1595, therefore, Ricci, who gave his name Matteo the Chinese form of 'Ma Dou', addressed himself to the higher ranks of diplomats and bureaucrats, and succeeded in penetrating the imperial city at Peking. Ricci made a formidable contribution to Chinese scholarship and was the author of more than twenty works in Chinese. The Jesuits' proficiency in astronomy, mathematics and the physical sciences was greatly appreciated by the Chinese, especially in connection with the establishment of an accurate calendar, around which rotated the whole of Chinese social and religious life. Involvement in these aspects of Chinese cultural life carried considerable risks of misinterpretation, and we do not know how it would have developed, since it came to an end after Ricci's death.

It seems, nevertheless, that Ricci and his fellow Jesuit missionaries were embarked on a profound dialogue with the religious culture of the Chinese, and that they were aiming at nothing more nor less than inculturation in the true sense of the word. The goal was to achieve a Christian reinterpretation of Chinese culture which would, in turn, provoke a Chinese interpretation of Christianity presented in this sympathetic Chinese form. It is, perhaps, a measure of the success of this policy that three thousand people had been baptized by the time of Ricci's death in 1610.

The tragedy which followed Ricci's death was that the whole ambitious scheme was rejected by Church authority because of a dispute over the meaning of certain cultural elements which, while they were important to the Chinese, were of marginal interest to Christianity. It was also ironical that the controversy should have been a practical test of *Propaganda Fide*'s own principle of accepting every aspect of culture not clearly opposed to Christian faith and morality.

The controversy concerned the so-called 'Chinese rites' which Ricci accepted as compatible with Christian faith and morals. These, in Ricci's understanding, were threefold. Firstly, there was his approval of the application of the traditional Chinese title 'Lord of Heaven' to the God of Christianity. Secondly, there was the honour paid to the founding philosopher, Confucius, through periodic rituals; and finally there was the cult of the familial dead which was characterized by prostrations, the burning of incense and the offering of food at graves. Ricci authorized the cult of Confucius and of the familial dead in 1603, as probably not superstitious. At least, in his view, there was no evidence of superstition. After his death, Ricci's view was challenged by missionaries of other congregations. In many cases their condemnation embraced a mass of superstitious practices which Ricci had never allowed. In fact, those who attacked the Chinese rites were unable or unwilling to make the kind of distinctions that Ricci himself made.

Charles Maigrot, the Vicar Apostolic of Fukien, began the indictment in 1693, and this was the start of a lengthy and complex judicial process which continued into the following century. A special commission of Cardinals was appointed to examine the case, and Pope Clement IX issued a decree condemning the Chinese rites in 1704. This condemnation was finalized by Pope Benedict XIV who closed the discussion with his decree *Ex Quo Singulari* in 1742. The condemnation included many practices that were never originally at issue and which were seen as opposed to Christian doctrine.

Two hundred years later these adverse decisions were rescinded, and the wisdom of Matteo Ricci was belatedly recognized. In 1935 Pope Pius XI approved the cult of Confucius as essentially non-religious, and therefore not opposed to Catholic doctrine. Four years later, in 1939, Pope Pius XII issued his *Instructio Circa Quasdam Caeremonias Super Ritibus Sinensibus*. This instruction approved traditional Chinese funeral rites and the cult of the familial dead. Within a few years Communism came to power in China, and Catholics were persecuted very largely because of their foreign characteristics and connections. In Taiwan, after the Second Vatican Council, the Catholics of Nationalist China were able to celebrate their ancestral cult in the context of the Christian liturgy itself. One cannot help wondering what the history of the Church in mainland China would have been if the Catholic authorities had been sufficiently mature theologically to accept Matteo Ricci's experiment during, or soon after, his own lifetime.

The reversal of the Church's position on the question of the Chinese rites holds an abiding interest for other newly evangelized peoples who have ancestral cults. Chief among the latter are the numerous ethnic groups of Africa who venerate their ancestors. In some cases such veneration may amount to an illicit form of spirit-worship, especially where human ancestors have become divinities. But in the majority of cases it is a practice that is fairly easily reconciled with Christian faith and practice. A good example of such a reconciliation is the new Catholic funeral rite of Zimbabwe.

Roberto de Nobili in India

Roberto de Nobili was a Jesuit missionary to India. Born in 1577, he was the son of an Italian count. In India he used his noble origins in order to commend his teaching to the upper castes. Like Ricci in China, he aimed at the conversion of the élite, and penetrated the world of scholarship and learning. He was the first European to acquire a first-hand knowledge of Sanskrit and to read the Hindu Scriptures, the Vedas and the Vedanta, in their originals. He adopted the costume and mode of life of a Hindu holy man and was called *Rajah Sannyasi* or 'noble holy man'.

Christianity in India was confronted by the rigid Hindu caste system, and this posed a dilemma for the missionaries. To concentrate their efforts upon the 'untouchable' outcastes was to preclude for ever the possibility of influencing the élite. De Nobili's plan was to penetrate the caste system itself and to approach the very highest caste of the Brahmins. To do this, he had to approve a variety of cultural practices and to resort to *Propaganda Fide*'s distinction between civil and religious rites or customs. This distinction enabled de Nobili to authorize much of Brahmin culture as compatible with the Gospel.[5]

The success of de Nobili's mission strategy was demonstrated when Sivadarma, an eminent Brahmin scholar, was converted to Christianity and allowed to retain his former way of life. When de Nobili finally left Madras, there were more than four thousand Christians. However, his approach was soon challenged by church authorities and he was censured in 1610. De Nobili appealed to Rome and a final verdict was given in his favour shortly after the founding of *Propaganda Fide* in 1623. Nevertheless, he had been forbidden to baptize during the thirteen years of the judicial process. Moreover, the Church in India abandoned his experiment after his retirement and death in 1656. It was only in our own century, in the wake of the Second Vatican Council, that Christian *sannyasi* reappeared and Christian *ashrams* or prayer centres were set up on the Hindu model.[6]

Pedro Paez in Ethiopia

Christian Ethiopia was cut off from contact with European Christendom by desert, distance and Islam. It was only in the middle of the fifteenth century that any real knowledge of Ethiopia reached Europe at all. Ethiopian delegates attended the Council of Florence in 1441, as a result of papal negotiations with the Coptic Patriarch of Alexandria and with the Ethiopian community in Jerusalem. Early in the sixteenth century a Franciscan mission was sent to Ethiopia from Jerusalem, but little could be achieved while Europe was in the throes of the Reformation.

It was in the first decade of the following century that a Jesuit mission was sent to Ethiopia. Pedro Paez arrived there in 1607 as part of this mission. This Spanish missionary was extremely tolerant of Ethiopian Christian culture. He accepted the Ethiopic liturgy, and succeeded in persuading the Negus to profess the two natures of Christ and to legislate for the reunion of the Ethiopian Church with Rome. The Jewish Sabbath was also abolished and thousands of Ethiopians were baptized, made their confessions and received communion at the hands of the missionaries.[7]

All of these achievements were destroyed by the successor of Paez, the Portuguese Jesuit 'Patriarch', Mendez, who arrived in the country in 1625 together with eight missionaries. Mendez was an uncompromising Latinizer. He not only insisted on the Latin language, but also on the Roman calendar and on communion for the faithful under one kind. Furthermore, he ordered the rebaptism of all Ethiopian Christians, the reordination of all Ethiopian priests, the ceremonial washing of altars, and the removal from church buildings of the relics of Ethiopian saints.[8]

As a result of this incredible assault on the ancient culture and rites of the Ethiopian Church, there was an immediate return to schism and a definitive revival of Ethiopian hatred for Rome and all that Rome stood for. The massacre of Latin missionaries followed, and it was only in the nineteenth century that Catholic missionaries adopted the Ethiopian rite and began to ordain priests and bishops accordingly.

Lessons of the Counter-Reformation Missions

Catholics were first in the mission field after the discovery of the new continents by the Spaniards and Portuguese. This was partly because the geographical discoveries, and the missions that followed them, antedated the Reformation. However, even after the Reformation the newly-founded Protestant Churches were slow to undertake missionary work. They were essentially a protest against Catholicism, and they saw their work as one of reforming the Church in Europe. Other factors inhibited Protestant missionary work, such as their theology of election and predestination which seemed to dispense with the need for missions. One factor that has already been mentioned was the Protestant identification with the national cultures of Europe. This meant that Protestants tended to limit their horizons to national frontiers, or at most to the colonial territories of their nationalities when forced to flee from persecution at home. The Protestant colonization of North America, for example, was not at first prompted by any zeal for the evangelization of Amerindian peoples. It was only with the Pietism of the eighteenth century that genuine Protestant missions began to emerge. One of the earliest Protestant missionary founders was Count Nicholas Louis Zinzendorf of the Moravian Brethren, whose missionary zeal was aroused by an encounter with Jesuit missionaries from Peking in the early eighteenth century.[9]

The Catholic missions of the Counter-Reformation period were indeed a striking witness to the universalist faith of the Christian Gospel. In particular, the contribution of the newly founded Society of Jesus was outstanding. For the first time in its history the Church was directly confronted by cultures that had never been in contact with Graeco-Roman civilization, or, as in the case of Ethiopia, with a culture long cut off from that tradition.

Faced with seemingly self-sufficient non-Western cultures, Jesuit missionaries, such as Ricci, de Nobili or Paez, realized immediately that their only course was to try and penetrate these cultures from within. They did not need to have a sophisticated understanding of inculturation to tell them this. Evangelization from within a culture necessitated a profound dialogue with that culture, a capacity for clear discernment, and the assumption that the missionary's goal was a new cultural creation in Christ.

The missionaries of the Counter-Reformation, and even more so their superiors at home, lacked an adequate theology of revelation-salvation to cope with this new strategy. They also lacked a multicultural vision of the Church. Indeed the reigning theology was designed to create a rigid uniformity in the face of the Protestant threat, and to counteract the fissiparous tendencies of the Reformation. It ran exactly contrary to the needs of the missionaries in the field, who were obliged to fall back on rule-of-thumb distinctions, such as that adopted by *Propaganda Fide*, between civil and religious culture. Such distinctions were not only unrealistic, they were not even consistent-

162

ly applied. Ecclesiastical authorities did not, in fact, believe in them when the moment of truth arrived.

The great Jesuit missionaries, Ricci, de Nobili, Paez and others, were not theoretically or theologically equipped, let alone supported, by the Church of their time, to carry their inculturation through successfully. But their abortive endeavours were a sign of the Church's yearning for a more fully developed Catholicity. As such, they were, and still are, an inspiration for missionaries of later centuries, and they have received a belated recognition from a Church that has benefited by theological hindsight. In the following chapter we carry the story a stage further, and take a look at the missionaries, both Catholic and Protestant, of the nineteenth century, and their growing awareness of the need for a positive approach to non-Christian cultures. In point of fact, as we shall see, the questions posed by the Counter-Reformation missionaries refused to go away.

References

1 Azevedo 1982, p. 17.

2 *S.C. de Propaganda Fide, Collectanea*, Rome 1907, *Cap.* X, No. 300, p. 103.

3 Turner and Turner 1978, pp. 40–103.

4 Standaert 1985, pp. 6–12. Much of my information concerning Ricci in China comes from this article.

5 Cf. Rocarés 1967.

6 Cf. the work of Dom Bede Griffiths as a Christian *sannyasi*.

7 Cf. Coulbeaux 1928.

8 *Ibid.*

9 Hutton 1922, chapter one.

12

Mission and culture in the nineteenth century

Vatican I and Anti-Modernism

Pope Pius IX reigned from 1846 to 1878, the longest pontificate of any of the successors of St Peter. Politically, his pontificate was a disaster. Shortly after his election, Mazzini's short-lived Roman republic drove him into exile, and at the end of his reign the *Risorgimento* deprived the Church permanently of the Papal States. In almost every country of Europe the public position of the Church was assailed by liberal and secularizing governments. Yet Pius IX's thirty-two years were of immense significance to the Church.

In the first place, they were years of extraordinary expansion. The industrial revolution sharpened the competition between the European powers, and this competition spilled over into the exploration and colonization of vast areas of the earth. The improvement in the means of travel and communication facilitated this process. The interior of Africa was explored and annexed by Europe, likewise Australasia and the islands of the Pacific. In North and South America also the frontiers of Western culture were pushed into the furthest interior. Christian missionaries accompanied or followed, or even in some cases preceded, these movements. Secular governments reaped advantages from missionary expansion, and, as Gambetta is alleged to have told Cardinal Lavigerie, anticlericalism was 'not for export'.

The Church thrived on opposition. Discriminatory laws at home actually encouraged the foundation of foreign missionary institutes. As Pope and Church were deprived of their political influence, their moral stature grew, and the structures of Christian communion became stronger and more centralized. This centralization was accompanied by the greatest expansion the Church had yet known. Once again Christianity was confronted with a vast spectrum of non-Christian cultures, and once again the questions posed by the Jesuit missionaries of the sixteenth century were to be repeated.

Although the Christian missionaries of the nineteenth century were to experience considerable difficulty in freeing themselves from ethnocentric prejudice at a time of aggressive European nationalism, the scientific approach to cultures was already present among them in embryo. The human sciences were young, and were often possessed of an evolutionary and atheistic bias. However, it was the missionaries and not the early anthropologists who were in the field, and who made systematic observations long before fieldwork was begun by social scientists. And if they did not find contemporary sociological theory of much help, they did not ignore it altogether. Long before the development of the science of linguistics, missionaries were collecting and recording the languages of preliterate societies on a massive scale. Language is, of course, a key to the understanding of culture, and in our own time the science of linguistics has become an inspiration and a model for structural anthropology. Missionary emphasis on language was necessary for serious evangelization, but it was also an important preparation for the later study of cultures.

Unfortunately, missionaries were hampered less by their ignorance of the infant human sciences than by the theology in which they had been trained. Before long, they became experts in the social institutions and practices of the people they served, but the theology they had imbibed during their training prevented them from making any positive use of their newly acquired knowledge. It was as if they were studying non-Christian cultures only to condemn them, or at least to bypass them.

This nineteenth-century theology was reactionary and integralist, the over-cautious response to contemporary liberalism and to the anti-religious tendencies of evolutionary and empirical science. Its most extreme expression was Pius IX's *Syllabus of Errors*, issued in 1864, a list of current errors condemned by the Pope in his various writings. These errors included modern liberalism, socialism, the rejection of the temporal power of the Pope, the subjection of the Church to the authority of the State, Bible societies, and religious freedom. Although we have come to accept many of these things as compatible with Catholicism today, their condemnation by Pius IX has to be seen against the background of a movement to remove the

Church from influencing the life of individuals, families and nations. The Pope's attack on rationalism was also a direct preparation for the constitution *Dei Filius* of the First Vatican Council.

The First Vatican Council met in 1869, and its second session was suspended in 1870 by the outbreak of the Franco-Prussian War which was accompanied, among other things, by the final loss of the Papal States. The Council promulgated two documents, *Dei Filius* and *Pastor Aeternus*, the latter being the definition of papal infallibility. *Dei Filius* studied the interrelationship of faith and reason and was principally concerned to refute Traditionalism. This was itself a reaction to eighteenth-century rationalism, and proposed that knowledge of God derived from a primitive revelation. Vatican I taught that this knowledge could be discovered by the light of reason alone.

Nineteenth-century Catholic theology placed considerable emphasis on deductive reasoning, and Thomistic philosophy was virtually equated with reason itself. The Church adopted a policy of strict fidelity to the philosophy and theology of St Thomas Aquinas and used Thomism as a restraint on further exploration. Having demonstrated the supernatural origin of revealed truth, it brought reasoning to bear on these assertions. As Gabriel Daly has pointed out, its methods were, in fact, rationalist, not to say, positivist.[1] They were also extrinsicist, since there was no need to posit any intrinsic relationship between revealed truth and the nature of the believer. Although 'pure nature' does not, in fact, exist, nineteenth-century neo-Thomism continued to stress the dichotomy between natural and supernatural. The definition of *Dei Filius* tacitly prescinds from the real order of things.

Nineteenth-century theology was unable to distinguish clearly between meaning and contingent formulation. It sought eternal, unchanging truths, and, as Bernard Lonergan has pointed out, its extrinsicism separated the objectivity of these truths from the very way in which objectivity is reached — the self-transcendence of the existing subject.[2] This explains its hostility towards Modernism, as well as towards history and cultural pluralism. Anti-Modernism became the bulwark of classicist theology, as well as the last and most formidable obstacle to inculturation. It was finally undermined by critical history and by the objective missionary experience of cultures.

Modernism was the name given, at the close of the nineteenth century, to the teaching of a group of theologians, liturgists, philosophers and historians who made the mistake of supposing that the contemporary advances of science and rational philosophy had relegated religion to the expression of inner experiences which had no objective basis. The so-called 'Modernists', however, raised many questions which neo-Thomism was unable to answer in the light of its own argument and conceptual scheme. These questions concerned two issues already mentioned: the fact that nature is already graced, and that certainty of objective truth is gained by self-transcendence. They also included the claim that neo-Thomism exempted revelation from the laws of history, and that a philosophical theology contradicted the symbolic mode according to which God's self-revelation makes itself known to humanity.

The Church failed at first to meet the challenge of Modernism. Its extrinsicism and 'supernatural rationalism' led it to deny the relevance of religious experience or of any contingent historical and cultural factors. The condemnation of Modernism by Pope St Pius X in 1907 meant that the Modernists' questions remained unanswered. It also meant that the claims of history, culture and religious experience were ignored. A missionary who subscribed wholeheartedly to his anti-Modernist oath might find it difficult to identify a 'preparation of the Gospel' in non-Christian cultures, or he might be guilty, as some missionaries were, of looking for Thomistic definitions of God in such cultures.[3] Anti-Modernism, therefore, precluded the possibility of a multicultural Church, and its reinforcement of theological intellectualism rendered popular culture irrelevant.

Vatican I and its anti-Modernist aftermath found juridical expression in the 1917 Code of Canon Law. The Code imposed a practical uniformity on the universal Church, which the authorities were enabled to enforce through modern means of travel and communication, although, inevitably, remote mission territories could not always enjoy the full benefit of the law, and a growing body of special mission faculties came into existence. It says a great deal for the missionaries that, in spite of these handicaps, they were able eventually to cultivate the mentality that gave rise to the mission documents of the Second Vatican Council. They were assisted, no doubt, both by the resurgence of some of the Modernists' questions in the New Theology of the 1940s and 1950s and in Vatican II itself, and also by the cultural awakening of the colonial peoples at their political independence after the Second World War. The relics of anti-Modernism, and the classicism it sought to defend, still remain in the end-of-the-twentieth-century Church, and constitute most of the obstacles to a whole-hearted commitment to inculturation.

Nineteenth-Century Missionary Founders and Culture

The founders of Catholic missionary institutes in the nineteenth century all realized, in their various ways, the importance of indigenous cultures, and exhorted their followers to study them and conform to them as far as possible. Most of these founders turned their attention wholly or initially towards Africa, which was the principal field open to evangelization at the time.

Francis Libermann, the convert Jew from Alsace, founded his Congregation of the Immaculate Heart of Mary in 1841. This congregation was fused in 1848 with the Congregation of the Holy Ghost, originally founded in 1703 by Claude Francis Poullard des Places, and Libermann was appointed superior general of the joint institute. Its members have become known as Holy Ghost Fathers or Spiritans. An example of his teaching on culture is provided by the following quotation from one of his letters to his missionaries in Africa.

> Do not judge according to appearances nor to what you have been accustomed in Europe. Forget Europe with its customs and its spirit. Become Negroes with the Negroes, and then you will regard them as they should be regarded. Become Negroes with the Negroes, to form them as they should be formed, not after the fashion of Europe, but by letting them keep what is proper to them. Act towards them as servants towards their masters. Adopt their customs and manner and habit, as servants do those of their master. Perfect them, sanctify them, show them their lowliness and make them, slowly but surely into a People of God. That is what St Paul refers to as becoming all to all, to win all to Jesus Christ.[4]

Libermann died on 2 February 1852, during the recitation of Vespers, at the words of the *Magnificat*: 'He has put down the mighty from their seats and exalted the humble'.

Melchior de Marion Brésillac, a French nobleman from Languedoc, served first of all in India as a priest of the Paris Foreign Mission Society. While serving this mission, he was appointed bishop in 1846, but resigned seven years later for two reasons. The first reason was that his clergy did not share his missionary policy towards the Hindu caste system, and de Marion Brésillac saw the importance of a unanimous stand on the issue if he was to obtain clear and favourable directives from Rome in the matter. The other reason for the bishop's resignation was the opposition of the missionaries to his plan for the training of indigenous clergy.

Back in France, de Marion Brésillac founded the Society of African Missions at Lyons in 1856. Although his initial document describing the aims of the society had a monocultural ring about it and spoke of 'spreading the religion of Jesus Christ, and with it civilization, among those abandoned tribes',[5] both he and his closest collaborator, Augustine Planque, were convinced that the eventual evangelizers of Africa would be the Africans themselves, and that the training of an indigenous clergy was a priority. De Marion Brésillac died of yellow fever in Sierra Leone, little more than a month after landing there in 1859.

Cardinal Charles Lavigerie, Archbishop of Algiers and Carthage and 'Primate of Africa', founded the Society of Missionaries of Africa (White Fathers) in 1868, and the Missionary Sisters of Our Lady of Africa (White Sisters) in the following year. Like other missionary founders, he laid emphasis on the formation of an indigenous clergy and on the evangelization of Africa by the Africans themselves. His scheme for training African doctor-catechists in Malta was a concrete realization of this principle. On the subject of the missionary approach to local culture, he was more than usually explicit. Missionaries must not only learn the local language in order to communicate with the people, they must speak it amongst themselves. The children they educate must be allowed to remain truly African and to keep their customs and way of life. Missionaries themselves must enter scientific and cultural observations in a journal. In his instructions to the first caravan of missionaries departing for Equatorial Africa in 1878, the Cardinal wrote:

> To descriptive accounts must be added historical material, and this will be the missionaries' main work once they have arrived and have settled in their final mission stations. I insist very much on this recommendation because it could be of very great interest, even for theology. European tales and missionary teachings have not yet given rise among the natives to legends which it will be difficult later on to disentangle from their own, original traditions. These are what it is interesting to collect before they are altered. To do this, the old people must be asked to narrate all their legends carefully, all the historical narratives of the tribe, its origin and that of the human race, of the world, primitive revelation and, in general, all that can confirm the accounts of our Holy Writ or the teachings of Christianity on the origin of the human race, its fall, etc.[6]

The Cardinal went on to ask his missionaries to record their descriptions of customs, dress, dwellings and cultivation in detail. He also insisted that Christian evangelization should take place within the social and political structures of the people, and it should be noted that, in the 1870s, there were, as yet, no European colonies in Equatorial Africa. But it was to the subject of language that he always returned. He even threatened ecclesiastical penalties if missionaries failed to learn the local vernacular and to speak it among themselves.[7]

Cardinal Lavigerie took a particular interest in the Greek-Melkite Church of the Middle East. He had come across the Melkites when visiting the area on behalf of the Schools of the Orient as a young priest. Later, as Archbishop of Algiers, he was offered the custody of the shrine of St Anne in Jerusalem, and he saw it as a way of helping the Melkites re-establish themselves *vis-à-vis* the Latins. His missionaries opened an apostolic school for these Eastern-rite Christians and the Cardinal wrote to them as follows:

> The Eastern Apostolic School of St Anne's has been founded in these conditions. As a result it must maintain an absolutely Eastern character in the education of its pupils, if it is to respond to the thinking behind its foundation. The Eastern Rite alone is to be used for the public liturgical celebrations which the pupils attend. Oriental languages, that is to say, Arabic and Greek, together with French, are the only languages to be studied in the house. The children must never be made to adopt the Latin Rite. Even if they wish to enter the Society of Missionaries responsible for their education, they must keep their rite. In a word, the Apostolic School of St Anne's, founded exclusively for Orientals, must make everything conform to this goal. It must remain absolutely Eastern, not only in its worship and teaching, but also in its material way of life, such as clothing, sleeping arrangements and food.[8]

The Cardinal often returned to the danger of Latinization:

> Efforts must be made to follow only the authorized usages of the Greek liturgy and not to change or add anything. Just as our influence is enhanced by keeping this rule scrupulously, so it is lost through trying to introduce changes or additions borrowed from the Latin rite.[9]

Inevitably, the 'Scramble for Africa', which had begun before the

Cardinal's death in 1892, introduced a policy of aggressive cultural alienation, very different from the advice Lavigerie gave to his missionaries in the last years before colonization. It was not always possible for the missionaries to dissociate themselves from such a colonial policy, but the Cardinal's wise counsels were not forgotten, and they acquired new significance with political independence in the mid-twentieth century.

Daniel Comboni founded the society now known as the Combonian Missionaries of the Sacred Heart (Verona Fathers) in 1867, and its sister-congregation, the Pious Mothers of the Negroes (Verona Sisters), seven years later. These foundations followed upon Comboni's first, abortive experience as a missionary on the Nile. As a preparation for the foundation of these institutes, Bishop Comboni drew up his *Plan for the Regeneration of Africa* in 1865, and it is this document, more than any other, which contains his thinking on missionary strategy.

Comboni's plan rested on two premises which are not as true today as they were in the nineteenth century. The first was that Europeans could not live in Central Africa for any length of time, and the second was that Africans could not be successfully trained as priests and teachers in Europe. These premisses, however, allowed Comboni to draw a conclusion which was profoundly appropriate for reasons connected with inculturation. This conclusion was his principle of 'the regeneration of Africa by means of Africa herself'.

> Settlements will have to be established where young Africans can be trained in their own environment, but preserving their racial characteristics. Moreover, the chosen locations must be such that white missionaries will be able to perform their work as educationists with the minimum danger to their health and lives.[10]

This ultimate vision of saving Africa with Africa has encouraged the Combonian missionaries to respect the cultures of the peoples to whom they were sent and to foster the development of self-sufficient communities. Another principle dear to Bishop Comboni, which has come to be realized by the missionary society he founded, is that of internationality. The missionaries should be 'neither Spanish, nor French, nor German, nor Italian, but Catholic'.[11] Moreover, all the resources and agents for evangelization were to be mobilized to bring about the regeneration of the continent. Daniel Comboni was spared the sufferings endured by his missionaries during the revolt of the Mahdi, since he died in 1881, the first year of the insurrection.

171

The Catholic missionary founders of the nineteenth century had advanced ideas about the attitude which their missionaries should adopt towards indigenous cultures. They recommended a movement of evangelization from within those cultures. Yet it is not clear that they advocated a local cultural form for liturgy, catechetics, theology or secondary ecclesial structures, let alone that they already envisaged the reality of a multicultural Church. Theirs was a broader form of *Propaganda Fide*'s principle of 1659 that non-religious cultural practices compatible with the Gospel should not only be tolerated but upheld. Lavigerie, however, does seem to have been groping towards a 'seeds of the Word' approach to African religious traditions. Moreover, the insistence of the founders on their followers learning the vernaculars and acquainting themselves with local culture was to bear eventual fruit.

In spite of the exhortations of their founders, missionaries generally have a bad reputation among the modern Third World generation, Christian and non-Christian. They are regarded as cultural iconoclasts who, more than anyone else, alienated people from the religious roots of their traditional culture. The accusation goes much deeper than to condemn missionaries for their occasional, high-handed destruction of non-Christian sacred places and institutions, in the tradition of St Gregory the Great. It is the claim that missionary Christianity destroyed a religious cultural system which it had no right to destroy and which it did not attempt to replace. Some critics would say that missionaries should have stayed at home. This is not a realistic conclusion if it is meant that traditional ethnic religions would have been thereby preserved, for it ignores the much more drastic impact of modernization. What the accusation means, perhaps, is that missionaries did not enter into dialogue with non-Christian cultures and did not practise inculturation.

Such a charge would be substantially correct, although it is made with the benefit of obvious hindsight. Missionaries were equipped to study languages and respect cultures. They were exhorted to do so by their founders, but they were hindered from real dialogue by their theology; not merely by an undeveloped theology of salvation and the Church, but by the very nature of contemporary classicist theology itself. That this theology was eventually replaced by a modern view, which accepted the claims of history and culture and which rendered inculturation possible, is largely due to the cultural observations and labours of nineteenth- and early twentieth-century missionaries.

Protestant Cultural Approaches to Mission

Protestant missions got under way in the eighteenth century, with the Danish Halle Society and the Moravian Brethren, but, as in the case of Catholic missions, the real expansion occurred in the nineteenth century.[12] The Churches of the Reformation were often tightly wedded to a European national culture and this was an obvious handicap for a dialogue with non-Western cultures. On the other hand, they possessed organizational advantages that Catholics did not enjoy. Their mission boards were often independent of Church structures at home, and their missionaries sometimes frankly envisaged the proliferation of local churches independent of the sending Church. Henry Venn, Secretary of the evangelical, Anglican, Church Missionary Society, spoke as early as 1854 of the local church as 'self-governing, self-supporting and self-propagating', and of the 'euthanasia' of mission. Other mission bodies wanted the minimum of ecclesiastical structure, and tolerated, if they did not actually encourage, secessions. There is no doubt that this attitude encouraged the proliferation of new religious movements that adopted an indigenous cultural form.

There are a number of famous names associated with Protestant missionary activity. One of the earliest was that of William Carey (1761–1834), founder of the English Baptist Society and for many years head of the Baptist mission at Serampur in India. His work for the Bengali language makes him a latter-day Cyril or Methodius. He produced grammars, dictionaries and translations, and even published Hindu Scriptures in the original Sanskrit. He also trained Indians as missionaries.

Another famous name is that of John William Colenso (1814–83), Anglican Bishop of Natal. Colenso did not insist on the divorce of secondary wives when polygamists were baptized. But this leniency in the African cultural sphere shocked his contemporaries less than his controversial biblical commentaries. Although he was solemnly excommunicated by the Archbishop of Cape Town, the Judicial Committee of the British Privy Council delivered a verdict in his favour, and he retained the cathedral and assets of the Natal diocese. After his death his followers continued with the 'Church of England in Natal', and the schism only formally ended in 1911. Although such figures drew attention to cultural aspects of missionary work, they cannot be said to have envisaged inculturation in the sense of Christianizing a whole culture from within.

173

The successes and failures of those missionaries who did attempt something approaching inculturation are less well known. An area that was particularly fruitful in such experiments is the East African country now known as Tanzania, formerly German East Africa and later the mandated territory of Tanganyika. It provides us with an outstanding example of missionary attempts at cultural dialogue.

The first case is that of Bishop Vincent Lucas of the Anglo-Catholic Universities Mission to Central Africa. Lucas was the first Bishop of Masasi, a mission in south-eastern Tanzania that had been originally founded in 1876. Under considerable pressure from local congregations and African clergy, and convinced, himself, of the need for a positive approach to traditional rites and religious practices, Lucas created Christian funeral and Rogation rituals, using the local cultural idiom of funerary practices and fertility rites. With the same encouragement, he then attempted the insertion of traditional puberty rites for boys and girls into a Christian liturgical context and into the psychological process of religious awakening as experienced by young Christians.

The Christianization of these initiation rites challenged the authority of the traditional chiefs who had controlled them hitherto, and it also aroused the opposition of white missionaries. The puberty rites were never structurally linked to the Church's sacramental system, and they never passed fully under the Church's control. They have remained as an alternative and competitive form of a traditional institution. However, the Catholic missionaries in the area followed Bishop Lucas' example and developed their own form of the rites. While opinion remains sharply divided on the issue, valuable lessons can be drawn from the experience. T. O. Ranger has concluded that it became a 'key point of interaction between Christian and traditional ideas, between modern and traditional roles, rather than merely an experiment in adaptation'.[13]

The other Tanzanian examples are from German missionaries, Moravian and Lutheran.[14] German Protestant missiology at the time accepted virtually the same distinction as Catholic Counter-Reformation missiology, namely the distinction between religious and civil aspects of culture. The Greek term *adiaphora* was used to refer to all customs and cultural institutions which were neither intrinsically good nor bad. They included such things as beer-drinking, circumcision, traditional medicine, payment of bride wealth and many other practices. The missions were expected to influence and regulate such things but not to hand down rulings about them. That right belonged

174

to the civil community. It is possible that the questioning of Western cultural superiority after the First World War encouraged a greater openness among German missionaries towards African values.

Traugott Bachmann served as a Moravian missionary at Rungwe from 1892, and at first demanded of converts a complete break with their cultural tradition. Under the influence of the local Christians, he began to realize that such things as bridewealth, child-rearing customs and the social position of women were compatible with the Christian Gospel. He even accepted polygamy, but was reluctant to approve of beer-drinking. Except in the matter of polygamy, most Moravian missionaries followed his lead.

Bruno Gutmann, the Lutheran pioneer, arrived on Mount Kilimanjaro in 1902. He followed the sociological theory of F. Tonnies who distinguished between *Gemeinschaft* and *Gesellschaft*, that is, between community organisms and primal ties on the one hand, and social organizations like the Church on the other. Gutmann held that primal ties, such as clans and age-groups, were of divine dispensation and even a preparation for the Gospel itself. He took over the Chagga age-group pattern of 'shield-comradeship' and tried to link circumcision with Confirmation. Gutmann, far-sighted though he was, did not succeed in convincing his fellow missionaries of the validity of his experiments. However, George Fritze, another Lutheran on Kilimanjaro, started Confirmation 'camps' in 1932, but also failed to link circumcision with Christian initiation. Anna von Waldow, a Lutheran missionary at the Coast between 1932 and 1940, tried to do for female puberty rites what Fritze had failed to do for the male rites.

Although their fellow missionaries were often opposed to the initiatives of these pioneers, opposition also came from progressive African converts and from African Christian leaders whose leadership positions were threatened by the changes. It was the ethnically conservative group among the Christians who accepted, and sometimes inspired, them. It must also be said that the Protestant 'cultural approach' was partly inspired by eighteenth-century romanticism concerning the 'noble savage', the idea of a simple, unspoilt, God-given culture which was to be conserved and shielded from modern influences. It was a point of view shared by Catholic missionary anthropology of the early Vienna school, a progressionist theory that was not devoid of the theological traditionalism condemned by the First Vatican Council. Ultimately education and modernization put an end to the cultural approach in this form.

175

The nineteenth and early twentieth centuries offer us a picture of the ferment of ideas and experiences which preceded the Church's adoption of an empirical approach to cultures. We are now in a position to consider the evolution of the Church's thinking about inculturation in the mid-twentieth century, and we possess many, if not all, the elements needed to evaluate this process and its conclusions.

References

1 Daly 1980.

2 Lonergan 1973, p. 338.

3 Cf. Schönenberger 1961; also for a discussion of Modernism, Shorter 1983, pp. 163–6.

4 Russell 1981, pp. 58–9.

5 *Ibid.*, p. 74.

6 Duchêne 1907 (1950), pp. 115–116.

7 *Ibid.*, p. 135.

8 *Ibid.*, p. 185.

9 *Ibid.*, p. 190.

10 Russell 1981, p. 223.

11 Gilli and Chiocchetta 1977, p. 243.

12 The Society for the Propagation of the Gospel had already been founded at the very beginning of the eighteenth century and was at work on the North American frontier.

13 Ranger 1972, p. 247.

14 Fiedler 1974.

PART FOUR

THE TEACHING OF
THE CATHOLIC CHURCH ON
INCULTURATION TODAY

13

Evolution of the Church's thought before Vatican II

Up to this point, our enquiry has led us from an analysis of the sociological implications of inculturation to the theological foundations of the concept and the history of its realization in the mission of the Church. All of this discussion can now enable us to understand and to evaluate the various official statements on the subject emanating from the contemporary Church. In examining these statements we, of course, enjoy the benefit of hindsight. Papal, conciliar and synodal declarations testify to an evolution of thought, a process which is doubtless far from complete. It is, however, of the first importance that we discover the mind of the Church's teaching authority on the subject of inculturation, for it is in the light of its doctrine that we should judge the Church's actual praxis.

The present chapter demonstrates that the dawn of a multicultural ecclesiology preceded the Second Vatican Council, while Chapter 14 shows how the concept of inculturation made progress in the Council itself. The concept became fully fledged in the teaching of Paul VI, especially after the 1974 Synod, as Chapter 15 points out. Chapter 16 considers John Paul II's intense interest in culture. The idea of inculturation has received its fullest theoretical expression in his addresses and writings, while the need for its implementation in practice has never been so acutely felt by theologians and churchmen in the Third World.

The Early Mission Encyclicals of this Century

The first modern mission encyclical issued by a Pope was the Apostolic Letter *Maximum Illud* of Pope Benedict XV, dated 30 November 1919.[1] Appearing, as it did, a year after the First World War, the encyclical was concerned to strengthen and co-ordinate the Catholic missionary effort at a moment of unprecedented expansion. There are three preoccupations relevant to our discussion. The first is the Pope's demand for effectiveness, his desire that 'the preaching of the Gospel should come within everyone's hearing more successfully and quickly'.[2] In order to achieve this, the Pope asked heads of missions in a particular country to collaborate with one another and negotiate common interests together.[3] This was an important step towards the eventual foundation of episcopal conferences. It was also a precondition for a common cultural policy in newly-formed colonial states, and for establishing the identity of a local church.

The second preoccupation of Benedict XV was with the training of an indigenous clergy. Although the Pope insisted that this training be as full, and as adequate in extent of studies and length of years, as was given to priests in Europe, he wanted to make sure that the local clergy took eventual responsibility for the running of their own church, and that they were fitted for this task.

> Nor should the indigenous priest be trained for the sole purpose of assisting foreign missionaries in a subordinate ministry, but he must be fitted for his divine task and rendered able one day to undertake with credit the administration of his own people.[4]

This was, yet again, an important precondition for an eventual dialogue between faith and culture.

Finally, the Pope strongly opposed any cultural domination by Catholic missionaries. Like Abraham, they were to forget their own country.

> Some of the mission accounts published recently make very painful reading for us, as we find therein an anxiety not so much to extend the Kingdom of God as to increase the power of the missionary's own country. We are surprised that it does not occur to the writers to what extent the mind of the heathen is in danger of being thus repelled from religion. Not in this way does the Catholic missionary act who is worthy of the name; but, bearing perpetually in mind that he is the ambassador not of his own country but of Christ, he should so comport himself that everyone can recognize in him a minister of a religion which embraces all men who adore God in spirit and truth, is a stranger to no nation, and where there is neither Gentile nor Jew, circumcision nor uncircumcision, Barbarian nor Scythian, bond nor free. But Christ is all and in all.[5]

With this allusion to Colossians, the Pope went on to exhort the missionary to a profound knowledge of the vernacular. 'He should not rest satisfied with a superficial knowledge, but it should be thorough enough for a fluent and elegant command.'[6] He should be endowed with all the necessary qualities and versed in all the relevant sciences. He should, says the Pope, be 'accomplished in every department of culture'.[7] Moreover, he should be humble in front of the local people and neither despise them nor scorn them, let alone treat them harshly.

Benedict XV was reiterating the advice of the missionary founders. Although a discussion of inculturation would have been theologically premature in 1919, the implications of such advice were beginning to accumulate.

Seven years later, in 1926, Pope Pius XI, who became known as the 'Pope of the Missions', issued his encyclical letter *Rerum Ecclesiae*.[8] Although it was written in the heyday of colonialism, it was strongly prophetic. The Pope first of all referred to the missionary exhibition which had recently been held in the grounds of the Vatican. This exhibition, which included specimens of Christian art from mission countries, was already an unconscious instance of inculturation. It was to have repercussions in a number of countries for the decoration of churches, the foundation of workshops in the liturgical arts and the establishment of academies of fine art. In Africa, it was particularly the Church in Zaire which started such centres in the 1920s and 1930s, largely under Benedictine influence.[9]

After making a point to which the Second Vatican Council would later return with considerable emphasis, namely that the whole Church is responsible for propagating the Faith, the Pope turned again to the question of an indigenous clergy. After repeating the exact words of Benedict XV, already cited above, the Pope added:

> What is the object of these holy missions, we ask, except that the Church of Christ may be instituted and established in these boundless regions, and by what means shall the Church be built up today among the heathens, except from those elements out of which it was formerly built up among us; that is, unless it is composed of people and clergy and religious orders of men and women recruited from its own region? Why should the native clergy be prevented from cultivating their own field — that is, from governing their own people?[10]

181

Pius XI then went on to develop the point, already made by his predecessor, that the indigenous priest was more in touch with his own people than the foreign missionary, who, more often than not, had an 'imperfect knowledge of the language'.[11]

After this, the Pope made a far-sighted statement about the possibility of decolonization. Although the thought is church-centred and priest-centred, the idea of cultural development is present, albeit in a monolithic form.

> [Suppose] that the native population, raised to a higher degree of culture and political development in order to gain its freedom, wants to drive out of their territory all governors, armed forces and missionaries belonging to the occupying foreign power, and that it cannot do so otherwise than by force. What then, we ask, would be the disaster that would threaten the Church throughout all that territory, unless full provision has been made for the needs of the Christian populace by a network of native priests throughout the whole country?[12]

From this distant prospect Pius XI drew several conclusions: the need for seminaries, the foundation of native religious and contemplative orders and the multiplication of catechists. He also spoke of the need for equality between missionary and indigenous clergy in a culturally significant passage.

> He errs grievously who considers such natives as of an inferior race and of obtuse intelligence. For long experience has shown that the peoples who inhabit the remote regions of the east and of the south frequently are not inferior to us, and can even hold their own very well in keenness of mind. But if you find extreme slowness of mind in the case of men who live in the very heart of barbarous regions, this is due to the conditions of their lives, for since the exigencies of their lives are limited, they are not compelled to make use of their intelligence. But you, venerable brethren, beloved sons, can testify to the truth of what we say, and we ourselves can testify, since we have under our very eyes the example of certain natives who, as students in the colleges of Rome, are not only the equals of the others in ability and in the results obtained, but frequently even surpass them.[13]

Pius XI was concerned with intellectual equality among individuals of different races and conditions of life. He did not go so far as to explore these conditions. It was left to his successor to discern a plurality of cultures or ways of life, and to the Pope who followed — John XXIII — to assert a basic equality among these diverse cultures.

The Recognition of Cultural Pluralism by Pius XII

An important landmark in the development of the theology of incul-turation was the address given by Pope Pius XII to the Pontifical Mission Aid Societies in 1944.[14] It is important because it appears to be the first recorded instance in which the Church officially recog-nized the plurality of cultures. However, Pius XII spoke with two voices on the subject of culture. In spite of the 1944 speech, he gave the impression, on other occasions, of a monolithic Christian culture which was effectively a hybrid.

Already at this time the concept of missionary adaptation was beginning to enjoy a fairly wide currency. It was linked with the reality of acculturation, which the Church was starting to experience consciously. There was a reluctance to admit the plurality, let alone the equality, of cultures. Hence the ambiguity in official statements. Normally there was no question of evangelizing human cultures themselves. The one Catholic Faith had to be extrinsically adapted in order to render it acceptable to different groups of people. To employ a commercial metaphor, the same product was to be 'packaged' in various ways, in order to sell it successfully in different countries.

However, the aim was ultimately to produce a monolithic, Catholic, or Christian culture. To explain this, theologians had recourse to the grafting metaphor employed by St Paul in the Epistle to the Romans.[15] Paul had spoken of the Romans as a 'wild olive' grafted on to a 'cultivated olive'. Since he also spoke of the Jews as a 'natural branch' that had been cut off and that could be grafted on to the olive tree again, it is clear that the tree itself did not represent the religious culture of Judaism; nor, indeed, was Paul speaking primarily about cultures at all. The context was one of faith and fidelity, and the olive tree, in Paul's analogy, represented the tradi-tion of faith in God's promises that went back to Abraham. What bound the cultures together in Paul's day, as in our own, was the bond of faith.[16]

Pope Pius XII resorted to the missiological reinterpretation of Paul's analogy in his encyclical letter *Evangelii Praecones* of 1951.[17] He also quoted extensively from his 1944 address in this encyclical, but the context was that of the monolithic hybrid, and he thus robbed his earlier contribution of its impact.

After defining the object of missionary activity in ecclesiocentric terms as 'to establish the Church on sound foundations among non-Christian peoples and place it under its own native hierarchy',[18] the Pope went on to tackle the question of culture. In using the Pauline grafting metaphor, he made an interesting innovation by reversing the signification of tree and branch. Instead of the wild branch being grafted on to the cultivated tree, the cultivated branch was to be grafted on to the wild tree and this would have the effect of transforming the whole tree. All the wild trees of the forest are thus tamed and gathered into the 'higher culture'. Carrying the analogy to its logical conclusion, it is interesting to speculate about the cultivated branch or 'good scion'. Presumably, the Pope believed that it had a previous, independent existence in the older Christian culture of the West.

> The Church from the beginning down to our own time has always followed this wise practice: let not the gospel, on being introduced into any new land, destroy or extinguish whatever its people possess that is naturally good, just or beautiful. For the Church, when she calls people to a higher culture and a better way of life under the inspiration of the Christian religion, does not act like one who recklessly cuts down and uproots a thriving forest. No, she grafts a good scion upon the wild stock that it may bear a crop of more delicious fruit.[19]

Pius XII then evoked the past missionary policy of the Church, and it is immediately clear that he did not set his sights much higher than Gregory the Great's forcible appropriation of cultural institutions or *Propaganda Fide*'s seventeenth-century distinction between civil and religious culture.

> Human nature, though owing to Adam's fall it is tainted with original sin, has in itself something that is naturally Christian; and this, if illumined by divine light and nourished by God's grace, can eventually be changed into true and supernatural virtue.
>
> This is the reason why the Catholic Church has neither scorned nor rejected the pagan philosophies. Instead, after freeing them from error and all contamination she has perfected and completed them by Christian revelation. So likewise the Church has graciously made her own the native art and culture

which in some countries is so highly developed. She has care-fully encouraged them and has brought them to a point of aesthetic perfection that of themselves they probably would never have attained. By no means has she repressed native customs and traditions but has given them a certain religious significance; she has even transformed their feast days and made them serve to commemorate the martyrs and to celebrate mysteries of the faith.[20]

Although his generalization about the Church's past attitudes towards native customs and traditions is remarkably bland, the sincerity of Pius XII on this matter is unquestionable. We should not forget that he was the Pope who belatedly approved the Chinese rites after the Church's condemnation of them.

The Pope continued for several more paragraphs to speak of 'civilization' and 'customs', quoting first of all from his first encyclical *Summi Pontificatus* of 1939: 'Whatever there is in native customs that is not inseparably bound up with superstition and error will always receive kindly consideration and, when possible, will be preserved intact.'[21] It was at this juncture that he introduced a lengthy quotation from his 1944 address to the Pontifical Mission Aid Societies. There is no doubt that these words introduce the concept of cultural pluralism in unmistakable terms, and that a distinction is implied between European culture and the Gospel. They sound odd after all that has gone before.

The herald of the gospel and messenger of Christ is an apostle. His office does not demand that he transplant European civilisation and culture, and no other, to foreign soil, there to take root and propagate itself. His task in dealing with these peoples, who sometimes boast a very old and highly developed culture of their own, is to teach and form them so that they are ready to accept willingly and in a practical manner the principles of Christian life and morality; principles, I might add, that fit into any culture, provided it be good and sound, and which give that culture greater force in safeguarding human dignity and in gaining human happiness. Catholic inhabitants of missionary countries, although they are first of all citizens of the Kingdom of God and members of his great family, do not for all that cease to be citizens of their earthly fatherland.[22]

After this, the Pope understandably recalls his predecessor's missionary exhibition.

In 1957, Pius XII published his encyclical letter *Fidei Donum*.[23] This was an appeal to the entire Church to provide missionary priests for Africa on the eve of political independence. It did not deal directly with questions of faith and culture. It did, however, introduce the invidious concept of 'young churches'. This is a concept which was to enjoy a long history and which is still among us. It conveys the impression that a particular church, because it has been hierarchically established relatively recently and still requires the assistance of missionaries and financial support from abroad, is not in control of its own affairs and is not able to establish its own priorities. This notion of ecclesial juniority or adolescence can always be exploited in the interests of centralization and uniformity. It is essentially a 'neo-colonial' concept. If Cardinal Newman found the regime of *Propaganda Fide* theologically burdensome in nineteenth-century England, it is understandable that African and Asian churches today should wonder about the criteria of ecclesial adulthood.[24]

Pius XII was a scholarly pontiff who reflected and spoke publicly on a great many issues of the day. Many of the roots of Vatican Two are to be found in his pontificate: the recognition of diverse literary forms in the Bible, liturgical reform, the emphasis on the laity, and so on. On the question of faith and culture, we see his ideas developing towards a modern, empirical view. This view became explicit in the writings of his successor John XXIII.

John XXIII and the Equality of Cultures in the Church

Pope John XXIII's encyclical *Princeps Pastorum* of 1959 reiterates the themes of previous mission encyclicals: the training of a local clergy, decolonization and the training of lay leaders.[25] On one significant point, however, it represents a theoretical leap forward. This is on the question of a multicultural Church and of equality among the participating cultures.

Earlier in the same year, the Pope had delivered an address to participants in the Second International Congress of Negro Artists and Writers, and this occasion had inspired him to comment about the Church's multiculturalism.[26] He inserted the same passage into his mission encyclical immediately after a quotation from Pius XII's *Evangelii Praecones*, the passage inspired by Gregory the Great's policy of transforming pagan festival days into commemorations of the martyrs. It is a startling juxtaposition.

Whenever authentic values of art and thought can enrich the culture of the human family, the Church is ready to encourage and give her patronage to these products of the spirit. As you know, she does not identify herself with any one culture to the exclusion of the rest — not even with European and Western culture, with which her history is so closely linked. True, her divinely appointed task is not directly concerned with these things, but with religion and man's eternal salvation. Nevertheless, the Church in her unfailing youth, continually renewed by the breath of the Holy Spirit, is ever ready to recognise and acknowledge — and indeed to sponsor whole-heartedly — everything that can be set to the credit of the human mind and spirit. And it is a matter of no consequence that these things may not always spring from Mediterranean lands, which in God's providence formed the cradle of her infancy.[27]

A full ecclesiology of the multicultural Church is not worked out, but the germ is here. The Church's cultural pluralism is clearly affirmed. Moreover, says the Pope, the Church does not identify with any particular culture to the exclusion of the rest. The cultures of Europe and the West are not privileged, even the historic cultures of the Mediterranean. Presumably, Pope John was not denying the special prerogative of the cultures of the Bible, but there could be no more emphatic statement of cultural equality in the contemporary Church. Pope John was a church historian, and this statement seems to indicate a readiness on his part to undertake a rereading of Church history.

The notion of particular churches and their cultural character was to be developed by the Second Vatican Council and by Paul VI's *Evangelii Nuntiandi* of 1975. However, Pope John XXIII made a further personal contribution to an understanding of the dialogue between faith and culture in his famous opening address to the Council, on 11 October 1962. As Peter Hebblethwaite has commented in his biography of the Pope, the speech contained four themes: the Council as a celebration of faith, an optimism in the Spirit, an up-dating of the language of authentic doctrine, and a 'merciful' approach to those guilty of errors.[28]

Our interest centres on the third theme which the Pope climaxes with a celebrated and much re-edited sentence. Hebblethwaite has re-established the Pope's actual words from the Latin transcript provided by Vatican Radio.

Starting from a renewed, serene and calm acceptance of the whole teaching of the Church in all its scope and detail as it is found in Trent and Vatican I, Christians and Catholics of apostolic spirit all the world over expect a leap forwards in doctrinal insight and the education of consciences in ever greater fidelity to authentic teaching. But this authentic doctrine has to be studied and expounded in the light of research methods and the language of modern thought. For the substance of the ancient deposit of faith is one thing, and the way in which it is presented is another.[29]

In making this — at the time, controversial — distinction between the 'substance' of the deposit of faith and its manner of presentation, Pope John XXIII was, in fact, saying that dogmas or faith-statements are culturally conditioned expressions of revelation. It was a distinction which would reappear in the documents of the Second Vatican Council, in *Evangelii Nuntiandi* and especially in *Mysterium Ecclesiae*, the Declaration issued in 1973 by the Congregation for the Doctrine of the Faith. This document acknowledges that statements of the faith are influenced by the presuppositions, the concerns, the thought-categories and the available vocabulary of the culture in which they were composed.[30] A cultural rereading of the history of dogma is therefore indispensable, and an invitation to reformulate dogma in accordance with the dictates of different cultures is thereby implied.

In the years immediately before the Second Vatican Council it was becoming clearer that 'adaptation' was not simply a form of ecclesiastical diplomacy or missionary strategy. Once the cultural diversity of humanity was acknowledged, it could be seen that adaptation was a necessary condition of Catholicity. The one Gospel of salvation had to be proclaimed to people of varying cultures and be understood and lived by them. Adaptation was demanded by the nature of evangelization itself and it was necessarily a permanent feature of missionary activity.

It became fashionable to speak about a *praeparatio evangelii*, or 'preparation of the Gospel', the idea that peoples had been providentially prepared by God for the proclamation of the Gospel, and that there were elements in their cultures which were useful for understanding and expressing the teaching of the Gospel. This patristic concept needed to be complemented by other more dynamic approaches of the early Fathers, since, taken by itself, it suggested that such cultural elements lost their usefulness once the Gospel had been proclaimed and that they were superseded.

In the French language, however, a more suggestive image was in widespread use on the eve of the Council. This was the phrase *pierres d'attente*, which refers to 'toothing stones', or pieces of projecting masonry which are waiting for another section of wall to be built on to them. Although the image is not very lively in itself, it has the merit of expressing continuity with the cultural past, even if that past is not seen to influence the shape of the 'building' to come. The problem of 'adaptation' was not yet viewed from within the cultures themselves. Nor was there yet a holistic understanding of these cultures.

The Second Vatican Council opened on 11 October 1962. Unlike its predecessor of 1869, the non-Western cultures were not exclusively represented by missionary bishops. Of the 2,540 Council Fathers a high proportion were natives of Latin America, Africa, Asia and Oceania. There were also the representatives of the Eastern rites who celebrated their liturgies in the Vatican Basilica during the Council sessions. The cultural diversity of the Church was distinctly visible at Vatican Two.

However, it was not until more than a decade after the start of the Second Vatican Council, in the forum provided by the Synods of Bishops and the various regional and continental episcopal associations, that the voice of the 'Third Church' began to have an impact. For the development of the concept of inculturation, the Synod of 1974 was crucial. Until that moment, the inadequate notion of 'adaptation' prevailed. The Second Vatican Council was obliged to work with this notion. Not only was it the only available conception; but it conformed more easily to the culture-bound structures of Catholic communion, for it remained at the level of acculturation — the exchange of cultural elements within a Latin, or Western, Church. The mission documents of Vatican Two witness to the inadequacy of the conception, and the story of the dialogue between faith and culture — both at the Council and afterwards — has been one of the struggle to transcend it.

In the chapter that follows we shall consider the fortunes of the notion of adaptation at the Second Vatican Council, and, in particular, the Council's approach to culture as a whole. It will be seen that, while most of the necessary elements are present, they were not fully co-ordinated or applied.

References

1 *Maximum Illud*, Hickey 1982, pp. 30–47.

2 *Ibid.*, p. 33.

3 *Ibid.*, pp. 34–5.

4 *Ibid.*, p. 35.

5 *Ibid.*, pp. 37–8; Col 3:11.

6 *Maximum Illud*, Hickey 1982, p. 39.

7 *Ibid.*, p. 40.

8 *Rerum Ecclesiae*, Hickey 1982, pp. 50–71.

9 Badi-Banga Ne-Mwine 1982.

10 *Rerum Ecclesiae*, Hickey 1982, p. 61.

11 *Ibid.*, pp. 61–2.

12 *Ibid.*, p. 62.

13 *Ibid.*, p. 64.

14 *AAS* 1944, p. 210.

15 Rom 11:16–24.

16 Cf. Shorter 1972, pp. 57–8.

17 *Evangelii Praecones*, Hickey 1982, pp. 75–103.

18 *Ibid.*, pp. 83–4.

19 *Ibid.*, p. 97.

20 *Ibid.*, pp. 97–8.

21 *Ibid.*, pp. 98–9.

22 *Ibid.*, p. 99.

23 *Fidei Donum*, Hickey 1982, pp. 107–128.

24 Coulson 1981, pp. 43–4. The paternalism implicit in the phrase 'young churches' has many precedents, including even that of the letters of St Paul.

25 *Princeps Pastorum*, Hickey 1982, pp. 132–63.

26 *AAS* 1959, p. 260.

27 *Princeps Pastorum*, Hickey 1982, p. 143.

28 Hebblethwaite 1984, p. 430.

29 *Ibid.*, pp. 431–2.

30 Cf. Dulles 1978, p. 53.

14

The Second Vatican Council and inculturation

The Practical Question of Liturgical Reform

The Second Vatican Council began its work with a discussion on the renewal of the liturgy. In fact, *Sacrosanctum Concilium*, the Constitution on the Sacred Liturgy, was the first conciliar document to be approved and promulgated (in 1963). Liturgy was given priority because it was a practical question, and its early discussion was an earnest of the Council's pastoral concern. The preconciliar Liturgy Commission was also one of the few that had done its work to the satisfaction of the Council Fathers. Thus it came about that the renewal of the Church's worship was delineated before establishing its *locus*, which is the Church itself, and before discussing the consequences for evangelization of a new ecclesiology. This was a fateful decision, imposed by circumstances, which later meant that liturgical renewal was sadly out of step with the Church's thinking on evangelization and culture.

The key passage of the Liturgical Constitution is number 38, which provides for a single, reformed Roman Rite, with the possibility of 'legitimate variations and adaptations' foreseen by the liturgical books. However, as we already saw in Chapter 2, the Latin of this rite could be translated into the local vernacular, according to the policy and approval of the local episcopal conference.[1]

Provided that the substantial unity of the Roman rite is preserved, provision shall be made, when revising the liturgical books, for legitimate variations and adaptations to different groups, regions and peoples, especially in mission countries. This should be borne in mind when drawing up the rites and determining the rubrics.[2]

191

Although the revision was to be made for the benefit of different groups, regions and peoples, the Council did not envisage the possibility of creating new rites. On the contrary, the preservation of the 'substantial unity of the Roman rite' was the *conditio sine qua non* of all liturgical renewal. Notable liturgists, such as A. Chupungco and E. Uzukwu, have argued that liturgical inculturation demands the creation of new rites, and, in the early days after the Council, it was even assumed by the Sacred Congregation for Divine Worship that such was the ultimate goal of liturgical renewal.[3] The revision of the Roman rite and its translation into the vernacular was merely a dress rehearsal for a truly creative stage. An instruction on translation, issued in 1967, stated:

> In a really renewed liturgy we shall not be content with texts translated from another language. New creations will be needed. It remains true that the translation of texts from the Church's tradition is an invaluable exercise and necessary training for the drawing up of new texts, with the result that the new forms adopted should in some way grow organically from forms already existing.[4]

The Second Vatican Council paid extensive tribute to the diversity of Eastern rites in its Decree on Eastern Catholic Churches, *Orientalium Ecclesiarum*, noting that such diversity does not harm, but actually contributes to the unity of the Universal Church.[5] Although the decree emphasized the apostolic and patristic, rather than the cultural, origins of the Eastern rites, it compared the development of their liturgical and spiritual traditions to the contemporary need for adaptation.

> Between those churches there is such a wonderful bond of union that this variety in the Universal Church, so far from diminishing its unity, rather serves to emphasize it. For the Catholic Church wishes the traditions of each particular church or rite to remain whole and entire, and it likewise wishes to adapt its own way of life to the needs of different times and places.[6]

We already noted in Chapter 5 that the Dogmatic Constitution on the Church, *Lumen Gentium*, located the primary reality of Church in the so-called 'particular church'. It is perhaps significant that this phrase was applied in *Orientalium Ecclesiarum* to the churches of Eastern rite. *Lumen Gentium* itself went even further and compared the collegiate action of episcopal conferences of Latin rite to the development of

Eastern rite churches.[7] However, the liturgical constitution had been drafted and discussed before any of these later statements of the Council were made, and the proviso of maintaining the substantial unity of the Roman rite was not changed. It was easy, therefore, for the central authority to appeal to this condition when it decided to inhibit experimentation and diversification.

The intention of *Sacrosanctum Concilium* is not in doubt. As a general rule, it offered an extrinsic adaptation of the Roman rite — a choice of ceremonial or of readings and prayers. As an exception, it foresaw 'a more radical adaptation' in mission lands, which amounted to acculturation, the insertion of elements from non-Western cultures into the Roman (or Western cultural) rite.[8] Those who, in the post-conciliar euphoria, tried to follow the Council's more mature, cultural insights in matters liturgical, were certainly not faithful to the spirit of the Liturgical Constitution.

The Constitution offered one instance of the 'more radical adaptation' (acculturation) that it proposed for mission lands:

> In mission countries, in addition to what is furnished by the Christian tradition, those elements of initiation rites may be admitted which are already in use among some peoples insofar as they can be adapted to the Christian ritual in accordance with Articles 37–40 of this Constitution.[9]

The articles in question, of course, include the stipulation that the substantial unity of the Roman rite be preserved.

Nowhere in the constitution is it suggested that a Eucharistic prayer could be created locally and receive approval. This was eventually conceded in *Eucharistiae Participationem* of 1973, after a specially appointed commission had examined the spate of unauthorized Eucharistic prayers which had appeared in almost every part of the world.[10] As a result, Eucharistic prayers have been approved for Germany, the Philippines, Switzerland, Australia, the Netherlands and Brazil, among others. Very few have been submitted, let alone approved, from 'mission lands'. An Indian Eucharistic Rite was drawn up, but not, at first, submitted, and among several African Eucharistic rites, the best known — that of Zaire — was finally submitted for approval in 1983. Cardinal Malula of Kinshasa told Pope John Paul II, on the occasion of the *ad limina* visit of the Zairean Bishops in that year:

One of the major preoccupations of all the bishops of Zaire is without doubt the search for ways of creating a liturgy that responds to the most profound aspirations of Africans. In the case of Zaire, we are concerned with the rite still under experiment, known as the Zairean Rite of the Mass. The complete dossier concerning this question has been lodged with the competent dicastery.[11]

Mgr Virgilio Noè, the secretary of the Congregation for Divine Worship, declared in October 1986 that the Zairean 'Rite' would be the first to receive official approval, and that there were other 'rites' under consideration from India, the Philippines and Latin America. A commission of the Sacred Congregation for Divine Worship had reached agreement with an *ad hoc* committee of the Zaire Episcopal Conference.[12] At the time of writing, this approval has not yet been given, nor is it clear what the relationship of these 'rites' is to be towards the Roman rite.

The ardent desire for liturgical inculturation — a new liturgical creation — has to compete with the view of liturgy as a field for the exercise of hierarchical power. In so far as the bishop sees his role as the principal guarantor of an authentic liturgy circumscribed by Church Law, inculturation cannot fail to be discouraged. As E.-J. Pénoukou has rightly pointed out, an up-dated model of the bishop must be linked to an up-dated model of the Church.[13] He must not merely be conducting a holding operation for a Church closed in on itself. He must become a prophet and a privileged instrument of inculturation. A multicultural Church requires culturally conscious leaders, bishops who are authentic Africans, Indians, Melanesians or whatever.

More hopeful signs of a trend towards liturgical pluriformity in the Church were given at the Congress of Presidents and Secretaries of National Liturgical Commissions which was held in Rome in October 1984. There it was stated that the Roman rite should be a *terminus a quo* for initiatives taken primarily by the particular churches themselves. The members of the congress were asked to use the existing possibilities for renewal more fully before passing on to creativity. There was also a request for liturgically-trained personnel to assist the particular churches in their task. The congress appeared to assume that creativity and pluriformity in liturgy were the eventual goals of liturgical renewal.[14] The Second Vatican Council, in its Liturgical Constitution, only recommended acculturation in exceptional circumstances. Inculturation was not even considered. If the

Church is moving theoretically towards liturgical inculturation today, it is because other conciliar documents struck a chord in the hearts of non-Western worshippers, and because the use of the vernacular encouraged the hope of more thoroughgoing adaptation.

Cultures in the Mission Documents of the Council

In Chapter 7 we discussed the contribution of the Council's Dogmatic Constitution on the Church, *Lumen Gentium*, to the development of salvation theology. We also noted the Council's positive appraisal of non-Christian cultures in its Declaration on the Relation of the Church to Non-Christian Religions, *Nostra Aetate*. Here we shall concentrate on the mission documents: The Decree on the Church's Missionary Activity, *Ad Gentes* and The Norms for Implementing the Decree.[15]

It is difficult to exaggerate the importance of *Ad Gentes* for the development of modern mission theology. By the time the Council reached its third session, it had been decided not to produce a comprehensive mission document at all. Instead, thirteen propositions were presented to the Council, which were rejected after Bishop Donal Lamont's famous intervention comparing them to the 'dry bones' of Ezekiel's prophecy.[16] It was decided to abandon the propositions and draft a decree on the Church's missionary activity in time for the fourth and final session of the Council. In this way, *Ad Gentes* was born, and became one of the four final documents to be approved by the Council in December 1965.

Coming as it did in the Council's final session, the decree was able to benefit from earlier discussions, particularly from that on the Church itself, *Lumen Gentium*. After a first chapter of doctrinal principles, the decree discusses the nature of missionary work. From the outset stress is laid on human communities and their socio-cultural traditions as the focus of missionary interest. In this context the analogy of the Incarnation is used for the first time. Later, in the same chapter, the appeal is made to St Justin's 'seeds of the Word'.

There are two billion people — and their number is increasing day by day — who have never, or barely, heard the Gospel message; they constitute large and distinct groups united by enduring cultural ties, ancient religious traditions, and strong social relationships. Of these, some belong to one or other of the great religions, others have no knowledge of God, while others expressly deny the existence of God and sometimes even attack it. If the Church is to be in a position to offer all men the mystery of salvation and the life brought by God, then it must implant itself among these groups in the same way that Christ by his incarnation committed himself to the particular social and cultural circumstances of the men among whom he lived.[17]

In order to bear witness to Christ fruitfully, they [Christians] should establish relationships of respect and love with those men, they should acknowledge themselves as members of the group in which they live, and through the various undertakings and affairs of human life they should share in their social and cultural life. They should be familiar with their national and religious traditions and uncover with gladness and respect those seeds of the Word which lie hidden among them.[18]

In speaking of the Church's presence among these human groups as an implantation or incarnation, and as a commitment to their social and cultural traditions, the Council already envisaged an interior transformation of cultures. In reviving the concept of 'seeds of the Word', the decree visualized a positive dialogue with them.

Lumen Gentium had introduced the idea of 'particular church'; *Ad Gentes* now devoted an entire chapter to particular churches.[19] It is in this chapter that the decree makes its most important affirmations about culture. Although there is much ecclesiocentric and even Eurocentric language, with talk of 'implantation' and 'young churches' for example, the impression is given that the identity and relative autonomy of particular churches is bound up with culture. The opening paragraph of the chapter appears hesitant about the Church's conformity to culture, which is in contrast with the chapter's more positive conclusion.

This work of implanting the Church in a particular human community reaches a definite point when the assembly of the faithful, already rooted in the social life of the people and to some extent conformed to its culture, enjoys a certain stability and permanence; when it has its own priests, although insufficient, its own religious and laity, and possesses those ministries and institutions which are required for leading and spreading the life of the people of God under the leadership of their own bishop.[20]

The grafting metaphor even reappears in the reversed form used by

Pius XII, and is, of course, open to the same objections mentioned in Chapter 13.

> The communion of the young churches with the whole Church must remain intimate, they must graft elements of its tradition on to their own culture and thus, by a mutual outpouring of energy, increase the life of the mystical Body.[21]

However, the local culture provides the basis for the operation, which is also presented in terms of mutuality and partnership.

The final paragraphs of the chapter constitute the key passage of the entire document, invoking the economy of the Incarnation and calling for 'a more profound adaptation'.[22] The image of the 'seed' is used differently here, as a symbol of the proclamation of the Gospel which takes effect by making the customs, traditions, arts and sciences of different peoples a part of itself, just as a seed grows through absorbing moisture. This also happened, says the decree, in the economy of the Incarnation, according to which the Messiah-King was given all the nations of the world as an inheritance, the reference being to Psalm 2 in which the Messiah is depicted as a warrior receiving the submission of his enemies. We discussed the causal link between the Paschal Mystery and inculturation in Chapter 6, and it would seem that, with this juxtaposition of Incarnation and Messiah-King, the decree is appealing to the universal lordship of the Risen Christ, in spite of the unfortunate violent symbolism of the Psalmist. The phrase 'economy of the incarnation' may therefore apply to the whole mystery of Christ, unlike the decree's earlier reference to the Incarnation which restricts it to the earthly Christ's cultural education and commitment. We have here, then, an eloquent description of the manner in which the Gospel makes itself at home in a culture, and, as it were, takes cultural 'flesh'.

> The seed which is the word of God grows out of good soil watered by the divine dew, it absorbs moisture, transforms it, and makes it part of itself, so that eventually it bears much fruit. So too indeed, just as happened in the economy of the incarnation, the young churches which are rooted in Christ and built on the foundation of the apostles, take over all the riches of the nations which have been given to Christ as an inheritance (cf. Ps 2:8). They borrow from the customs, traditions, wisdom, teaching, arts and sciences of their people everything which could be used to praise the glory of the Creator, manifest the

197

grace of the Saviour, or contribute to the right ordering of Christian life.[23]

In spite of its suggestiveness, the passage is not devoid of ambiguity. While the Gospel certainly lives and grows through its cultural application and relevance, it is proclaimed and implanted through the instrumentality of an alien culture. The passage prescinds from the reality of cultural interaction. The reference to Psalm 2 was first made by *Lumen Gentium* in a slightly different context, that of the Church's universality.[24] There it was said that, in the Church, the different nations belong to Christ the King in the unity of the Spirit. The image was not primarily applied to the process of inculturation in a particular church.

The final paragraph, however, of the *Ad Gentes* text we are considering describes a process of theological investigation which leads to the creation of local churches with their own cultural traditions. Although it is still not yet fully explicit, it suggests an ecclesiology of cultural pluriformity.

> To achieve this, it is necessary that in each of the great socio-cultural regions, as they are called, theological investigation should be encouraged and the facts and words revealed by God, contained in Sacred Scripture, and explained by the Fathers and Magisterium of the Church, submitted to a new examination in the light of the tradition of the universal Church. In this way it will be more clearly understood by what means the faith can be explained in terms of the philosophy and wisdom of the people, and how their customs, concept of life and social structures can be reconciled with the standard proposed by divine revelation. Thus a way will be opened for a more profound adaptation in the whole sphere of Christian life. This manner of acting will avoid every appearance of syncretism and false exclusiveness; the Christian life will be adapted to the mentality and character of each culture, and local traditions together with the special qualities of each national family, illumined by the light of the Gospel, will be taken up into a Catholic unity. So new particular churches, each with its own traditions, have their place in the community of the Church, the primacy of Peter which presides over this universal assembly of charity all the while remaining intact.
>
> And so it is to be hoped, and indeed it would be a very good thing, that episcopal conferences should come together within

the boundaries of each great socio-cultural region and by a united and co-ordinated effort pursue this proposal of adaptation.[25]

The decree went straight to the heart of the problem in requesting a theological renewal as the precondition of a more profound adaptation. This appeal, together with the proposal of wide-ranging cultural research, was taken up in the document known as *Ecclesiae Sanctae* of 1966. This document provided norms for the implementation of three conciliar decrees, among them the Decree on the Church's Missionary Activity, *Ad Gentes*.

Ecclesiae Sanctae insists that mission theology, the missionary nature of the Church and the principles of modern salvation theology should be an indispensable part of the ordinary seminary curriculum.[26] It also provides for the setting up of regional episcopal associations as 'organic groups, according to the socio-cultural areas'.[27] In a few cases, such associations were already in existence before the Second Vatican Council. This provision, however, gave an impetus to their development in the post-conciliar years and ensured their forceful contribution to the theology of inculturation in the 1970s. The regional associations helped to orchestrate and co-ordinate Third World contributions to the meetings of the Synod of Bishops, particularly that of 1974 on evangelization, which marked an important step in the development of inculturation theology.

Ecclesiae Sanctae requested the episcopal conferences to set up study-groups, the task of which would be:

To examine the thought of the people on the universe, on man and on his attitude towards God, and to undertake theological reflection on what is good and true in their culture.

Such theological study is a necessary foundation for deciding what adaptations are to be made and in the decision concerning these adaptations the study groups mentioned above will take part. These adaptations cover, amongst other things, methods of evangelization, forms of worship, religious life and ecclesiastical legislation.[28]

The mention of ecclesiastical legislation is an interesting follow-up to a statement of *Ad Gentes* itself.

The faith should be imparted by means of a well adapted catechesis and celebrated in a liturgy that is in harmony with the character of the people; it should be embodied by suitable canonical legislation in the healthy institutions and customs of the locality.[29]

In the event, the idea of a local embodiment of canonical legislation has been superseded, as we have already seen in Chapter 5, by a newly codified universal law. The setting-up of study groups never took place as a regular measure, although certain episcopal conferences and some associations appointed *ad hoc* committees to investigate cultural questions, such as marriage or initiation. Tanzania was one of the exceptions in so far as its episcopal conference created a national committee for cultural research in 1975.

More significant has been the contribution of pastoral institutes which *Ecclesiae Sanctae* invited to collaborate in establishing methods of evangelization and catechesis.[30] According to these norms, the study groups, had they come into permanent existence, would have played a central role in forwarding liturgical proposals to Rome and in helping seminaries to adapt their programmes of studies to local contexts and priorities.[31] It is sad to reflect on the general failure to adhere to these norms, and on the somewhat haphazard way in which cultural adaptation has, in fact, taken place.

Culture in the Pastoral Constitution on the Church in the Modern World

The Council's mission documents, vibrant and innovative as they are, did not offer any definition or analysis of culture, although they made frequent reference to it. The Pastoral Constitution on the Church in the Modern World, *Gaudium et Spes*, however, devoted the entire second chapter of Part Two to the subject of culture, which it defined in general terms as 'all those things which go to the refining and developing of man's diverse mental and physical endowments'.[32]

The document takes a larger than sociological view of culture, but it admits that the individual achieves full humanity only through culture, and that there is a plurality of cultures.

> For different styles of living and different scales of values originate in different ways of using things, of working and self-expression, of practising religion and of behaviour, of establishing laws and juridical institutions, of developing science and the arts and of cultivating beauty. Thus the heritage of its institutions forms the patrimony proper to each human commun-

ity; thus too, is created a well-defined, historical milieu which envelops the men of every nation and age and from which they draw the values needed to foster humanity and civilization.[33]

Once again, let us note in passing that the Council seems to go out of its way to stress that law is culturally defined.

The constitution then considered the question of modernization and the way in which industrialization and urbanization are bringing 'mass cultures' into existence. It takes a frankly optimistic view of these developments and even suggests that:

. . . a more universal form of culture is gradually taking shape, and through it the unity of mankind is being fostered and expressed in the measure that the particular characteristics of each culture is preserved.[34]

The Fathers are on surer ground when they note that human beings are realizing their responsibility for the progress of culture, and that, in the exchange between cultures, there is a danger of cultural domination. They are also right to note that difficulty of harmonizing modernity and cultural tradition, and the growth of inequality in sharing the benefits of culture. Although the word 'culturalism' is not used, they also correctly note the danger of cultural autonomy that creates a humanism often hostile to religion. However, they also point to the positive service which culture and technology can render to truth and goodness.[35]

The key passage of the entire document is number 58, which discusses the relationship between the Gospel and culture. The first paragraph shows how God's self-revelation in the Old and New Testaments, and the Church's proclamation of Christ's message through the centuries, have used human cultures. However, it manages to avoid mentioning the necessity of culture as a medium for the Gospel, and conveys the impression that the freedom and autonomy of God's Word depend on a contingent relationship between the two.

There are many links between the message of salvation and culture. In his self-revelation to his people culminating in the fullness of manifestation in his incarnate Son, God spoke according to the culture proper to each age. Similarly the Church has existed through the centuries in varying circumstances and has utilized the resources of different cultures in its preaching to spread and explain the message of Christ, to examine and understand it more deeply, and to express it more perfectly in the liturgy and in various aspects of the life of the faithful.[36]

The constitution goes on to affirm that the Church is not tied exclusively to any one culture, but can enter into communion with different forms of culture. In so doing, it enriches itself and the cultures concerned. Quite correctly, the passage expresses the mutuality of the evangelization process. The Church enters into communion with a culture; the Church is thereby enriched along with the culture. However, there is an artificiality in speaking of the Church as if it were culturally disembodied. The Church in alien cultural form enters into communion with an unevangelized culture; the Church both in its alien cultural form and in its new cultural form is enriched.

> Nevertheless, the Church has been sent to all ages and nations and, therefore, is not tied exclusively and indissolubly to any race or nation, to any one particular way of life, or to any customary practices, ancient or modern. The Church is faithful to its traditions and is at the same time conscious of its universal mission; it can, then, enter into communion with different forms of culture, thereby enriching both itself and the cultures themselves.[37]

What happens when the Gospel enters into communion with a culture? It continually renews, corrects, purifies, completes and restores the culture in question. It causes its spiritual qualities to blossom from within. This seems to be more than a hint of what we really mean by inculturation.

> The good news of Christ continually renews the life and culture of fallen man; it combats and removes the error and evil which flow from the ever-present attraction of sin. It never ceases to purify and elevate the morality of peoples. It takes the spiritual qualities and endowments of every age and nation, and with supernatural riches it causes them to blossom, as it were, from within; it fortifies, completes and restores them to Christ. In this way the Church carries out its mission and in that very act it stimulates and advances human and civil culture, as well as contributing, by its activity, to man's interior freedom.[38]

The document goes on to speak of the human right to culture and its implementation. Although culture is a human right, it is not in itself an absolute, and must be subordinated to the human being's integral development, which, of course, includes the fulfilment of his spiritual and religious needs.

> For the reasons given above the Church recalls to mind that culture must be subordinated to the integral development of the human person, to the good of the community and of the whole of mankind. Therefore one must aim at encouraging the human spirit to develop its faculties of wonder, of understanding, of contemplation, of forming personal judgements and cultivating a religious, moral and social sense.
>
> Culture, since it flows from man's rational and social nature, has continual need of rightful freedom of development and a legitimate possibility of autonomy according to its own principles. Quite rightly it demands respect and enjoys a certain inviolability, provided, of course, that the rights of the individual and the community, both particular and universal, are safeguarded within the limits of the common good.[39]

The right to culture, however, as the constitution reminds us, is the right to a developed culture, and a developed culture entails cultural education.

> Hence it is necessary to ensure that there is a sufficiency of cultural benefits available to everybody, especially the benefit of what is called 'basic' culture, lest any be prevented by illiteracy and lack of initiative from contributing in an authentically human way to the common good . . .
>
> We must do everything possible to make all persons aware of their right to culture and their duty to develop themselves culturally and to help their fellows.[40]

The document finally considers the relevance of the sciences, literature and the arts to the life of the Church, and, in particular, to theology and those engaged in theological studies.[41] Altogether, *Gaudium et Spes* offers a comprehensive outlook on culture and its relationship to Christianity, and demonstrates the complexity of the phenomenon.

Apart from the Pastoral Constitution on the Liturgy, which is ecclesiologically immature, the other Council documents considered here represent a decisive starting-point for the development of a theology of inculturation. Essential elements are contained in them which have been recognized and used by theologians and missiologists. However, the theory is not fully explicit, and there is a frequent obscurity of ideas and language which may leave the reader with the impression that the concept of a monolithic hybrid Church is still being maintained. Careful reading of the texts shows that this is not the case. The documents of the Second Vatican Council made a new technological departure possible. We see this especially in the collegial dynamic of Pope and bishops during the rest of the pontificate of Paul VI.

References

1 *Sacrosanctum Concilium*, 35.

2 *Ibid.*, 38.

3 Cf. Chupungco 1982; Uzukwu 1982.

4 *Notitiae*, 44, 1969, p. 12.

5 *Orientalium Ecclesiarum*, 2.

6 *Ibid.*, 2.

7 *Lumen Gentium*, 23.

8 *Sacrosanctum Concilium*, 40.

9 *Ibid.*, 65.

10 *Eucharistiae Participationem*, 6; cf. Flannery 1975, p. 235.

11 *Documentation Catholique*, 1983, p. 513.

12 *DIA*, AF/10/1219, 31 October 1986, 476/86; 933/86.

13 Pénoukou, 1984.

14 *AFER*, Vol. 27, No. 1, February 1985, p. 50.

15 *Ecclesiae Sanctae*, cf. Hickey 1982, pp. 166–72.

16 Lamont in Stacpoole 1986, pp. 270–82.

17 *Ad Gentes*, 10.

18 *Ibid.*, 11.

19 *Ibid.*, Chap. III.

20 *Ibid.*, 19.

21 *Ibid.*, 19.

22 *Ibid.*, 22.

23 *Ibid.*, 22.

24 *Lumen Gentium*, 13.

25 *Ad Gentes*, 22.

26 *Ecclesiae Sanctae*, 1.

27 *Ibid.*, 18.

28 *Ibid.*, 18.

29 *Ad Gentes*, 19.

30 *Ecclesiae Sanctae*, 18.

31 *Ibid.*, 18.

32 *Gaudium et Spes*, 53.

33 *Ibid.*, 53.

34 *Ibid.*, 54.

35 *Ibid.*, 56–7.

36 *Ibid.*, 58.

37 *Ibid.*, 58.

38 *Ibid.*, 58.

39 *Ibid.*, 59.

40 *Ibid.*, 60.

41 *Ibid.*, 61.

15

Inculturation in the teaching of Paul VI

The Message to Africa and the Kampala Address

Even before the end of the Second Vatican Council important contributions to the development of a theology of inculturation were associated with the name of Pope Paul VI. Mention has already been made in Chapter 10 of his Address to the Eastern Rite Bishops in the Church of St Anne, Jerusalem, on 4 January 1964. Later in the same year, during the third session of the Council, the Pope visited India for the Thirty-eighth International Eucharistic Congress, held in Bombay. It was in connection with this congress that an important conference on 'Christian Revelation and Non-Christian Religions' was held from 25 to 28 November 1964. This conference helped to publicize the advances in salvation theology which were being incorporated into the Council texts.[1]

On 29 October 1967 Pope Paul VI issued *Africae Terrarum*, a message to the hierarchy and people of Africa.[2] The abiding importance of this letter consists in the fact that it not only deals with the Christian reinterpretation of African values in principle, but also identifies them in practice. Having referred to the history of ancient Christian Africa and to the Coptic and Ethiopic rites, and having, also, expressed the hope of an effective dialogue with Islam, the Pope went on to consider certain general ideas which typify African religious cultures:

> We think it profitable to dwell on some general ideas which typify ancient African religious cultures because we think their moral and religious values deserving of attentive consideration.[3]

The Pope then enumerated four typical values.[4] The first was the African's spiritual view of life, centred on the perception of God

206

permeating the whole of existence; the second was respect for the
dignity of man; and the third was the sense of the family. While on
the latter topic, Paul VI noted the role played by the father in the
African family and explicitly included the matrilineal father in this
positive appreciation. Finally, the Pope spoke about the African
tradition of community life. He concluded his survey with the following remarks:

> Today, Africa has met with progress which is taking her
> onwards to new forms of life made available by science and
> technology. All this is not in contradiction with the essential
> values of moral and religious tradition of the past, which we
> have briefly described, the values that belong in a way to the
> natural law which is implanted in the heart of every man and
> is the foundation for a well-ordered life with his fellow men in
> every generation.
>
> For this reason, while these values which have been handed
> down ought to be respected as a cultural legacy from the past,
> there is no less a duty to give them new meaning and new
> expression. In the face of modern civilization, however, it is
> sometimes necessary to 'know how to discriminate: to assess
> critically, and eliminate those deceptive goods which would
> bring about a lowering of the human ideal, and to accept those
> values that are sound and beneficial, in order to develop them
> alongside their own, in accordance with their own genius'
> (*Populorum Progressio*, 41). New forms of life will thus spring
> from what is good in the old and the new alike, and will be seen
> by younger generations as a solid and real inheritance.
>
> The Church views with great respect the moral and religious
> values of the African tradition, not only because of their
> meaning, but also because she sees them as providential, as the
> basis for spreading the gospel message and beginning the esta-
> blishment of the new society in Christ. This we ourselves pointed
> out at the canonization of the martyrs of Uganda, who were the
> first flowering of Christian holiness in the new Africa, sprung
> from the most vigorous stock of ancient tradition.
>
> The teaching of Jesus Christ and his redemption are, in fact,
> the complement, the renewal, and the bringing to perfection, of
> all that is good in human tradition. And that is why the African
> who becomes a Christian does not disown himself, but takes up
> the age-old values of tradition 'in spirit and in truth' (John
> 4:24).[5]

Paul VI was clearly alluding here to the process now known as inculturation. It is interesting that he spoke about modernization in the same breath with which he spoke about giving new meaning and new expression to ancient cultural values. His quotation from *Populorum Progressio* was taken from a passage dealing with the materialistic threat to culture.

Two years later, on 31 July 1969, Paul VI made one of his most important speeches on the subject of the dialogue between faith and culture. The speech was made on the first day of his visit to Uganda to consecrate the altar of the shrine of the African martyrs at Namugongo. The context was the closing of the first plenary assembly of the Symposium of Episcopal Conferences of Africa and Madagascar. This newly founded episcopal association had been the forum for some plain speaking by African bishops in the preceding week. Cardinal Paul Zoungrana of Upper Volta (now Burkina Faso) had made the following forthright declaration:

> Our very being must not be conferred upon us from outside; the Gospel is a germ of life and the Church of Africa must develop itself and build itself up thanks to its own apostolic priorities.[6]

The Pope delivered his address to the bishops in the Cathedral of Kampala Archdiocese on Rubaga Hill, before a large congregation of clergy, religious and laity. Expectations were high, and many were disappointed with this keynote address of the first papal visit to Africa. However, it was a document that repaid careful study, and it was realized soon afterwards that Paul VI had quietly and unobtrusively made several important points.

The Kampala Address falls into two parts. The first part, which does not concern us directly, deals with the African Church's coming of age, and of its own missionary responsibility. The second part deals with evangelization and the problem of cultural adaptation. Paul VI described the problem in the following terms:

> A burning and much-discussed question arises concerning your evangelizing work, and it is that of the adaptation of the gospel and of the Church to African culture. Must the Church be European, Latin, Oriental . . . or must she be African? This seems a difficult problem, and in practice may be so, indeed.[7]

The way in which the question is posed is interesting. The alternatives are not only 'European' or 'African', but even 'Latin' or 'Oriental'. That is to say, the Pope considers alternatives of rite, as well as of culture. It is worth remembering this starting-point, when considering his reply. Nowhere does Paul VI rule out explicitly the possibility of an African rite or rites.

The Pope's reply, however, to this difficult question is rapid and twofold. In the first place, the African Church must be Catholic.

> That is, it must be entirely founded upon the identical, essential, constitutional patrimony of the self-same teaching of Christ, as professed by the authentic and authoritative tradition of the one true Church. This condition is fundamental and indisputable. We must, all of us, be both jealous and proud of that faith of which the apostles were the heralds, and of which the missionaries were scrupulous teachers. You know that the Church is particularly tenacious, we may even say conservative, in this regard. To make sure that the message of revealed doctrine cannot be altered, the Church has even set down her treasure of truth in certain conceptual and verbal formulas. Even when these formulas are difficult, at times, she obliges us to preserve them textually. We are not the inventors of our faith, we are its custodians. Not every religious feeling is good, but only that religious sentiment which interprets the thought of God, according to the apostolic teaching authority established by the sole master, Jesus Christ.[8]

Catholicity demands, therefore, a common bond of faith, founded upon the teaching of Christ, professed by the authentic tradition of the Church and guaranteed by its divinely instituted teaching authority, or *magisterium*. The message of revealed doctrine cannot be altered, and its meaning is preserved by the Church in certain conceptual and verbal formulas. The Pope is careful not to say that the formulations cannot be changed, only that the formulas are preserved, even when they are 'difficult'.

The second part of the Pope's reply to his initial question is a cautious declaration of cultural pluralism:

> The expression, that is, the language and mode of manifesting this one faith, may be manifold. Hence, it may be original, suited to the tongue, the style, the character, the genius, and the culture, of the one who professes this one faith. From this point of view, a certain pluralism is not only legitimate, but desirable. An adaptation of the Christian life in the fields of pastoral, ritual, didactic and spiritual activities is not only possible, it is even

favoured by the Church. The liturgical renewal is a living example of this. And in this sense you may, and you must, have an African Christianity.[9]

The Pope, therefore, envisaged an extensive dialogue between faith and culture in every field of the Church's activity, and saw the liturgical renewal as evidence of its beginning. He then went on to make a remark which shows that he was aware of the reciprocal character of the evangelization process, even if, like the documents of Vatican Two, he makes abstraction of the reality of acculturation. He told the African bishops:

Indeed, you possess human values and characteristic forms of culture which can rise up to perfection such as to find *in* Christianity, and *for* Christianity, a true superior fullness, and prove to be capable of a richness of expression all its own, and genuinely African.[10] [Italics not in the original.]

The prepositions 'in' and 'for' are crucial, and it is clear from them that the Pope expected African culture to make a positive contribution to Christianity.

Paul VI thought that this process would take considerable time. It would include the exercise of drawing from the Church's patrimony those treasures which can be considered universal and which can be most easily assimilated by the African mind. It was to be an exchange which enhanced the originality of African culture. Furthermore, there was to be an 'incubation' of the faith within that culture. Finally, the Pope used an image of pluriformity in unity to describe the Church. It was, he said, 'a chorus of voices'.

Such an exchange of the highest expressions of Christian thought nourishes any particular culture without altering its originality. It will require an incubation of the Christian 'mystery' in the genius of your people in order that its native voice, more clearly and frankly, may then be raised harmoniously in the chorus of the other voices in the universal Church.[11]

After exhorting the African bishops to set up centres of pastoral training, the Pope reminded them of the dangers of religious pluralism, of turning Christianity into a folk-lore, of racialism and of egoistic tribalism. Their task was to formulate Catholicism in terms congenial to their own culture. Also to bring to the Church 'the precious and original contribution of *negritude*.[12] 'The African Church', said the Pope, 'is confronted with an immense and original undertaking.'[13]

The 1974 Synod of Bishops

The theme of the 1974 Synod of Bishops was 'Evangelization', and the reflection on this topic which the Synod stimulated was directly responsible for the maturation of the concept of inculturation. Paul VI's words at Kampala had already provided a stimulus for the African bishops, in particular, and their intervention proved decisive at the Synod. At its third plenary assembly, the Symposium of Bishops of Africa and Madagascar made the following declaration:

> In the context of a development of Africa which may be truly African, the Symposium intends to encourage any kind of study or research capable of enriching our knowledge of African anthropology, sociology, traditional religions, rites and ceremonies of African societies. It wishes this research not to be merely theoretical, nor to fall into 'antiquarianism', but to contribute African solutions to problems of development and evangelization. It wishes that experts involved in this research, as experts and as Christians, may be convinced that they thus make an original and necessary contribution to the life of the whole Church.[14]

During 1973 the Bishops of Eastern Africa (AMECEA) held their plenary assembly on the theme: 'Planning for the Church in Eastern Africa in the 1980s'. It turned out to be an event of considerable pastoral importance for the countries of East and Central Africa, for it launched the programme of building small Christian communities. During this assembly, Bishop Joseph Blomjous, who later coined the term 'interculturation', spoke about the African Church's need for a relative autonomy and a concrete African expression of its Christian life in liturgy, sacraments, catechetics, preaching, priestly formation, priestly life, spirituality, religious life and theology.[15] Several African bishops also made a plea for the preservation and Christianization of African culture. Bishop Medardo Mazombwe of Chipata, Zambia, declared:

> The main elements which make up a people's culture are art, music, language and literature, customs and morals. Our apos-

tolate requires continuous communication with the environment where we are and where we work.[16]

It was this need for continuous communication with the human environment that prompted the decision to create small Christian communities. Later plenary assemblies of AMECEA in 1976 and 1979 studied small Christian communities in greater detail. It was felt that with these communities it was now possible to experiment liturgically and to make the Gospel truly relevant to African culture and tradition. Small Christian communities were the best means for implementing Paul VI's conception of an 'African Christianity'.[17]

Among the reports on the experience of evangelization presented to the Synod, one of the most outspoken was that compiled by Bishop J. D. Sangu of Mbeya, Tanzania. It cited the small Christian communities as places of 'intense vitality' and laid particular emphasis on liturgical renewal. In this respect, the report stated:

> The African is proud of his culture and religious traditions. Since there has been great confusion between Christianity and western culture, the African is thinking of going back to his traditional practices. War is being waged on religious colonialism in Africa.[18]

After quoting Paul VI's words about an African Christianity, the Bishop continued:

> In spite of this, some bishops' conferences in Africa have to complain about too much control from Rome, in matters of liturgical adaptation.[19]

Finally, on this question, the report stated:

> It is then necessary to foster the particular incarnation of Christianity in each country, in accordance with the genius and talents of each culture so that a thousand flowers may bloom in God's garden.[20]

During the 1974 Synod itself, the Bishops of Africa and Madagascar made a collective statement, concerning what they termed 'the task of religious acculturation'. Their intervention was prompted by the feeling that Christian life in Africa was very often lived merely at the surface, without any dialogue between the Gospel and the genuine values of traditional religion.

> We must bring to our Catholic faith, not only those cultural and

artistic experiences which are part of our heritage — a real, even though as yet, modest Africanization — but also a theology which enables us to tackle the challenges arising out of our historical background and the ongoing evolution of our society.

Our theological thinking must remain faithful to the authentic tradition of the Church, and at the same time be attentive to the life of our communities and respectful of our traditions and languages, that is of our philosophy of life. (*Ad Gentes*, 22; *Unitatis Redintegratio*, 14, 17.)

Following this idea of mission, the Bishops of Africa and Madagascar consider as being completely out of date, the so-called theology of adaptation. Instead, they adopt the theology of incarnation. The young churches of Africa and Madagascar cannot refuse to face up to this demand. They accept the fact of theological pluralism within the unity of faith, and consequently they must encourage, by all means, African theological research. Theology must be open to the aspiration of the people of Africa if it is to help Christianity to become incarnate in the life of the peoples of the African continent. To achieve this, the young churches of Africa and Madagascar must take over more and more the responsibility for their own evangelization and total development. They must combine creativity with dynamic responsibility.[21]

The Pope's reply to this declaration was as astonishing as it was uncharacteristic. In a few chilly sentences of his closing discourse Paul VI seemed to undermine the promise of the Kampala address. In Kampala he had spoken of the desirability and necessity of 'a certain pluralism', now he condemned the talk of diversified theologies as 'dangerous'. Adaptation was merely a question of verbal translation. The Pope seemed no longer to uphold the distinction between the faith itself and its mode of expression. 'The content of the faith is either Catholic or it is not.'

We sincerely rejoice at the increasing vitality of the particular churches and of their ever more manifest will to assume all their proper responsibilities. At the same time we hope proportionate care will be taken so that in the furthering of this essential aspect of ecclesial reality, no harm will come to the firmness of the *communio* with the other particular churches and with the successor of Saint Peter, to whom the Lord has entrusted the serious and enduring role — one full of love — of tending his lambs and sheep (Jn 21:13–17), of confirming his brethren (Lk 22:32) and of being the foundation and sign of the unity of the Church (Mt 16:18–20).[22]

It is evident from this passage that the Pope was alarmed at the tone of the African and other interventions, and that he feared for the bond of communion, uniting the particular churches. Perhaps, also, he saw in them a challenge to papal authority. It is possible, too, that, in reacting so sharply, he hoped to stem the tide of pluralism and slow down the process of what was now called 'incarnation'. These must have been among the reasons for the gloomy words that followed.

> Thus we consider necessary a word on the need of finding a better expression of faith to correspond to the racial, social and cultural milieux. This is indeed a necessary requirement of authenticity and effectiveness of evangelization; it would nevertheless be dangerous to speak of diversified theologies according to continents and cultures. The content of the faith is either Catholic or it is not. All of us, on the other hand, have received the faith of a constant tradition: Peter and Paul did not transform it to adapt it to the Jewish, Greek or Roman world; but they watched vigilantly over its authenticity and over the truth of its single message presented in a diversity of languages. (Ac 2:8)[23]

There is obviously a confusion of thought here. Diversified theology does not entail a departure from the Church's constant tradition. Nor does it imply a transformation of its content. The African bishops had spoken of 'theological pluralism within the unity of faith'. Moreover, language has profoundly cultural implications. The Pope referred to the outpouring of the Spirit at Pentecost in a diversity of tongues. Whatever historical event may or may not underlie this passage of Acts, and whatever the nature of the manifestation to which it refers, there is, as we have seen in Chapter 9, abundant evidence for the beginnings of a dialogue between faith and culture in the New Testament. The theology of the early Christian communities was certainly diversified by more than verbal translation. As it happens, however, there is no need to spend any more time on Paul VI's closing address to the 1974 Synod of Bishops, because, in the synodal document which he issued the following year (*Evangelii Nuntiandi*), he took a much more subtle and comprehensive view of language. In fact, it is clear that the 1974 Synod occasioned, in this document, the fullest and most positive, official statement of the *magisterium* on inculturation.

The Apostolic Exhortation on Evangelization in the Modern World

The 1974 Synod asked Paul VI to embody the fruits of their discussions in a document of his own. This the Pope did at the end of the Holy Year, 1975. The Apostolic Exhortation *Evangelii Nuntiandi* was promulgated on the Feast on the Immaculate Conception, 8 December. The document offers an advanced theology of a multicultural Church which has probably not been surpassed by any other official statement. It also offers an analysis of how a given culture appropriates the Gospel. In this analysis, the emphasis is placed on the evangelized, rather than on the evangelizing, or missionary, culture. This means that there is a certain sociological unreality about it. However, as a basic statement of the issues involved, it is unrivalled. Subsequent papal and synodal statements have been no more than additions or corrections.

The first part of the exhortation traces the Church's evangelizing mission back to Christ the evangelizer. In the second part, the Pope answers the question: 'What is evangelization?' His answer is that it means bringing the Good News of Christ into all the strata of humanity, so that humanity itself becomes a new creation. This leads naturally to a discussion of the evangelization of culture. Number 20 is worth quoting in full.

> All this could be expressed in the following words: what matters is to evangelize man's culture and cultures (not in a purely decorative way as it were by applying a thin veneer, but in a vital way, in depth and right to their very roots), in the wide and rich sense which these terms have in *Gaudium et Spes*, always taking the person as one's starting-point and always coming back to the relationships of people among themselves and with God.
>
> The Gospel, and therefore evangelization, are certainly not identical with culture, and they are independent in regard to all cultures. Nevertheless, the Kingdom which the Gospel proclaims is lived by men who are profoundly linked to a culture, and the building up of the Kingdom cannot avoid borrowing the elements of human culture or cultures. Though independent of cultures, the Gospel and evangelization are not necessarily incompatible with them; rather they are capable of permeating them all without becoming subject to any one of them.
>
> The split between the Gospel and culture is without a doubt the drama of our time, just as it was of other times. Therefore,

215

every effort must be made to ensure a full evangelization of culture, or more correctly of cultures. They have to be regenerated by an encounter with the Gospel. But this encounter will not take place if the Gospel is not proclaimed.[24]

The Pope was clearly concerned to safeguard the autonomy of the Gospel *vis-à-vis* cultures. Quite correctly he states that it is not tied exclusively to any one culture, and that evangelization consists in penetrating to the depth of culture. Neither is the Gospel 'subject' to culture, but permeates and elevates culture. However, he appears reluctant to admit the extent to which the process of evangelization is dependent on culture in actual fact. The Gospel is addressed to people who are 'profoundly linked' to culture and it 'borrows the elements of human culture'. Although the Pope admits that the Kingdom which the Gospel proclaims is lived by men who are profoundly linked to culture, he does not say, in so many words, that those who *proclaim* the Gospel are so linked. Nevertheless, that must be the obvious inference, since proclamation and witness of life are inseparable. There is a tendency, in the passage, to personify the Gospel and to make it sound like an independent agent.

After speaking of the methods, content and beneficiaries of evangelization — with basic Christian communities placed among the latter, Paul VI turned to the workers for evangelization. Since the individual churches are the primary agents of this mission, the exposition is basically ecclesiological, and cultural adaptation is treated within this ecclesiological setting. After speaking of the universal Church, the Pope dealt with the individual churches and warned against 'federal' interpretations. The particular (or individual) church is the Catholic Church in a particular place and time.

> Nevertheless this universal Church is in practice incarnate in the individual Churches made up of such or such an actual part of mankind, speaking such and such a language, heirs of a cultural patrimony, of a vision of the world, of an historical past, of a particular human substratum. Receptivity to the wealth of the individual Church corresponds to a special sensitivity of modern man.
>
> Let us be very careful not to conceive of the universal Church as the sum, or, if one can say so, the more or less anomalous federation of essentially different individual Churches. In the mind of the Lord the Church is universal by vocation and

mission, but when she puts down her roots in a variety of cultural, social and human terrains, she takes on different external expressions and appearances in each part of the world.[25]

The Pope then went on to warn particular churches against cutting themselves off from the Universal Church, and stressed the need of continual attention to both the universal and the particular poles of the Church.

The most important passage for our purposes is undoubtedly the paragraph that follows (number 63). Its strength lies in the analysis of the inculturation process as having three basic phases: assimilation, transposition and proclamation; in the enumeration of its fields of application; and in a more profound understanding of language as 'anthropological and cultural'. The weakness of the passage lies in the concept of the Gospel emerging from a world of essences, and in the assumption that evangelization (or the Church) is doing things for the people. Ultimately, inculturation can only be understood in terms of a real world of culture and history and as the outcome of community action. It is not a few evangelizing experts who are going to conduct the process on behalf of the community. Their role is one of stimulation, canalization and prophetical expression. A very serious lacuna in the whole treatment of the subject is also the lack of reference to the Bible or to biblical cultures.

> The individual Churches, intimately built up not only of people but also of aspirations, of riches and limitations, of ways of praying, of loving, of looking at life and the world which distinguish this or that human gathering, have the task of assimilating the essence of the Gospel message and of transposing it, without the slightest betrayal of its essential truth, into the language that these particular people understand, then of proclaiming it in this language.
>
> The transposition has to be done with the discernment, seriousness, respect and competence which the matter calls for in the field of liturgical expression, and in the areas of catechesis, theological formulation, secondary ecclesial structures and ministries. And the word 'language' should be understood here less in the semantic or literary sense than in the sense which one may call anthropological and cultural.
>
> The question is undoubtedly a delicate one. Evangelization loses much of its force and effectiveness if it does not take into

consideration the actual people to whom it is addressed, if it does not use their language, their signs and symbols, if it does not answer the questions they ask, and if it does not have an impact on their concrete life. But on the other hand evangelization risks losing its power and disappearing altogether if one empties or adulterates its content under the pretext of translating it; if, in other words, one sacrifices the reality and destroys the unity without which there is no universality, out of a wish to adapt a universal reality to a local situation. Now only a Church which preserves the awareness of her universality and shows that she is in fact universal is capable of having a message which can be heard by all, regardless of regional frontiers.

Legitimate attention to individual Churches cannot fail to enrich the Church. Such attention is indispensable and urgent. It responds to the very deep aspirations of peoples and human communities to find their own identity ever more clearly.[26]

In these last two paragraphs, Paul VI broached the subject of what later came to be called 'culturalism' — sacrificing the content of the Gospel to incompatible cultural values or rendering the Gospel subject to culture. He also introduced the idea of the mutual enrichment of particular churches. This idea, which he pursued in the following number of the document (number 64), is a development of *Gaudium et Spes*, 58. Mutual enrichment requires a 'profound openness towards the universal Church'. Such reciprocity presupposes the forum of a universal communion.

> The more an individual Church is attached to the universal Church by solid bonds of communion, in charity and loyalty, in receptiveness to the Magisterium of Peter, in the unity of the *lex orandi* which is also the *lex credendi*, in the desire for unity with all the other Churches which make up the whole — the more such a Church will be capable of translating the treasure of faith into the legitimate variety of expressions of the profession of faith, of prayer and worship, of Christian life and conduct and of the spiritual influence on the people among which it dwells. The more will it also be truly evangelizing, that is to say capable of drawing upon the universal patrimony in order to enable its own people to profit from it, and capable too of communicating to the universal Church the experience and the life of this people, for the benefit of all.[27]

In this vision of exchange between the churches that make up the

Church universal, the *magisterium* of Peter is seen as the guarantor of unity and authenticity. The particular churches are required to be 'receptive' to this *magisterium*. In the following paragraph Paul VI returns to the theme of his closing address at the Synod of Bishops: the role of Peter's successor as principle of unity and charged with the 'grave responsibility of preserving unaltered the content of the Catholic faith which the Lord entrusted to the Apostles'.[28]

> While being translated into all expressions, this content must be neither impaired nor mutilated. While being clothed with the outward forms proper to each people, and made explicit by theological expression which takes account of differing cultural, social and even racial milieux, it must remain the content of the Catholic faith just exactly as the ecclesial *Magisterium* has received it and transmits it.[29]

In speaking of the Petrine office, Paul VI placed all the emphasis on the ministry of teaching and safeguarding the revealed truth. It is a pity that the Petrine role of listening to the particular churches and of guaranteeing their freedom of expression and initiative has not been equally stressed, either by Paul VI or his successors. What needs to be spelt out more fully is the papal role in the partnership and mutuality of the evangelization process. How far, it may be asked, does the Pope participate in the two-way process? Is he, in fact, and is his office, enriched?

Evangelii Nuntiandi paved the way for the theological reflection on inculturation which followed in the late 1970s. At the 1977 Synod of Bishops on Catechesis, there were many interventions on this theme. Among the most important were those of Cardinal Jaime Sin of the Philippines, who noted the Church's recognition of cultural pluralism and the shift in salvation theology, and of Fr Pedro Arrupe SJ, who used the actual term 'inculturation' in the *aula* and spoke of the necessity of a balanced pluralism in the Church.[30]

During the Synod Paul VI gave his final message to Africa when receiving the African Bishops in audience. He spoke of the cultural originality of Africa which must be 'enlivened from within' by the Catholic faith. The faith 'grafted on to the venerable ancestral trunk' would 'give quality and taste to the fruits of the tree'.[31] Notwithstanding the poverty of the metaphor, there was no doubt that the Pope meant the Church to be, in his own words, 'entirely at home in Africa'.[32] Although ambiguities remained, Paul VI's teaching on the evangelization of culture represented a very notable advance.

References

1 Neuner 1967.

2 Hickey 1982, pp. 176–97.

3 *Africae Terrarum*, 7.

4 *Ibid.*, 8–12.

5 *Ibid.*, 13.

6 Gaba Pastoral Paper No. 7, 1969, p. 17. The author was present at this first SECAM Assembly and at all the functions of the subsequent papal visit. He helped to draft some of the documents connected with both events, and was a member of the organizing committee.

7 Hickey 1982, p. 203.

8 *Ibid.*, p. 203.

9 *Ibid.*, pp. 203–4.

10 *Ibid.*, p. 204.

11 *Ibid.*, p. 204.

12 *Ibid.*, p. 204.

13 *Ibid.*, p. 204.

14 *AFER*, Vol. 14, 1972, No. 1, pp. 362–3.

15 *AFER*, Vol. 16, 1974, Nos. 1 and 2, p. 38.

16 *Ibid.*, p. 216.

17 *AFER*, Vol. 18, 1976, No. 5, pp. 250–54.

18 Hickey 1982, p. 218.

19 *Ibid.*, p. 219.

20 *Ibid.*, p. 234.

21 *AMECEA Documentation Service*, 11/74/2, pp. 2–3.

22 *L'Osservatore Romano*, N. 45, 7 Nov. 1974, p. 9.

23 *Ibid.*

24 *Evangelii Nuntiandi*, 20.

25 *Ibid.*, 62.

26 *Ibid.*, 63.

27 *Ibid.*, 64.

28 *Ibid.*, 65.

29 *Ibid.*, 65.

30 *AFER*, Vol. 20, 1978, No. 1, pp. 32–3.

31 Hickey 1982, p. 248.

32 *Ibid.*, p. 248.

16

John Paul II
and inculturation

Catechesis in Our Time

Pope John Paul II has travelled further and visited more countries than any other Pope. His addresses, letters and speeches are also more numerous than those of his predecessors. His worldwide pastoral journeys confront him with the reality of cultural pluralism, and they also demand of him an enormous output of teaching. In the circumstances he is often called upon to deal with the subject of faith and culture. Consequently, he cannot avoid a great amount of repetition. Even the most superficial acquaintance with his teachings shows that there are recurring themes which are repeatedly adapted to different audiences. There is no question, therefore, of enumerating all the many occasions on which he has spoken about the relationship of faith and culture. Nor is it necessary to refer to all of the synodal documents, which, in spite of the regular call for inculturation at the Synod of Bishops, reflect, for the most part, the concerns and presuppositions of traditional theology. The most that needs to be done in this chapter is to study some of the original passages which have served, as it were, as a blueprint for the Pope's other speeches and writings.

The extreme frequency of the Pope's pastoral journeys make it well-nigh impossible for him to be fully receptive to all the different insights and priorities of the local churches he visits, though he, himself, often singles out a particular or controversial issue, such as polygamy, birth-control, food aid or minority rights, usually restating official teaching in traditional form. His concessions to local culture are largely a question of outward gesture, wearing a monkey-skin cape in Nairobi, drinking *kava* in Fiji, rubbing noses with Maoris in New Zealand, or walking a 'dreamtime trail' with Australian aborigines. Official policy (interpreted in this instance by the Pronuncio to Zaire) prevented him from celebrating Mass according to the Zaire rite in Kinshasa in 1980. The stated objective of the papal journeys is to confirm the faith of his brethren, and this takes the form of imposing the universal papal *magisterium*, in a bid to strengthen the bond of communion.

Nevertheless, John Paul II has a real and abiding interest in culture. This interest stems first of all from his preoccupation with man and with the human phenomenon. Culture, especially Christian culture, enables man to be fully human. The Pope's interest also flows from the strugggle of his own Christian Slavonic culture with the culture of atheistic Marxism. This leads him to view the non-Christian partner in the intercultural dialogue with suspicion, as a potentially alienating force. It means further that, while his enunciation of the principles involved is theologically and sociologically exact — more so, even, than was the case with Paul VI — he seems to be sceptical in practice about the outcome of the dialogue which the emergent local churches of the Third World wish to conduct with their own non-Christian traditions. This scepticism is seldom directly expressed. It is more often conveyed by a choice of phrase or the tone of a passage. It is probable that this personal viewpoint has much to do with the growing discrepancy between official teaching on inculturation and actual ecclesial policy.

Pope Paul VI and Pope John Paul I both died in 1978, before the final document of the Synod of Bishops of 1977 could be drawn up. It was left to John Paul II to sum up the thinking of the Synod in his Apostolic Exhortation *Catechesi Tradendae*, 'Catechesis in Our Time', which was issued in October 1979. As we saw in the previous chapter, the participants at the Synod laid considerable emphasis on culture, and it was not surprising, therefore, to find an important section on the subject in the Pope's exhortation.[1]

In this section, the Pope began by quoting a statement he had made to the Pontifical Biblical Commission earlier in the same year.[2] It was a statement that contained, for the first time in a papal document, the word 'inculturation' itself. As we have already seen, it had been used in the *aula* of the Synod in 1977. The Pope used it in conjunction with 'acculturation', and it is impossible to tell whether he thought the terms were interchangeable, or whether he was alluding to the essential connection between the two. The passage went on to refer to the privileged place of biblical cultures in the dialogue between Gospel and culture, and to the historical character of the whole process of inculturation. This was a valuable corrective to *Evangelii Nuntiandi* which had seemingly ignored both these aspects. After this, John Paul II condemned culturalism with the aid of a phrase from the Letter to the Corinthians, which he was to use many times afterwards.[3] The whole passage, in fact, has been inserted into numerous subsequent speeches and addresses.

As I said recently to the members of the Biblical Commission: 'The term *acculturation* or *inculturation* may be a neologism, but it expresses very well one factor of the great mystery of the Incarnation'. We can say of catechesis, as well as of evangelization in general, that it is called to bring the power of the Gospel into the very heart of culture and cultures. For this purpose, catechesis will seek to know these cultures and their essential components; it will learn their most significant expressions; it will respect their particular values and riches. In this manner it will be able to offer these cultures the knowledge of the hidden mystery and help them to bring forth from their own living tradition original expressions of Christian life, celebration and thought. Two things must, however, be kept in mind.

On the one hand the Gospel message cannot be purely and simply isolated from the culture in which it was first inserted (the Biblical world, or more concretely, the cultural milieu in which Jesus of Nazareth lived), nor, without serious loss, from the cultures in which it has already been expressed down the centuries; it does not spring spontaneously from any cultural soil; it has always been transmitted by means of an apostolic dialogue which inevitably becomes part of a certain dialogue of cultures.

On the other hand, the power of the Gospel everywhere transforms and regenerates. When that power enters into a culture, it is no surprise that it rectifies many of its elements. There would be no catechesis if it were the Gospel that had to change when it came into contact with the cultures.

To forget this would simply amount to what Saint Paul very forcefully calls 'emptying the cross of Christ of its power'.

It is a different matter to take, with wise discernment, certain elements, religious or otherwise, that form part of the cultural heritage of a human group and use them to help its members to understand better the whole of the Christian mystery. Genuine catechists know that catechesis 'takes flesh' in the various cultures and milieux . . .[4]

In this last paragraph the Pope seems to illustrate the passage from acculturation to inculturation, the difference between using certain cultural elements to assist in the understanding of Christianity and the actual 'taking flesh' of Christianity in a culture or milieu. However, he does not go any further in the analysis of this incarnation, but begins to draw examples, of which the only explicit one is that of modern youth culture (or more correctly, sub-culture). The Pope condemns even a purely linguistic adaptation in so far as it endangers the faith. Perhaps he has in mind those who advocate the use of a Marxist terminology.

> . . . one has only to think of peoples with their great differences, of modern youth, of the great variety of circumstances in which people find themselves today. But they refuse to accept an impoverishment of catechesis through a renunciation or obscuring of its message, by adaptation, even in language, that would endanger the 'precious deposit' of the faith, or by concessions in matters of faith or morals. They are convinced that true catechesis eventually enriches these cultures by helping them to go beyond the defective or even inhuman features in them, and by communicating to their legitimate values the fullness of Christ.[5]

This important text sets the tone for all the Pope's later utterances on the subject of inculturation. He does not spontaneously refer to the cultural values of the Third World, nor does he fail to convey a certain scepticism by insisting on the dangers, rather than on the advantages, of inculturation.

The First African Journey

During his journey to Africa in 1980, John Paul II spoke to the bishops of Zaire on the subject of 'the inculturation of the Gospel, the Africanization of the Church'.[6] The positive content of his address is largely supplied by quotations from the Second Vatican Council, Paul VI's Kampala Address, *Evangelii Nuntiandi* and the passage just cited from *Catechesi Tradendae*. Much of the rest tends to be prudential and cautionary. The Pope feels that there is much to do before we can speak of inculturation, and he compares the situation of twentieth-century Africa to that of medieval Poland.

> Africanisation covers wide and deep fields, which have not yet been sufficiently explored, whether it is a question of the

language to present the Christian message in a way that will reach the spirit and heart of Zaireans, of catechesis, theological reflection, the most suitable expression in liturgy or sacred art, community forms of Christian life.

It is up to you, bishops, to promote and harmonise the advance in this field, after mature reflection, in concerted action among yourselves, in union also with the universal church and with the Holy See. Inculturation, for the people as a whole, cannot be, moreover, but the fruit of gradual maturity in faith. For you are convinced as I am that this work, for which I am anxious to express to you all my confidence, requires a great deal of theological lucidity, spiritual discernment, wisdom and prudence, and also time.

Allow me to recall, among other examples, the experience of my own country. In Poland, a deep union has been established between the ways of thinking and living that characterise the nation and Catholicism; this impregnation took centuries. Here, taking into consideration a different situation, it should be possible for Christianity to unite with what is deepest in the Zairean soul for an original culture, at the same time African and Christian.[7]

After citing Paul VI's concern for safeguarding the unity of faith and his own remarks in *Catechesi Tradendae* in the context of theological inculturation, John Paul II reviews the other fields: catechesis, liturgy and ethics. For catechesis there must be presentations 'better suited to the African soul'. In liturgy, enrichment is possible, but the substantial unity of the Roman rite must be preserved. In the ethical field, the resources of the African soul were already highlighted by Paul VI in *Africae Terrarum* and are, in any case, better known to the Zairean bishops than to anyone.

The Pope then made an important theological criticism of the analogy of Incarnation.

. . . there is always a conversion to be effected, in regard to the person of Christ, the only Saviour, and his teaching, such as the Church transmits it to us: it is then that the liberation, the purification, the transfiguration, the elevation that he came to bring and that he realised in his paschal mystery, takes place. It is necessary to consider both the incarnation of Christ and his redemption.[8]

Finally, in this matter of inculturation, John Paul II exhorted the Zairean bishops to have perfect cohesion among themselves and a trusting communion with the Holy See where, he assured them, their concerns would meet with understanding. Citing the example of Poland once more, he laid great stress on the Polish virtue of 'solidarity'.

> Each Church has its problems, but everywhere, I am not afraid of repeating, as I said to the Polish bishops: 'It is this unity which is the source of spiritual strength'.[9]

It is clear that the recent history of the Pope's own homeland predisposes him to view diversity and local autonomy as signs of weakness. In this view, the Church is perhaps to be seen as a counterweight to the Marxist, ideological bloc.

Four days after the address to the Zairean bishops, the Pope was in Kenya, where he also addressed the local hierarchy on the subject of inculturation. After again quoting *Catechesi Tradendae*, he spoke of inculturation in personal terms. Christ was the Christian term of inculturation. It was a happy conception which later became a commonplace of papal addresses in various countries.

> There is no question of adulterating the Word of God, or of emptying the cross of Christ of its power, but rather of bringing Christ into the very centre of African life and of lifting up all African life to Christ. Thus, not only is Christianity relevant to Africa, but Christ, in the members of his Body, is himself African.[10]

John Paul II struck an even more positive note when he spoke to a group of Zairean bishops in 1983 on the subject of African theology. He began by tracing the history of the early Church, recalling how first Greek, and then Latin, culture had to be confronted and how a variety of local churches came into existence, as a result.

> This diversity sometimes became so sharp that tensions and schisms resulted. Nonetheless, the coexistence of these diverse churches remains the most typical and, in many respects, the most exemplary, manifestation of a legitimate pluralism in worship, discipline and theological expressions, as is indicated in the decree *Unitatis Redintegratio* of Vatican II [cf. nos. 14–18].[11]

The Pope noted that a clear distinction between the three, interrelated, levels of faith, culture and history is necessary for anyone who wants to study closely the way Christian life can be inculturated.

Although he emphasized once again the role of bishops in controlling the process of inculturation, John Paul II had some refreshing things to add. Too much emphasis should not be placed on the *magisterium*. Believers, and especially theologians, have a vital role to play in the development of the Church's understanding of Revelation, as *Dei Verbum* reminds us. Moreover, such insights must be communicated to the universal Church which is enriched thereby.

> There was perhaps a time when some put too much stress on the authority of the *magisterium* in the organic life of faith. Vatican II has clearly shown that the understanding of Revelation develops not only by 'the preaching of those who have received, along with their right of succession in the episcopate, the sure charism of truth', but also by 'the contemplation and study of believers' and 'the intimate sense of spiritual realities which they experience' (*Dei Verbum*, 8). For their part, theologians have had their important place in the Church recognized. They are the official 'co-adjutors' of the *magisterium*, above all in approaches to new questions and in the scholarly deepening of the study of the sources of faith . . .
>
> But do not forget that it is to you, the bishops, united with the successor of Peter, that it belongs to make the final decisions about the Christian authenticity of such ideas and experiments. The charism of our ordination is at stake here, for we are Teachers and Fathers in the faith. Besides, one of the criteria of your discernment must be the possibility of communicating with the other local churches. Rightly proud of your African identity, you also have the duty of sharing with the other Christian communities about the ways you express and live the faith. In doing this, you both guarantee the unity of the Church and you contribute to a mutual enrichment.[12]

After this, the Pope considered the tasks of African theology, disarming in advance the criticism that his remarks might be considered too negative.

> These remarks are not meant in any way to be negative. We are trying to lay the foundations for an authentic African contribution to theological research, and to investigate the conditions for a fruitful and beneficial inculturation of Christianity in Africa

— which is a valid concern of yours. This is not a matter just for Christian life in Africa: no, it is a way of enriching the entire Church by fresh approaches to the mystery of God, as a living out of spiritual and moral values which manifests the whole Christian way of life in practice, in action.[13]

The tasks were twofold: a doctrinal reflection on African identity, and a study of the fundamental data of Christianity. On the first subject, the Pope immediately pointed to the danger of culturalism and made a significant comparison with so-called 'Christian Marxism'.

There is room here for many different and more or less legitimate doctrinal positions. You are certainly aware of a danger: that of building up a philosophy and theology of 'African-ness' which would be solely indigenous and stripped of any true and deep link with Christ. In such a case, Christianity would be merely a nominal reference, an element that is added on in an artificial way. Medieval Europe had this experience, with the Aristotelians who were Christian only in name, like, for example, the Averroists against whom St Thomas Aquinas and St Bonaventure had to struggle vigorously. At the present time, the same danger can be seen in the efforts being made to develop so-called Christian Marxism or Christian Hegelianism.[14]

Even more significantly, John Paul II goes on to quote Paul VI's pessimistic closing speech to the 1974 Synod on the dangers of theological pluralism, and to oppose this to Paul's later exhortation on reconciliation of 1975.[15] This had spoken of dogma being 'unfolded' through the pluralism of research and thought, and of this pluralism recognizing 'a legitimate right to be oneself in the Church', a sign of the Church's cultural richness. John Paul II, however, considers that there are languages and systems

which are so impoverished and closed that they make any satisfactory translation and interpretation of the Word of God quite impossible.[16]

African theologians are on safer ground if they

make use of a culture to retranslate in new words and in new perspectives the biblical revelation that has been handed down to us.[17]

This constitutes, in the mind of the Pope, the second and more preferable task of African theology, one founded directly on the Bible, the Councils and the *magisterium*. However, he mentions some other concrete problems that command the attention ot the theologian in Africa: the family, justice, development, economic progress, evangelization and the sects 'which nibble away here and there at Catholic unity'.[18] John Paul II's thinking on culturalism was to be developed more particularly in connection with the Pontifical Council for Culture.

The Council for Culture and the Apostles of the Slavs

On 20 May 1982 John Paul II founded the Pontifical Council for Culture and, in a personal letter to Cardinal Agostino Casaroli, directed him to preside over its organization. As the letter shows, the Pope believed that culture was a fundamental dimension of humanity, and that in promoting both the dialogue between cultures, and the dialogue between cultures and the Gospel, the ideological divisions of mankind could be overcome and the threats to human existence removed. The emphasis is once again on unity, as opposed to diversity.

> Since the beginning of my pontificate, I have considered the Church's dialogue with the cultures of our time to be a vital area, one in which the destiny of the world at the end of this twentieth century is at stake. There in fact does exist a fundamental dimension capable of strengthening or shaking to their foundations the systems into which mankind as a whole is organized, and of liberating human existence, individually and collectively, from the threats which hang over it. This fundamental dimension is man, in his totality. Now man lives a fully human life thanks to culture . . .
>
> For this reason, I have decided to found and institute a Council for Culture, capable of giving the whole Church a common impulse in the continuously renewed encounter between the salvific message of the Gospel and the multiplicity of cultures, in the diversity of cultures to which she must carry her fruits of grace.[19]

The Council was charged with the defence of the cultural inheritance of humankind, threatened by materialistic and dehumanizing values, and also with the evangelization of cultures. It is clear that the ongoing dialogue between faith and the Western cultures of modernity was in the forefront of the Pope's mind. However, there is much in the letter to Cardinal Casaroli and in the Pope's subsequent communications to the Council which is relevant to inculturation in the Third World. In particular, the Pope saw an 'organic and constitutive link' between Christianity and culture.

> . . . the synthesis between culture and faith is not just a demand of culture, but also of faith. A faith which does not become culture is a faith which has not been fully received, not thoroughly thought through, not fully lived out.[20]

This is probably the clearest official Church statement of the relationship between faith and culture. It is characteristic of John Paul II's social and historical realism that he has expressed the relationship more clearly than his predecessors. However, one feels that he appreciates the synthesis in the historic cultures of Christian Europe, and fears for their future, while at the same time hesitating to risk the deposit of faith in a dialogue with the cultures of the non-Christian Third World.

In an address to the Council in January 1984, the Pope reiterated his fear of culturalism, and spoke of the culture of peace overcoming 'anti-culture'.[21] Three months later, similar concepts appeared in a speech given to the Jubilee of Youth. This time, the Pope saw it as a struggle between 'the culture of love' and 'the culture of death'.[22] John Paul II is constantly alive to the threat posed to the Gospel and to true culture by modern ideology and technology and also by nationalistic culturalism. In this struggle Gospel and culture are seen by him as allies.

The eleventh centenary of the missionary brothers, Saints Cyril and Methodius, gave John Paul II an occasion to commemorate them and their contribution to Slavonic culture in an encyclical letter entitled: *Slavorum Apostoli*, 'Apostles of the Slavs'. The encyclical letter represents the speech the Pope would have given, had he been able to visit the tomb of St Methodius in Czechoslovakia for the centenary celebrations. It was issued on 2 June 1985. In it John Paul II proclaims these saints as 'a model of what is called today *inculturation*'. He notes especially that Cyril and Methodius formed and developed Slavonic culture, in the act of evangelizing it. In Chapter 10 we discussed the mission of Saints Cyril and Methodius, and saw that it was not free of cultural domination or manipulation. Whatever benefits have accrued to modern Slavonic culture through the unification accomplished by these ninth-century missionaries, there is surely room for discussion about the appropriateness of their methods for us today. Once again, the Pope's attachment to the history and culture of his own people obscures the very real difference between the twentieth century and the medieval world.

On one point, the Pope was surely correct: Saints Cyril and Methodius possessed a strong sense of Catholicity, of unity in diversity. As the Pope wrote:

> The concrete dimension of catholicity, inscribed by Christ the Lord in the very make-up of the Church, is not something static, outside history and flatly uniform.[23]

The Pope recalled how, in Venice, St Cyril contrasted this concept of Catholicity with the narrow view of the Church held by the ecclesiastics assembled there. He had cried:

> And you are not ashamed to decree only three languages [Hebrew, Greek and Latin], deciding that all other peoples and races should remain blind and deaf? Tell me: do you hold this because you consider God is so weak that he cannot grant it, or so envious that he does not wish it?[24]

It was at this point that John Paul II hailed Cyril and Methodius as a model of inculturation.

> The work of evangelization which they carried out — as pioneers in territory inhabited by Slav peoples — contains both a model of what today is called 'inculturation' — the incarnation of the Gospel in native cultures — and also the introduction of these cultures into the life of the Church. By incarnating the Gospel in the native culture of the peoples they were evangelizing, Saints Cyril and Methodius were especially meritorious for the formation and development of that same culture, or rather of many cultures.[25]

In a letter to the clergy of Czechoslovakia, issued shortly before *Slavorum Apostoli*, John Paul II had spoken, not only of the two saints' 'dialogue with history', but also of their appreciation of the doctrinal and disciplinary unity of the Church.[26] They had suffered for their loyalty to the see of Peter. However, the Pope did not emphasize the fact that many of their sufferings had occurred at the hands of Latins, jealous for the integrity of this very Petrine jurisdiction.

The encyclical letter *Slavorum Apostoli* is a celebration of John Paul II's conception of culture. The most exalted form of culture is that which is permeated and developed by the Gospel. The Pope does not deny the name of 'culture' to those not yet evangelized, but the gulf that lies between them and evangelized cultures, and also their potential antagonism to the Gospel, places them lower down on the cultural scale. St Justin's concept of the 'seeds of the Word' is not found in the Pope's writings, nor does he often dwell on the Christian potentialities of non-Christian culture. Could there be here a yearning for a vanished Christian monoculturalism?

Before and After the Extraordinary Synod

In January 1985 Pope John Paul II announced that he was summoning an Extraordinary Synod of Bishops at the end of the year, the purpose of which was to celebrate the twentieth anniversary of the conclusion of the Second Vatican Council and to deepen the application of its teaching. Four months before the meeting of the Extraordinary Synod, the Pope undertook another journey to Africa, his third, which took in a first visit to Cameroun and a second visit to Kenya for the forty-third International Eucharistic Congress. The journey was an opportunity to speak again about inculturation, and also, perhaps, to offer orientations for the coming Synod. The two most relevant addresses were those to the University of Cameroun and to the Catholic Higher Institute of Eastern Africa in Nairobi.

In Cameroun the Pope struck a positive note. He remarked that the African's cry for liberation included the yearning for freedom from cultural exploitation. This freedom was guaranteed by the Christian faith, which can be assimilated into every language and tradition, the positive elements and spiritual values of which must be integrated and fulfilled.

> Therefore an unremitting effort of inculturation must be pursued in order that the faith may not remain superficial.[27]

Faith plays a prophetical and critical role. It consolidates what is human. It purifies culture, raises it up, prunes it of error and helps it expand and bear fruit.

In Nairobi, at the formal opening of the Catholic Higher Institute of Eastern Africa, the Pope struck a more sombre note. Indeed, the cheerlessness of the speech led a local newspaper to headline its report: 'Clergy cautioned on Cultural Values'.[28] The Pope saw the Institute as an instrument of the teaching office of the bishops of the region, and its pastoral and theological tasks were derived from this role. The speech was characterized by a new and analogous use of the term 'culture'. The Pope spoke several times of 'the theological culture' or 'the theological patrimony' of the Universal Church. By this he conveyed something more than the tradition or deposit of faith. He seemed, in fact, to be alluding to the theological aspect of what we called, in Chapter 5, the Church's cultural patrimony. In this case, it seems to have been the accumulation of orthodox theological speculation and formulation throughout history. The teaching office of bishops assisted by theologians must not only be exercised 'in enlightened dialogue' with that 'culture', but must be 'solidly grounded' in it. We have already seen, in Chapter 5, that such patrimony should not be allowed to become a culture in the strictly sociological sense. The Pope seemed to be telling his hearers in Nairobi that African theology must take this cultural patrimony, and not African culture, as its starting-point.

There were, however, unacceptable forms of 'theological culture'. One of these was a form of theological élitism which was not linked to pastoral concerns. Another more dangerous form was a 'pseudo-theological culture' which was inspired by 'the spirit of antichrist'. It did not serve the mystery of redemption nor the spirit of truth. It was on the side of the 'spirit of error'. In other words, it used the methodological criteria of other sciences, and did not take 'as its specific point of departure . . . the word of God transmitted in Tradition and in the Scriptures', with the Church's *magisterium* as 'a constant point of reference'. Once again, the Pope was giving strong expression to his fear of culturalism and of a culture without Christ.

There were, however, words of encouragement in the Nairobi speech. Among the pastoral tasks requiring the assistance of theologians were the strengthening of spiritual life, the consolidation of the family and the building of small Christian communities. Under the supervision of the bishops, there was to be an active dialogue between faith and culture, following the example of Saints Cyril and Methodius. These ideas were contained in the most positive passage of the address, which was qualified only by the stress on the Church's patrimony and by a subtle shift of emphasis from inculturation to acculturation in the final sentence. Here it was a question, not of introducing Christian values into the African way of life, but of introducing African values into the life of the Church.

This supervisory role of the Bishops is especially applicable in the important and delicate area of what has come to be known as 'inculturation'.

Throughout the course of the Church's history, teachers and missionaries have engaged in an apostolic dialogue between the Christian message of salvation and the cultures in which the various peoples express their characteristic spiritual and human experience. In my recent Encyclical Epistle in commemoration of the Eleventh Centenary of the evangelizing work of Saints Cyril and Methodius among the Slav Peoples, I thought it proper to draw attention to their magnificent example in this regard.

An active dialogue between faith and culture is necessary on all levels of the proclamation of the Christian message: in evangelization, in catechesis, and in theological reflection. As a requirement stemming from faith itself, the supreme criterion of this dialogue — also in the field of theological investigation — must be the power of the Gospel to transform, elevate and regenerate human life in every culture and in all circumstances.

The success of the local churches in incarnating the Gospel of Jesus Christ in the rich soil of your African cultures will depend on the extent to which your evangelizing and catechetical labours are solidly grounded in the theological patrimony of the universal Church. It will also depend on the extent to which your pastoral activities are accompanied by a serious reflection on the values which are present in each community and which can usefully be introduced into the life of the Church.[29]

Finally, John Paul II called upon the Catholic Higher Institute to implement for Eastern Africa the dynamism of the Second Vatican Council, the greatest concern of which, according to Pope John XXIII, was to safeguard and teach the deposit of Christian doctrine. Pope John's biographer has pointed out that, while this concern was voiced in the opening address of the Council, Pope John also told the bishops that the Council had not been called to re-state what had been repeatedly taught by the Church. Its 'salient point' was a great leap forward in the understanding of the Gospel and to clothe the traditional faith in new language.[30]

The Institute is called to assist the local Churches in the challenging dialogue between faith and culture, between the Church and human society, between the Kingdom of God and the temporal realities through which the human family moves towards its final destiny. The Institute has a role to play in implementing for Eastern Africa the dynamism of the Second Vatican Council. Let us never forget those words spoken by Pope John XXIII on the opening day of that collegial assembly: 'The greatest concern of the Ecumenical Council is this: that the sacred deposit of Christian doctrine should be more effectively guarded and taught' (11 October 1962). May the Institute always be found worthy of the extremely important responsibility to which it has been called![31]

When the Extraordinary Synod finally met in Rome at the end of 1985, it had little to say about inculturation itself. It did, however, draw a sharp distinction between inculturation and adaptation (acculturation).

Since the Church is a communion, which joins diversity and unity, being present throughout the world, it takes up whatever it finds positive in all cultures. Inculturation, however, is different from a mere external adaptation, as it signifies an interior transformation of authentic cultural values through integration into Christianity and the rooting of Christianity in various human cultures.[32]

The Synod then quoted Paul VI's words in *Evangelii Nuntiandi* concerning the danger of a split between Gospel and culture and the need of cultures to be reborn from their union with the Gospel.

The passage quoted above, from the final document of the Extraordinary Synod, was repeated again in full in the *Instruction on Christian Freedom and Liberation* which was issued by the Congregation for the Doctrine of the Faith in April 1986. Earlier, the document had spoken about the right to culture and the respect for cultural freedom. Too often culture is debased by ideology. At the end of the short section on inculturation it added a sentence which placed the dialogue between faith and culture in the context of liberation.

Enlightened by the second Vatican Council, the Church wishes to devote all her energies to this task, so as to evoke an immense liberating effort.[33]

It is not easy to summarize Pope John Paul II's contribution to the theology of inculturation. On the one hand, he has clarified the historical and social processes involved, and has warned against the very real danger of culturalism. On the other hand, he has carried the concept of inculturation to the extreme of exalting the idea of Christian culture in a way that reflects adversely on non-Christian cultures. The latter are seen as potentially, if not actually, hostile and threatening to the Gospel. In the final part of this book we shall try to assess the future of inculturation in the Church, and this will necessarily involve a further assessment of official positions taken during this pontificate. It is possible that the present Pope shares the scepticism of Cardinal Ratzinger with regard to Third World cultures in general and African culture in particular. In Cardinal Ratzinger's case, this derives from the Cardinal's belief that European thought has spread to the whole world, and from what he calls 'the *universal* significance of Christian thought as it has evolved in the West'. This, of course, is a position not far removed from monoculturalism.[34]

References

1 *Catechesi Tradendae*, 53.

2 AAS 71, 1979, p. 607.

3 1 Cor 1:17 (Revised Standard Version).

4 *Catechesi Tradendae*, 53.

5 *Ibid.*, 53.

6 *AFER*, Vol. 22, No. 4, August 1980, pp. 222–30.

7 *Ibid.*, 4–5.

8 *Ibid.*, 5.

9 *Ibid.*, 6.

10 *AFER*, Vol. 22, No. 4, August 1980, p. 198.

11 *AFER*, Vol. 25, No. 5, October 1983, p. 313–14.

12 *Ibid.*, p. 315.

13 *Ibid.*, p. 316.

14 *Ibid.*, p. 317.

15 *Ibid.*, p. 317; *AAS* 67, 1975, p. 13.

16 *AFER*, Vol. 25, No. 5, October 1983, p. 317.

17 *Ibid.*, p. 317.

18 *Ibid.*, p. 318.

19 *L'Osservatore Romano*, 28 June 1982, pp. 1–8.

20 *Ibid.*

21 Quoted in *Church and Cultures* (Bulletin for the Pontifical Council for Culture), No. 1, 1984, p. 3.

22 *L'Osservatore Romano*, 25 April 1984.

23 *The Tablet*, 6 July 1985, p. 708.

24 *Ibid.*

25 *Ibid.*

26 *L'Osservatore Romano*, 25 May 1985, p. 11.

27 *L'Osservatore Romano*, 9 September 1985.

28 *Daily Nation*, 19 August 1985.

29 *L'Osservatore Romano*, 26 August 1985, pp. 6–7, No. 7.

30 Hebblethwaite 1986, pp. 77–78.

31 *L'Osservatore Romano*, 26 August 1985, pp. 6–7, No. 7. The author was present as a staff-member of CHIEA when the Pope gave this uncompromising address.

32 *The Tablet*, 14 December 1985, p. 1328, No. D.4.

33 *The Tablet*, 5 April 1986, p. 391, No. 96.

34 Ratzinger 1985, p. 103.

PART FIVE

THE FUTURE OF INCULTURATION IN THE CATHOLIC CHURCH

17

Development or inculturation?

In Part Four of this book we traced the progress of the Church's official teaching on culture and inculturation, mainly in the letters and addresses of popes, in the conciliar and post-conciliar documents and the synodal statements. We have noted the impressive development of inculturation theology. At the same time, we have also noticed a spirit of caution, even a reluctance to put the theory into practice. This is chiefly implied by the heavy emphasis that is increasingly laid on the Church's cultural patrimony and on monocultural structures of universal communion which appear incompatible with the ideal of a multicultural Church.

The question of ecclesial communion in a multicultural Church will be discussed in the next chapter. In the meantime there is another related question, already hinted at in Chapter 4, which should logically be examined now. It concerns development and modernization, and the relevance of inculturation to these aspects of life in the particular churches of the Third World. As we already saw in Chapter 4, the association of the Church's mission with the processes of development and modernization helps to tilt the scales in favour of centralized structures and against local initiatives and resources.

We shall consider three points of view in this chapter: the view that inculturation is irrelevant to developing countries; the view that culture in a developing country is a 'will o' the wisp'; and the view that inculturation implies a liberation from socio-economic dependency on the West.

The Relevance of Inculturation for Development

As Adrian Hastings has remarked, theological conservatism is often found to be a good basis for social radicalism.[1] In circles concerned with development one sometimes hears the following thesis proposed.[2] Inculturation, it is said, was appropriate to the 1960s in Africa and the Third World generally. It belonged essentially to the euphoria of political independence and the spirit of hopefulness and freedom that prevailed after the Second Vatican Council. However, it was quickly found to be irrelevant. On the one hand, it soon became clear that the Vatican had no intention of allowing anything other than a trifling measure of creativity and diversity, particularly in the area of liturgical renewal. On the other hand, more urgent priorities came to the fore which demanded efficient handling, centralized administration and foreign funding.

Africa and other Third World countries began to feel the effects of economic recession in the 1970s. A series of droughts, famines, earthquakes and other natural disasters were compounded by the inefficiency of newly independent regimes and by the economic pressures exerted upon poor countries by rich ones. Nations that were periodically faced with food shortages were constrained to grow cash crops for export, rather than to feed, clothe and house themselves. Lack of interest and communication ensured that food-aid and other forms of relief arrived only after thousands had died or had been rendered homeless. In such circumstances, inculturation and such things as 'fiddling with the liturgy' became irrelevant. What was required was healthy socio-economic development and the channelling of relief and aid to people in need. Structures of self-reliance had to be created. Exploitation, inefficiency, and corruption had to be overcome.

This point of view sounds eminently rational; however, it does not explain the continued insistence on culture in African and Third World countries. This insistence cannot simply be written off as an opiate of the oppressed. It is also a point of view that underestimates culture itself, not to mention such areas of inculturation as liturgy, theology and catechetics.

In purely secular terms, culture is relevant to socio-economic development. This is a truth frequently emphasized by African statesmen. In the culturally heterogeneous and disorientated countries of Africa, social integration is a prerequisite for nation-building. In fact, cultural differences and antagonisms account for many of the structural and organizational weaknesses of these countries. Development programmes have all too often ignored socio-cultural factors at their peril, and social upheavals have resulted which have brought lasting damage and unhappiness. National identity is far from being un-related to national efficiency or national solvency. This is the reason why political leaders work hard to promote socio-cultural integration and to foster a pride in indigenous culture which will motivate the citizens and stimulate co-operation with people of other traditions.

Socio-economic development, as the Church teaches, is not enough. What is required is integral human development. It is not sufficient simply to improve material conditions or standards of living through development aid. What is required is to change people's hearts, to give them a confidence and a pride in themselves and an openness to one another. Only this can help them overcome the dehumanizing 'pathology' of poverty. Culture plays an important role in this. Anyone who has worked, for example, in the slums and shanty-towns of Africa, India or Latin America knows how cultural loyalties and cultural events and activities are cherished by the poor, not as a form of escapism, but as a form of self-consciousness and community consciousness. Culture is a positive factor in develop-ment.

In many cases modernization undermines morale and produces dehumanizing effects. The purpose of development should be the well-being of the human individual in community. The reinforce-ment and/or the development of culture can help individuals and communities adapt to new technologies and new social circumstan-ces. It can motivate them to co-operate with one another for the improvement of conditions and the creation of wealth.

The view that inculturation is irrelevant to human development not only underrates culture, it also misjudges the role of theology, liturgy and catechetics, to mention only three major fields of incul-turation. Theology is often regarded by modern man as an irrele-vance in itself. Indeed, the term is frequently used to refer to any useless theory, remote from the practical questions of ordinary life. Questions used to be dismissed as 'academic'. They are now dismissed as 'theological'. In many ways theologians have only themselves to blame for their failure to communicate. This failure is primarily due to their preference for what Newman called 'second order language', and to their incapacity to retranslate their notions into the 'first order language' of the ordinary man in the street. In Third World coun-tries, such as those of Africa, the language of classical theology is even more remote, being tied to a foreign cultural tradition.

There is now a general recognition of the need for a more function-al theology, and of a theological language that is imaginative — even narrative. There is also the acceptance of the need for Third World theologians to enter into dialogue with the life-situations and cosmological ideas of their own cultures. A growing number of theologians from Africa, India and elsewhere are doing precisely this. Although Cardinal Ratzinger, in 1985, dismissed African theology as 'more a project than a reality', the list of African theological writers was already a long one.[3] It included already, at that time, such names as: Sanon, Pénoukou, Tshibangu, Nyamiti, Mulago, Ngindu Mushete, Bimwenyi, Monsengwo, Adokonou, Ezeanya, Sempore, Ela, Uzukwu, Ukpong, Okolo, Magesa, Bukasa Kabongo, Bujo, Boulaga, Messi Metogo and many more (to mention only Catholics). The Ecumenical Association of Third World Theologians and its sister, the Ecumenical Association of African Theologians, have been making an important impact in the last ten years. By challenging and reinterpreting African cultural traditons, theologians are helping to make them more relevant, not less relevant, to modern life.

If this is already true of the work of theologians, it is even more the case in the field of catechetics. Modern catechetics has developed a typically 'life-centred approach'. It enables Christians to respond to God's self-revelation from within their own cultural traditions and life-situations, and it sheds the light of this revelation upon them. The story of modern catechetics is very largely one of the pursuit of relevance. It is also linked to the process of conscientization, enabling people to identify their own needs and concerns, as well as the deeper causes of their problems. Catechetics goes hand-in-hand with self-reliance and liberation.

Finally, as the place of privileged encounter between God and humanity, the place where actions express faith and faith is translated into action, liturgy is intimately related to human development. Before the current liturgical renewal, the relationship was not obvious. Today the links are very often explicit, not merely in the theme of a homily or the intentions of bidding prayers, but in the occasion, and even the form, of a celebration. Liturgy enables the whole of human life to become a means of divine worship. A truly inculturated liturgy not only does this more effectively, it can also enliven and transform a people's way of life by bringing it to God, thus making it more efficacious and creative. The thesis, therefore, that inculturation is irrelevant to development cannot be sustained. The whole purpose of inculturation is to make evangelization — the influence of the Good News — more effective in human development.

Cultural Development

As we have just seen, to doubt the relevance of inculturation for development is to question the relevance of culture itself. Here again, the plausible viewpoint is often put forward that culture nowadays is a 'will o' the wisp', impossible to identify, let alone identify with. Modern society is pluralistic, a cultural melting-pot. When we speak of a dialogue between faith and culture, whose culture are we speaking about? Are we referring to a minority normative culture owned by the ruling classes, or are we talking about one or other popular culture — perhaps even a recently imported culture?

It must be admitted that we have a difficulty here. The multicultural character of the Church is not one of a multitude of separate, well-defined, if not incapsulated, cultures. Too often, within a particular church, within the jurisdiction of a given episcopal conference, even within a single parish, there exists a variety of unintegrated cultures. Britain and France have become multicultural societies in themselves. Australia and New Zealand have acquired new cultures alongside their Aboriginal and European ones. Africa and the Indian sub-continent are experiencing greater social mobility and internal migration, particularly towards the towns, which bring indigenous peoples of different cultural and religious traditions into co-operation and/or conflict. Everywhere, a youth sub-culture has come into existence which seems to distance the generations more and more radically from one another.

The scandal of cultural diversity is most evident in urban areas, where the population is at its most dense. Here, there may not be so much an interaction between well-defined traditions, as a blurring of distinctions between them, especially among children of inter-ethnic and inter-faith marriages. What becomes of inculturation in situations such as these, particularly when to cultural disorientation are added all the problems of the Third World city, of human apathy and loss of hope?

This is a many-sided question which demands a variety of answers. To begin with, it is possible to exaggerate the negative aspects of multiculturalism and to overlook the more positive and integrating aspects. These were outlined in Chapter 4 under the terms: interdependence, congruence and incorporation. However, the meeting of vastly different cultures or religious systems may well result in cultural disorientation or apathy, to an impoverishment of humanity and a loss of cultural standards and values.

On the other hand, as we have already pointed out, people in Africa and elsewhere in the Third World are seldom completely cut off from their cultural roots. Cultural intransigence and tribalism are just as likely an outcome of this pluralism as loss of culture. In general, people find it difficult to relate to those of other cultures, and the alternatives of intransigence or drift illustrate the difficulty. They are not, however, the only courses open, as we demonstrated in Chapter 4.

It has never been pretended in this book that inculturation is easy, and obviously there are social situations which offer varying degrees of challenge to the Church where the evangelization of culture is concerned. In Africa, for example, it is one thing to envisage dialogue with a single ethnic culture in a relatively stable rural area, quite another to inculturate the Faith in a crowded urban squatter parish composed of a dozen tribal groupings. Up to the middle of this century, the average Australian Catholic parish was made up of Irish immigrants or their descendants. Today there may be Italians, Vietnamese, Koreans, and Singaporeans, as well as a few Aborigines. No one is claiming that such pastoral situations are easy to cope with, but these cultures must be evangelized. Equally, the very different needs of the youth and the parental generation have to be catered for. It is not even easy to distinguish the urban and rural apostolates any more. Often they are combined within the frontiers of a single parish.

It is clear from all this complexity that the work of inculturation involves a great measure of cultural education and cultural development. People must be helped not only to preserve their culture, but to adapt it to a changed social situation. They have to be helped to realize their cultural ideals, to learn about their culture and to develop it creatively. They also have to learn how to enrich, and be enriched by, people of other cultural traditions. Their task is to achieve at grass-roots level what is demanded at the level of the universal Church, a partnership in the faith. And there is no more effective means of helping a culture to develop than this shared faith.

In the final chapter of this book we shall examine the practical implications of cultural development in greater detail. Undoubtedly, small Christian communities can be an important instrument of cultural development, as they should be of inculturation itself. What is important for us to retain here, in a chapter on the relationship of inculturation to development, is the undoubted fact that integral human development necessarily includes cultural development, and that cultural development is epitomized by inculturation.

Inculturation and Liberation

In a recent book Jean-Marc Ela, the theologian from Cameroun, asks an important question concerning inculturation.[4] Is inculturation possible in Africa, as long as Africans are not in control of their own lives and destinies? Is inculturation to be the work of outsiders? Clearly, the answer is 'No'. For Ela, inculturation is not antiquarianism, but liberation. Missionaries cannot carry out inculturation. They are merely at the start of the process. They listen, stimulate and canalize. Africans themselves cannot carry out inculturation, as long as they are in cultural and socio-economic bondage to non-Africans. They are not free to be themselves. The Church in Africa, says Ela, may be growing in numbers, but it is not growing in awareness.

Ela is quite right to make this point, although, in the process, he tends to calumniate Western Christianity as a decadent and decomposing Church. It is not necessary to go as far as this in order to uphold the right of Christians in Africa to take their rightful place in the Church. The argument for African inculturation is not strengthened by denigrating the parent church of Europe. However, it *is* true that the structures of ecclesial communion are culturally biased in favour of Europe, and it *is* true that authority in the Church is in no hurry to put the theology of inculturation into pastoral practice.

It is also true that African cultural identity is by no means clearcut, and that there are still far too many traces of colonial, cultural domination in Africa. These are even reinforced by neo-colonial structures of dependence. It is not only cultural liberation of which Africa stands in need, but a real political, social and economic liberation. Africans, says Ela, should not accept to live the Gospel in a state of dependence which is connived at by the Church.

There is always a danger that in a situation of continuing dependence, the Church in Africa will opt for a second best, a second-rate inculturation, a kind of domesticated animal that is neither flesh, fish nor fowl. Ela already detects this tamed hybrid in the works of African theologians, and he calls it 'indigenism'. It is the preoccupation with the harmless, the superficial and the non-controversial. It is a nostalgia for the past and a flight from present realities. It is the Church's version of the tourist-spectacle which African culture has become. This kind of inculturation can too easily be appropriated by the bourgeois élite and be manipulated by oppressive régimes.

In the terms to which we have been accustomed in the course of this book, it could be said that Ela is asking the Church in Africa to go beyond the phase of acculturation and into a phase of genuine inculturation, in which the real way of life of contemporary Africans is enlivened by the Gospel. The elements of continuity with the past are there, but they are only a part of the whole reality. They must be taken together with all the new elements that make up the modern culture of Africa. This culture has to be freed by the Gospel. It is not only a question of liberating culture in the strict sense, though this, as the Vatican *Instruction on Freedom and Liberation* pointed out, is basic. It also implies liberation from the political, social and economic oppression to which Africa is still subjected. Politics, social facts, economics all affect culture in one way or another. None of these things are culturally neutral. As Ela says, the fundamental question that has to be asked is: How can we express our belonging to God in a continent that does not belong to itself?[5]

It is too easy to oppose liberation theology to the theology of inculturation, and to say, for example, that, while Latin Americans are only interested in liberation, Africans are preoccupied with inculturation. It may, of course, be true that Latin Americans are united in their legacy of Hispanic culture, and that the struggle against racism in South Africa is the only form of liberation that interests Africans nowadays. These facts account, perhaps, for the lack of interest in culture in one continent and the lack of interest in liberation in the other. However, it remains true that liberation and culture are related, and that inculturation must be placed in a context of liberation and integral human development. This is demanded by the Christian Gospel itself. The liberation of the poor and the oppressed is the fundamental condition for authentic inculturation. Otherwise the dialogue is not with the true Gospel of Jesus Christ.

All of this is not to say that inculturation is only realized when total liberation is achieved. That would be to turn it into a wholly eschatological phenomenon. What it means is that inculturation implies an active commitment to this liberation, that it becomes part of the on-going dialogue that constitutes inculturation. It is a commitment to the new creation which inculturation strives to bring into existence (cf. our basic definition of inculturation in Chapter 1). In Christian terms, this new creation is brought about by proclaiming and living the Gospel of Jesus Christ, and through a deep-rooted faith expressed in prayer.

Ela is one of those Third World theolgoians who blame the Church for conniving, consciously or unconsciously, at political and socio-economic oppression. The Church is committed to development, but within the unjust framework of exploitation and domination that characterizes the relations between the West and the Third World. In practice, modernization creates dependency and ultimately 'mal-develops' poor countries, enriching a small élite and forming a new internal dependency of the poor upon the rich minority. The poor countries of Africa and elsewhere do not want modernization at this price. It is not a development that is integral.

The Church has to be far more self-critical in its development activities. Moreover, it has to be considerably more vocal in its support for issues of justice and peace in the relations between rich and poor countries and between rich and poor classes. The critique of development-aid and the dependency it frequently creates is a necessary component of inculturation theology. The Church should not become the silent accomplice of totalitarian regimes, any more than of exploitive Western countries. The culture it espouses and transforms cannot be a manipulated culture, but a culture to which the poor can rightly and effectively aspire.

As we already pointed out, the Church in the West deploys material resources which make it the ally of powerful, capitalist countries and organizations. These resources also tilt the balance of power in the Church towards the West, and help to reinforce the Western cultural character of the structures of communion in the Universal Church. Radical Third World theologians are claiming a liberation from this cultural and economic captivity, as much as from its secular counterpart. On the other hand, Western Christianity has a duty to use its resources for the genuine benefit of the Third Church, but it must exercise this duty altruistically, otherwise it becomes guilty of an ecclesial neo-colonialism. It can never be repeated too often that aid must not be used to impose priorities from outside, or to supplant local processes and resources.

There is yet another form of dependency deplored by Jean-Marc Ela, the dependence of particular churches upon Rome. The relation-ship with the successor of Peter is a strictly necessary guarantee of Catholic communion, and an indispensable part of the hierarchical nature of the Church. However, the exercise of universal jurisdiction by the Pope and the receptiveness of particular churches to the papal *magisterium* should not imply a usurpation of the local church and its episcopal *magisterium*. Nor should it lead to the universalizing of the particular church of Rome. The Petrine ministry, as Pope Paul VI pointed out in *Evangelii Nuntiandi*, exists to guarantee the freeedom of each particular church to be itself, and to make an authentic inculturation possible.[6] Its primary purpose should certainly not be to make particular churches dependent. This is a topic which we shall explore more fully in the next chapter when we examine the competing demands of ecclesial communion and of multiculturalism in the Church.

References

1 Hastings, 1986, p. 583.

2 Dr Ian Linden, who heads the CIIR, seemed to be making a similar point in a CAMEC lecture on Indigenization in Africa in May 1985. However, the expression of this viewpoint is entirely my own here, and is not attributable to him.

3 Ratzinger, 1985, p. 191.

4 Ela, 1985.

5 *Ibid.*, p. 210.

6 *Evangelii Nuntiandi*, 64.

18

Ecclesial communion in the multicultural Church

Inculturation from Below

The mid-twentieth century has witnessed the acceptance by the Catholic Church of the concept of cultural pluralism. It has also seen the birth of a theology of the local or particular church. We are now confronted with both the theory and the incipient reality of a multicultural Church, a communion of particular churches, each representing a local form of inculturated Christianity. There is a growing demand among Christians of the Third World, especially in African countries, for inculturation to be taken seriously, for it to be implemented in certain specific areas, chiefly that of the liturgy. However, in practice the Church is seen to be dragging its feet. For example, the Zaire Mass appeared first in 1974. Yet it has taken more than twelve years for it to be presented to the appropriate dicastery and approved, and it is one of very few such projects even to reach this stage.[1]

Examples can be cited from other areas of Christian life. Episcopal conferences and associations in Africa have been discussing for decades the pastoral problems associated with marriage morality in the continent, yet we are nowhere near a solution to the customary marriage of Christians and other irregular situations. In 1982 Archbishop Emmanuel Milingo was removed from his archdiocese of Lusaka in Zambia. His healing and exorcizing activities, while responding to traditional needs and concepts, raised theological and pastoral questions for which the Church authorities had no immediate answer. The demise of popular devotions, such as the Holy Hour, the public recitation of the Rosary, Corpus Christi processions and the like, and the failure to replace them with anything else, has led in the archdiocese of Nairobi, Kenya, to a wave of Marian app-

251

aritions and other mystical phenomena which are strongly opposed by a large section of the clergy and which largely escapes their control.[2]

These are just a few signs of the failure or reluctance to inculturate. In fact, the structures of communion among the particular churches do not favour inculturation. Canon Law embodies Western cultural presuppositions. The papal *magisterium* can hardly be expected to reflect the cultural diversity of the whole Church, even though it is periodically supported by the Synod of Bishops. So far, the Second Vatican Council's concept of collegiality has only been realized in a one-sided manner. Much more is said about the particular churches being receptive to the papal *magisterium*, than about the Holy See supporting the *magisterium* of the local bishops and their efforts to inculturate the Gospel.

Much is said about the length of time needed for a genuine and orthodox inculturation. Pope John Paul II could not have been seriously suggesting that inculturation in the Africa of the 1980s should take as many centuries as Poland.[3] However, the Pope was perfectly correct in stressing that inculturation takes time. Nevertheless, this should not be used as an excuse for delaying the beginning of the process. Inculturation is not a purely intellectual problem. It concerns culture or the way of life of people. The only way in which inculturation can possibly be realized is through experimentation. If experimentation is prohibited, inculturation is delayed. Church leaders may be afraid of mistakes being made, or of losing control, but these are risks that have to be taken. Without the possibilty of making mistakes and of learning by mistakes, nothing can be achieved.

Fear of losing control seems to be very real among members of the Catholic hierarchy. In many Third World countries, especially those of Africa, the number of baptized is growing at a much faster rate than the number of priestly vocations, and the ratio of priests to people is becoming daily more unfavourable. To some extent this development can be offset by the amalgamation of parishes, the setting up of team ministries and the building of small Christian communities — perhaps even through the bolder step of experimenting with lay ministers like the *bakambi* in Zaire. However, it is undeniable that there is a problem of control. It is also undeniable that the explosion of multiple inculturations throughout the world is a frightening prospect for Church leaders who feel more at home in a monocultural system. There is a very real fear of Catholic communion disintegrating altogether, and it is likely that it is this fear which underlies official reluctance to encourage or even to countenance the putting of inculturation theory into pastoral practice.

In many parts of the Third World new religious movements are coming into existence, so-called 'sects' or 'independent churches'. Some are influenced by world trends of fundamentalism, pentecostalism and adventism. Others are simply new syncretic forms of ethnic religion which discover parallels with the Old Testament or with a highly selective understanding of the New Testament. Most are more or less guilty of culturalism, that is to say, they make far-reaching concessions to indigenous culture at the expense of Christian orthodoxy. Such movements attract people who live, as it were, on the margins of the modern world. Many of them are closed systems which do not offer any real hope of dialogue with other traditions or with modernity. However, they exhibit an obvious indigenous character, and they are in themselves a continuous indictment of a mainline Christianity that has failed to inculturate.

In 1985 four Vatican departments, the Secretariat for Promoting Christian Unity, the Secretariat for Non-Christians, the Secretariat for Non-Believers and the Pontifical Council for Culture, published a report on the response to a questionnaire concerning sects that was sent to all the episcopal conferences of the world.[4] The report sees these new religious movements as a pastoral challenge to the Catholic Church. These movements reveal a number of areas of need which are not being sufficiently catered for by the Church, for example, the need for participation and involvement, the need for a greater sense of community and the need for cultural identity. The report has this to say about inculturation:

> The question of inculturation is a fundamental one. It is particularly stressed by the responses from Africa which reveal a feeling of estrangement to Western forms of worship and ministry which are often quite irrelevant to people's cultural environment and life-situation. One respondent declared: 'Africans want to be Christians. We have given them accommodation, but no home . . . They want a simpler Christianity, integrated into all aspects of daily life, into the sufferings, joys, work, aspirations, fears and needs of the African . . . The young recognize in the Independent Churches a genuine vein of the African tradition of doing things religious.'[5]

Is there a danger that a more liberal policy of experimentation with a view to inculturation will lead to the disintegration of Catholic communion and the multiplication of sects? It is arguable whether the exercise of tight control by a dwindling power-structure, accompanied by the refusal to allow a full implementation of inculturation, will prevent the disintegration of communion. Even if sectarian secessions are forestalled — and this is unlikely — there is the danger of a development comparable to that of the African religions of Brazil, the probability of an outward conformity that conceals a far-reaching internal heterodoxy and syncretism.[6] Failure to inculturate is much more likely to force Christians back into the twilight, unevangelized world of the sects than the immediate implementation of inculturation.

In 1977 Andrew Hake, writing about the notorious squatter city of Mathare Valley in Nairobi, coined the phrase 'urbanization from below'.[7] If the urban poor are not admitted into the official sector of the city, they urbanize themselves and create their own city culture, their own 'self-help city'. An analogy can be drawn with the Church. If the Christians of the Third World are not allowed to be at home in the Church, there will be an 'inculturation from below', a 'self-help Church'.

Inculturation is essentially a community process. It can never be the responsibility of a few experts who then have the task of 'selling' it to the people. However, experts are needed, even sometimes missionaries from overseas, to give the community encouragement and to help it make the necessary discernment and the necessary critique of its own culture, and promote the discovery of the seeds of the Word. Experts are also needed to ensure the truly Christian character of the new creation which inculturation brings into existence. There is a sense in which all inculturation is 'inculturation from below'. However, it should not take place in opposition to the experts and representatives of the official Church, but in collaboration with them.

A Multicultural Patrimony

Pope John Paul II exhorted African theologians and catechetical experts to see that their work was solidly grounded in the theological patrimony or 'culture' of the universal Church.[8] We have already discussed the Church's cultural patrimony in Chapter 5. Since inculturation follows upon the ordinary processes of intercultural exchange or acculturation, and since Christianity is a historical religion that has been transmitted from culture to culture throughout history, it follows that there is an accumulated clutter of cultural elements from diverse sources which is circulating among the particular churches. Some of the elements are inessential, even trivial. Others are necessary and irreducible. We cannot, for example, dispense with the evidence of Jesus as a historical person, with his own historical culture. In knowing and relating to Jesus, we are also accepting to know and relate to his culture. Even though the Eternal Logos dwells at the heart of every human culture, we believe that the Word was made flesh, and there can be no authentic Christianity without reference to the historical self-manifestation of God in Christ, the Incarnation and the Paschal Mystery.

It follows that the actual historical and cultural events of Christ's life, death and resurrection cannot be changed. They are not myths that undergo successive transformations, as happens in some religions, even though our understanding of them makes progress in the Church. It also follows that the words and gestures — particularly those of sacramental worship — which claim to do as Christ did and as he commanded us to do, are tied to Christ's own cultural and historical situation and to the outlooks of the New Testament. We are not conscious of being able to change them. Similarly, in translating the Bible, we are not reinterpreting Scripture, but we should be as faithful as possible to its primary meaning.

Other elements in the Church's cultural patrimony are more or less useful, but not in themselves essential, because they belong to previous inculturations. Among them must be counted previous theological formulations and systems and even the wording of dogmatic definitions and faith-statements. Of course, it is necessary to study such previous formulations and to understand them, in order to arrive at the truth which they contain, a truth which must not be abandoned or contradicted. Their meaning is essential, but the forms in which it is expressed are contingent upon culture and history.

When the Pope bids African theologians ground their speculation solidly upon the Church's universal patrimony, he is certainly stressing the need to relate to the historical culture of Jesus Christ. He is also indicating the necessity of studying past theological formulations in order to arrive at an understanding of the deposit of faith. If his words were interpreted to mean that African theologians must make these formulations the starting-point of an inculturated theology, this would jeopardize the authenticity and originality of the new inculturation, and we would be back at the old idea of the Church as a monocultural hybrid.

Without prejudice to the autonomy of the tradition of faith, it is the local culture, and not Christianity's previous inculturations which should be made the starting-point of the new process. Specialists must be allowed to experiment in theological formulation, as in other areas. One of the basic conditions of successful inculturation is the guarantee of a supreme freedom in non-essentials.

'Grounding' inculturation in the Church's universal patrimony, on the other hand, may have a more subtle and a more actual and uncontroversial meaning. There are many important lessons to be learned from this patrimony. Firstly, the patrimony is universal. That means to say, it is both diverse and comprehensive. To take a monocultural view of the universal patrimony of the Church is patently false. In the light of the modern empirical understanding of culture, we can appreciate the multicultural character of this patrimony. It includes the legacies of multiple past inculturations — from the East, as well as from the West, all the cultures on which the varied Church traditions and rites have been based. The universal patrimony of the Church is not exclusively Latin. It is, for example, Greek and Slav, Coptic and Syrian. Its theological tradition is not merely Western, let alone Scholastic. Its liturgical expression and forms of spirituality are culturally diverse. In this patrimony pride of place must be given to patrology and the rich heritage of the early Fathers. If there is one thing which the universal patrimony of the Church teaches us, it is pluriformity.

Secondly, the universal patrimony of the Church offers us lessons in inculturation itself. In fact, the study of past inculturations may offer us models of how to proceed. It also offers us precedents to follow, in situations which are culturally comparable. Such precedents strengthen the hand of the expert in guiding a community and helping it to express its faith in its own cultural language. Among these precedents we must surely count former projects of inculturation which were not accepted at the time but which won the Church's recognition afterwards. The Chinese rites, for example, may be relevant to the Christianization of ancestor-veneration in Africa. The Church in Africa may even be able to make use of whatever facts historians are able to discover about the Church of the Kingdom of Kongo.

It is important to take a genuinely historical view of the cultural patrimony of the Church. Taking an outdated, classicist view is to deform the reality and impoverish Christianity. A historical view which takes full account of its cultural diversity helps to emphasize its relativity and contingency.

Ecclesial Partnership

As we already noted in Chapter 1, inculturation is 'interculturation'. It implies partnership and mutuality in the process of evangelization and in its outcome. One hears the phrase 'young churches' used too often when Westerners speak about Christianity in the Third World. These so-called 'young churches' would prefer to be called 'sister churches'. They would prefer a footing of equality with the other churches, even with those on which they are dependent for human and material resources. Only equality can ensure genuine mutual respect and the mutual enrichment of the particular churches which is the principal outcome of inculturation.

In collegiality, as we have already mentioned, the one-sided emphasis on the papal *magisterium* must be corrected, and the *magisterium* of the local hierarchy accorded greater recognition. A good example is provided, at the time of writing, by the project of the African Council. The idea behind this project first cropped up in discussions among African theologians in 1977 and was adopted by the bishops of Zaire in 1980, who first mentioned it to the Pope during their *ad limina* visit that year.[9] Two years later the standing committee of SECAM took up the question and the President of SECAM, Cardinal Zoungrana, discussed it with Pope John Paul II. In 1983 the African Council was again a subject of discussion between the Zairean bishops and the Pope, who agreed with the proposal in principle 'in one form or another'. In the same year, the SECAM standing committee commissioned the SECAM theological commission to carry out a study of the proposal, and in 1984 the Ecumenical Association of Theologians also took up the idea. In July of that year the SECAM theological commission presented their findings to the seventh plenary assembly of SECAM, held in Kinshasa. The bishops of the assembly favoured the proposal and decided to consult each episcopal conference in the matter.

In the meantime, Pope John Paul II made his third pastoral journey to Africa. On the journey out he spoke to journalists about the African Council and was reported as saying that, while he favoured the project itself, he thought the meeting should be called a 'synod' and not a 'council'. During 1985 and 1986, the Vatican decided to carry out its own consultation with the episcopal conferences and with experts of various kinds in Africa. At the eighth plenary assembly of SECAM held in Lagos in 1987 it was reported that the episcopal conferences of Africa were almost evenly divided over the project. Many on either side felt that more time was needed to prepare the Council. As a result, the project, while it has not been blocked, has at least been effectively shelved.

The African theologians strongly favour the term 'council' rather than 'synod'. This is because the 1983 Code of Canon Law provides for the Synod of Bishops as a purely consultative body, whereas the African bishops want a deliberative assembly *cum Petro et sub Petro*, which will have a decisive theological and juridical importance. The particular churches of Africa desire to meet together in Council in order to be more firmly rooted in their own cultural values. There are also precedents from Church history, especially that of the Plenary Council of Latin America which was held during the pontificate of Pope Leo XIII in 1899. It should also be noted that the Second Vatican Council spoke of 'councils' as well as 'synods':

> This sacred Ecumenical Synod (*sic*) expresses its earnest hope that these admirable institutions — synods and councils — may flourish with renewed vigour so that the growth of religion and the maintenance of discipline in the various churches may increasingly be more effectively provided for in accordance with the needs of the times.[10]

The stated aim of the African Council is to realize integral evangelization and to study all the tasks which belong to the duty of inculturation. These include relations with the universal Church, ecumenism, ministries, Church law, sacraments, mission and evangelization, means of social communication, political life, justice, spirituality and religious life. In short it is to deal with all the questions which are decisive for Christianity in Africa, and not only liturgy.

It can be seen, therefore, that the idea of the African Council is a fruit of the cultural patrimony of the Church, since it takes account of precedents in the Church's history. It is also an attempt to remedy the monocultural character of the Church's structures of communion and to redress the balance of collegiality which is tilted in the single direction of the papacy. It is also intended to be a major instrument of inculturation for the Church in Africa, once and for all giving the lie to those who claim that Christianity is foreign and Western. Much depends on the realization of this project of an African Council. The future of inculturation in Africa and in the Church as a whole may depend on it, perhaps the Church's credibility itself.

With the development of life-centred catechetics and the introduction of religious education programmes that take the context and culture of the student as their starting-point, it was soon found that this type of learning constitutes a challenge to authoritarian teachers and school structures. In exactly the same way, inculturation constitutes a challenge to authoritarianism and exaggerated centralism in the Church. There can be no question about it; inculturation assumes the existence of a multicultural, egalitarian Church, not one in which there are junior and senior partners. Inculturation implies that the particular churches enjoy a relative autonomy — an autonomy in everything that does not endanger the bond of faith and communion guaranteed, among other things, by the Petrine ministry.

A truly multicultural Church is one in which local solutions to pastoral problems and local formulations of doctrine and worship are favoured. More than this, it is one in which the priorities are decided locally. This means a generous measure of decentralization, and, in an age of instant communications and rapid travel, this should not be a frightening prospect. At the very moment of expansion and diversification, the Church possesses effective means to carry out the sharing of insights and the mutual enrichment which is one of the chief consequences of inculturation. This sharing is a new enhancement of Catholic communion itself. As long as communication flows in one direction only in the Church — from the centre to the periphery, from the West to the Third World — communion is a fragile reality. But, as soon as communication begins to flow in two (or more) directions at the same time, communion is immeasurably strengthened.

Ultimately, as the Fathers of Vatican II foresaw, local forms of canonical leglislation have to be drawn up in order to make inculturation a reality.[11] A more flexible approach to law in the Church, particularly in all that pertains to decision-making structures, as well as to liturgy and marriage, is an essential condition for a multicultural Church. This means a reform of the present order of things, and it is a matter for the hierarchy to decide. It is the duty of the other members of the Church, clergy, religious, laity, to bring it to the attention of the authorities. In the meantime they must work within the limits of the present dispensation.

This chapter has dealt with the structures of communion in the Catholic Church, and with the urgent need for their modification in a multicultural sense if inculturation is ever to become more than an elegant theory. Such a change affects the practical relationship between Pope and bishops, the way in which the Church's teaching and governing authority is exercised collegially. It is for this reason that the proposal of an African Council is of such extreme interest.

In the final chapter of this book we shall consider inculturation at the grass-roots, what can be done now at the lowest ecclesial levels to make the Church 'safe' for inculturation, and to change the mental climate of the Church in its favour. We have said that inculturation is essentially a community project. At the centre of the stage, in this matter of inculturation in Third World countries, is the basic Christian community. Programmes of Christian community-building, originally inspired by the Latin American experience, have been introduced into many countries of the Third World, sometimes — as in Eastern Africa — with the express intention of favouring inculturation at the grass-roots. In the final chapter, we shall determine the cultural priorities of the small Christian community and the way it can become an agent of inculturation.

References

1 *DIA*, 25 November 1986, 933.

2 The author has been commissioned by the Cardinal Archbishop of Nairobi to investigate these phenomena.

3 *L'Osservatore Romano*, 26 August 1985, pp. 6–7, No. 7.

4 SPCU, 1986. *Sects and New Religious Movements*, Nairobi, St Paul Publications.

5 *Ibid.*, pp. 17–18.

6 Cf. Bastide 1978.

7 Hake 1977.

8 *L'Osservatore Romano*, 26 August 1985, pp. 6–7, No. 7.

9 For information on the proposed African Council, cf. Acts of the Seventh Plenary Assembly of SECAM, Kinshasa 1984, pp. 180–94.

10 *Christus Dominus*, 36.

11 *Ad Gentes*, 19.

19

Inculturation at the grass-roots

Cultural Realism and Creativity

At the end of a book on the theology of inculturation, the question has to be asked: 'And what of us, Lord?' What can we, ourselves do to help inculturation make progress in the Church? What, especially, can be done at the level of the grass-roots? The short answer to these questions is: foster cultural awareness and stimulate community action.

Culture, as we saw right at the beginning, is about the conceptions which actually govern human thought and behaviour. As far as these conceptions substantially influence the ideas and actions of people, they are a social reality. Although our aim should not be cultural antiquarianism, we cannot ignore the fact that the ideal culture of the past influences people today. In Africa, above all, cultural roots are important. Performing a traditional dance or a traditional ritual, even in a modern setting, is a way of affirming identity. The idea of trying to recreate a past culture may be far from people's minds, yet the historical culture continues to exert an influence, as the culture of the Jewish homeland did upon the exiles of the Diaspora. A culture that is to all intents and purposes extinct can still operate normatively in the modern situation.

It is important not to be sceptical about the relevance of so-called 'vanishing cultures'. To take an interest in them is not necessarily to be guilty of folklorism or antiquarianism, any more than it is in the case of one who enjoys listening to Baroque music or sixteenth-century polyphony. If people are to develop their culture and enjoy the full benefit of culture, they must be allowed to study it. The ethnic cultures of the past must not become an exclusively 'highbrow' concern, the hobby of the bourgeois élite. Naturally, traditional culture is stronger in the rural areas than in the towns and cities, and in Africa particularly, townsmen look upon a journey to the countryside as a return to the sources of culture. To a greater or lesser degree this may be true. Cultural development demands that the experience of traditional culture, especially in family and community celebrations, be made available to people wherever they are. To promote cultural groups, cultural activities and the study of traditional culture is not counter-productive. In fact, the cultural link with the past is an important factor in modern social integration and cultural discernment.

Population mobility ensures that people, living today in a culturally heterogeneous society, are confronted with ways of life that differ from their own. The anonymity of urban existence may dilute this experience, but once again, programmes of cultural education and exchange can help people to appreciate the values and conceptions of other cultures. The Christian faith requires this at the microcosmic level, as well as at the universal level. In the same way it is required by nation-building. There are many opportunities in the life of a parish for cultural exchanges of this kind, especially in liturgical celebrations and in catechesis.

While the foregoing is true, realism demands that full account be taken of modern technological and urban culture. In Third World countries the modern or urban consciousness is affecting even the rural areas, possibly even more adversely than the towns and cities themselves. People accept modernization very easily, and it is a far less conscious reality than attachment to traditional culture. Once again, cultural education is necessary. People need to be helped to understand what is happening to them, to discern the positive and the negative elements and to counteract cultural impoverishment and dehumanization. They need to discover in their own traditions those ideas and values which are compatible with modern culture, or which can act as a corrective of its perverse effects. Cultural education, then, includes conscious reflection on modern processes of change.

The Church must be committed to cultural education if it takes inculturation seriously. It must help to give people the means of developing their culture: literacy, group-media of communication, such as printed publications, films and drama, the promotion of cultural groups and so forth. It must encourage people to be creative and to give expression to their understanding of a changed and changing situation. All of this is a precondition for the practice of inculturation itself.

Inculturation is not merely a dialogue between Gospel and culture, it is the Gospel bringing into existence a new cultural creation. It is essentially an instance of creativity. Creativity is not normally spontaneous, let alone *ex nihilo*! It is a question, very often, of perspiration rather than inspiration. That is why it is useful to study precedents, not only those from previous ages, but also contemporary examples of inculturation from elsewhere. One often hears the objection in Africa that such things as the Zaire Mass or the Zimbabwe funeral rite are too closely tied to a given culture for them to be acceptable to people elsewhere, say in Kenya or Nigeria. That is very likely true. The Zaire Mass has already been described in this book. The innovative character of the Zimbabwe funeral rite consists in the conditional invocation, and symbolic reinstatement, of the deceased according to Shona custom. Nevertheless, it must be said that there is nothing like the experience of a successful inculturation from elsewhere to stimulate creativity at home. The Tanzanian bishop who authorized the restricted celebration of the Zaire Mass in his diocese was trying to do just that.

Inculturation at the grass-roots means, among other things, stimulating liturgical and catechetical creativity in the community. In either case, a framework is needed at the outset, within which members of the community can exercise their gifts. Christian sacraments and celebrations have their own character and purpose which cannot be altered. This character and purpose must speak to the community through the forms and expressions of their own culture. Selecting the framework may be a task for the expert. In the case of the Ndzon Melen Mass in Cameroun, Fr Pie-Claude Ngumu took a local rite of reconciliation as his starting-point.[1] In the case of the Zimbabwe funeral rite, the framework was already provided by existing funerary custom among the Shona, as studied by anthropologists.[2] Turkana sacrifice was the point of departure for Fr Tony Barrett's Mass among the pastoralists of northern Kenya.[3]

A catechetical programme requires a syllabus or materials which take a cultural theme as the starting-point for each lesson and which are sufficiently flexible to allow the teacher to use the resources of his own and his pupils' experience. The themes have to be co-ordinated in a way that reflects the people's whole way of life and at the same time can be a vehicle for the whole message of salvation. The success of such a programme, however, depends as much on the class-room skills of the teacher, as it does on the adequacy of the syllabus, and teachers have to be trained.

If local churches are seriously committed to inculturation, then experts must be designated to offer the necessary stimulus for community creativity. Committees for liturgy and for liturgical music, for drafting religious education programmes for school and parish have to be set up. Moreover, institutes for pastoral training need to be given a free hand in the formation of community leaders who will thereby be encouraged to use their gifts creatively.

Inculturation as a Community Project

The building of small Christian communities was adopted as a pastoral priority by the bishops of Eastern Africa in 1973. They justified their decision in the following words:

> We believe that the Church in our countries, called to continue the prophetic mission of Christ, must defend those authentic human values which have been the basis of the life of our peoples. The Church must stand up against all that would tend to degrade the human person or lead to injustice, violence, oppression, racialism, wars and evils of all sorts.
>
> While the Church of Christ is universal, it is a communion of small local Christian churches, communities of Christians rooted in their own society. From the Bible we learn that such local churches are born through apostolic and missionary preaching. But they are meant to grow so that with time they become firmly rooted in the life and culture of the people. Thus the Church, like Christ himself, becomes incarnated in the life of the people. She is led by local people, meets and answers local needs and problems, and finds within herself the resources needed for her life and mission.
>
> We are convinced that in these countries of Eastern Africa it is time for the Church to become really 'local', that is: self-ministering, self-propagating and self-supporting. Our planning is aimed at building such local churches for the coming years.
>
> We believe that in order to achieve this we have to insist on building Church life and work on basic Christian communities, in both rural and urban areas. Church life must be based on the communities in which everyday life and work takes place: those basic and manageable social groupings whose members can experience real inter-personal relationships and feel a sense of communal belonging, both in living and working. We believe

that Christian communities at this level will be best suited to develop real intense vitality and to become effective witnesses in their natural environment.[4]

The bishops felt that building small Christian communities was the best way of safeguarding human values and of rooting the Church in the life and culture of the people. During the discussions that preceded the drafting of these guidelines, several bishops mentioned traditions of marriage and family life and one bishop spoke of the need to communicate with the social environment through the cultural channels of art, music, language and literature.

Three years later, in a study-session on the theme 'Building Small Christian Communities', the bishops of Eastern Africa began to realize the potential in small Christian communities for inculturation of the liturgy and for creative pastoral appproaches:

It now becomes possible to make serious research and experiments regarding the incarnation of worship into the life of the community. This will require study and research, consultation with the people of the community to determine their needs, actual implementation of these proposals and community evaluation. The suggested fields are the sacraments of Christian initiation, cultural values and marriage rites and new Eucharistic prayers. While all the above concern the celebration of the sacraments, it is presumed that similar study, research, consultation, experiments and evaluation will take place in matters of para-liturgy, sacramentals and devotions.[5]

Creative pastoral approaches are needed today to adequately respond to the life-situations of our peoples and communities. Better methods must be devised to incarnate the Gospel message into the local customs of our people, e.g. feasts and celebrations performed at different stages of man's development.[6]

A similar conclusion, though in less specific terms, was reached by the bishops at subsequent study sessions in Zomba, Malawi in 1979 and in Moshi, Tanzania in 1986.[7]

Following these declarations, attempts were made to implement them at national and diocesan levels. Sadly, however, relatively little has been achieved in the field of liturgy. Perhaps this disappointing outcome serves to drive home the lesson that implementation can only take place in and through the basic communities themselves.

The initiative must be given to the communities, granted that their leadership is sufficiently responsible and well-formed.

At the continental level, the bishops of Africa and Madagascar also endorsed the building of small Christian communities. At the Seventh Plenary Assembly of SECAM on 'The Church and Human Promotion in Africa Today', held in 1984, the resolutions included the following:

> In this effort to establish a link between Evangelization and man's promotion, we must rely especially on the activity and witness given by our small Christian communities . . . These communities can establish in a practical way the link between Christian life and the particular activities of human promotion that are needed in a specific neighbourhood, or a specific human group, or in a specific region.[8]

Ultimately, inculturation is a community project. The community provides the criteria of authenticity and success, because it is the life of the community which is in question. The community also provides the means of implementation.

Generally speaking, an inculturation that is clerically inspired and clerically controlled is not accepted. It is too cerebral, too remote from the real life of the community. Christians prefer forms which allow a full participation by laity of both sexes, and which capitalize the gifts that are found in the community. Clerical leadership and stimulation should aim at this. In the celebration of the sacraments and in the catechesis of adults and children there is ample scope for a sharing and an application of cultural values and expressions. Care, however, has to be taken that the shift is away from acculturation (the insertion of indigenous elements into patterns that are basically Western) and towards inculturation (the creation of indigenous patterns themselves).

The actual words and forms of the ceremonies of the Roman rite are still standardized and tightly controlled. In their present form they offer very little room for spontaneity. However, they can be made to fit into a particular socio-cultural setting created by the community. Local para-liturgical elements can precede and follow the celebration of the rite itself, or can be introduced into the rite where a measure of creativity is permitted, for example, in the offertory procession at Mass. This can be a first step towards a fuller inculturation, which will hopefully accelerate the production and approval of inculturated liturgical texts.

In Africa, for example, there is no reason why a more generous use should not be made of the dance-form in the present liturgy. Dancing normally accompanies song and all forms of ritual movement in African culture. One can go so far as to say that dancing itself can appropriate an alien ritual and make it obey the canons of African culture. This is evident in the Ndzon Melen Mass, where the stringencies of the Roman rite disappear in a liturgical choreography of purely local inspiration. To assist at the Ndzon Melen Mass, as the author did in 1973, is an exhilarating experience.

Community building involves discovering gifts and talents in individuals and putting them at the service of the whole community. People who are truly part of the community and sensitive to its ethos respond creatively to its needs and aspirations. The clergy and hierarchy are there to preside over the activity and help in the process of discernment. As one of the indispensable structures of communion, they help to guarantee the Christian authenticity of what is said and done in the community.

The basic Christian community is a free association of the baptized. It is Church, without being the whole Church. In most cases, the community of celebration is a larger grouping than the basic community, but the basic community should make a contribution from its own vitality and creativity to this more comprehensive, ecclesial level. In this way it can be a motor force for inculturation. The cumulative influence of basic communities will transform the local church.

Inculturation as a Way of Life

Small Christian communities are not intended as a substitute or supplement for an ordained ministry, however inadequate the latter may be. They are Church — ecclesial 'people-power'. They enjoy a freedom and a prophetical role comparable to that of religious orders. The latter, with their charisms of service to the community, are especially qualified to play a role in the building of these basic communities and in the training of their leaders. In fact, many religious orders began their history as a small community of lay people, offering a particular service to the Church. Small Christian communities are a way of being Church, a way that is promoted and preferred by Church leaders because it links the Gospel to real life situations and intensifies the process of evangelization. Ideally, evangelization should bring about a renewed humanity and a new human society, free of unjust and inhuman assumptions and structures. Evangelization is ultimately synonymous with inculturation, the renewal of culture itself, the redemption of a people's whole way of life.

Culture refers to the way of life of a people, to the ideas and images that orientate its thoughts and behaviour. Inculturation refers to the Christian renewal of culture, the transforming dialogue of culture with the Gospel, and indeed the person, of Jesus Christ. Inculturation can therefore be correctly called a way of life in itself, since this dialogue and this transformation have to be experienced and lived by people. It is lived and experienced primarily by people in community and especially in the basic communities which are at the hub of social and cultural life.

For the basic communities, then, inculturation must become a way of life. As agents of inculturation they are to bring the power of the Gospel to bear upon all the departments of social life and of the culture that animates it. This should be the case especially with marriage and family life. Married Christians and their children have to create new expressions of Christian family life and family apostolate which obey the norms of their contemporary culture. Small Christian communities can give societal support to these initiatives, and, hopefully, a more flexible and more localized Church Law can eventually reflect them. Christian communities can help families to become more aware of the cultural concepts and realities that affect them, and to translate into practice the ideals to which they aspire.

Then there is the equally delicate area of health and healing. In many Third World countries, and particularly in Africa, popular expectations and traditions are at loggerheads with Christian ideas and Western (often Church-sponsored) medical practice. On both sides the possibilities of misunderstanding are almost infinite. Pastoral care of the sick is one of the preoccupations of small Christian communities, and it is chiefly in this forum that discernment should be undertaken. Once again, it is likely that the initiatives taken by basic communities can further the dialogue between the Gospel and indigenous culture in this important area. The communities are closest to the problems which the official Church is struggling ineffectually to solve.

In Latin America the basic ecclesial communities were part of the struggle for social justice and liberation from the beginning. This has not been the case in Africa, although, even in the independent countries, there are many social inequalities and injustices that are ultimately connected with socio-economic dependency on rich nations. In Africa, the small Christian communities have a primarily pastoral role. However, as we saw in Chapter 17, inculturation demands a commitment to liberation from the cultural effects of foreign socio-economic domination. Small Christian communities have to join this struggle if they are to be effective agents of inculturation.

Not only should they care for the casualties of an unjust system: the destitute, the refugees, the morally disorientated, the untended sick, the prison populations, but they should try to understand the forces arrayed against the values of the Gospel and its seeds sown by the Logos in indigenous tradition. They should try to identify the culturally corrosive influences from abroad and the inhuman and un-Christian responses from within. Through concerted efforts with other small communities, they should try to bring about a change for the better, to dismantle unjust structures and to correct abuses in society. To do this they will have to be prepared to come out of the 'sacristy' and into the 'street'. They will have to lobby politicians and even to brave their displeasure. The exercise of Christian people-power is a necessary concomitant of inculturation.

One of the chief activities of small Christian communities is Bible reading and Bible sharing, trying to apply the Bible to everyday life. There are many dangers in this exercise, not least of all, fundamentalism. It is totally misleading to treat the Bible as a kind of encyclopaedia or question-box that offers immediate solutions to everyday problems. Reading the Bible with the community demands training and regular help from the expert, preferably also a reading scheme and discussion questions. Yet it is in this practice that we recognize inculturation at its most self-conscious. Through Bible reading the community makes contact with cultures far removed in space and time, cultures in which God revealed himself. Through Bible sharing the community discovers the signs of God's self-revelation in contemporary culture.

Bible reading in the community is the most privileged moment of inculturation. It is the moment when Christians strive to understand God's Word, to transpose it into their own cultural language and to proclaim it to their own human society. One sees the fruit of this reading of the Bible very often when communities re-enact the stories and parables of the Gospels or the Old Testament in biblical plays. The small anachronisms that they introduce into the drama are not so

269

much a sign of acculturation, as of the extent to which they reinterpret the stories for their own lives. Often the Christians themselves identify with the crowds in the Bible stories, with the travellers reporting to Bethlehem for registration by the government, with the shepherds, the Roman soldiers, the crowd at Pentecost. They are not introducing anachronisms into the Gospels, so much as inserting the Gospel into the context of their own lives and culture, and allowing it to challenge them. They really *are* the shepherds to whom the wonderful tidings were told. They really *are* the crowd, harassed and leaderless, hanging upon the lips of Jesus. They identify with the poor to whom God comes, and among whom he reveals himself. Reading and proclaiming the Word of God are the means by which Christians allow the Gospel to challenge and transform their lives, and to evoke a response within their own cultural context. This is the epitome of inculturation.

The official Church teaches the theology of inculturation with increasing exactness, and even sensitivity, but it does not appear eager to match praxis with theory. Its extreme caution and its policy of gradualness often discourage Christians in the local churches. The Church does not appear ready to enter upon a consistent and comprehensive programme of inculturation. This prospect is a cause of deep disappointment and misgiving to Third World Christians. It is also a possible source of danger — the danger of a superficial evangelization and of a threat to Catholic communion. For this danger to be averted, Christians at the grass-roots must nourish an optimistic faith in the Church's future capacity. This faith must sustain them in their own creativity and in their own initiatives. What they do now in their own small communities will eventually bear fruit for inculturation throughout the Church. At the present time of writing, the vocation of the small Christian communities is to be the keeper of the Church's conscience for inculturation.

References

1 Abega 1978.

2 *Information Service Catholic Secretariat*, Accra, 77/20–77/26; *Liturgy for Second Burial*, Harare, 1982.

3 Barrett 1977; cf. also the Irish missionary film (Kiltegan Fathers): 'Father of the Red Bull'.

4 *AFER*, Vol. 16, Nos. 1 and 2, 1974, pp. 9–10.

5 *AFER*, Vol. 18, No. 5, 1976, p. 252.

6 *Ibid.*, p. 253.

7 *AFER*, Vol. 21, No. 3, 1979, pp. 265–72; Vol. 28, Nos. 3 and 4, 1986, p. 269.

8 *Acts of Seventh Plenary Assembly of SECAM*, Kinshasa 1984, p. 228.

Bibliography

This is a list of works cited in the text, together with some items of suggested further reading.

Abega, P., 1978. 'Liturgical Adaptation' in Fashole-Luke *et al.*, pp. 597–605.

Aixala, J. (ed.), 1981. *Other Apostolates Today: Selected Letters and Addresses of Pedro Arrupe SJ*, St Louis.

Amaladoss, M., 1985. 'Culture and Dialogue', *IRM* Vol. 74, No. 294, April, pp. 169–77.

Appiah-Kubi, K., and Torres, S. (eds), 1979. *African Theology En Route*, New York.

Arrupe, P., 1978. 'Letter to the Whole Society on Inculturation', in Aixala (ed.), Vol. 3, pp. 172–81.

Aubert, J. M., 1986. *Inculturation de l'Église Catholique dans le Nord de Madagascar* (Document Interéglises, Centre de Recherches Théologiques Missionnaires), Paris.

Azevedo, M. de C., 1982. *Inculturation and the Challenges of Modernity*, Rome.

Badi-Banga Ne-Mwine, 1982. 'Expression de la Foi Chrétienne dans l'Art Plastique Zaïrois' in *Cahiers des Religions Africaines. Art Religieux Africain*, ed. Mbuyamba Lupwishi, Vol. 16, pp. 135–67.

Ball, J., 1986. 'Theological Trends: Missiology. The World Religions' in *The Way*, Vol. 26, January, pp. 53–60.

Banton, M. (ed.), 1966. *Anthropological Approaches to the Study of Religion*, London.

Barrett, T., 1977. *Incarnating the Church in Turkana*, Gaba Spearhead 52, Eldoret, Kenya.

Bastide, R., 1978. *The African Religions of Brazil*, Baltimore and London.

Beattie, J. H. M., 1964. *Other Cultures*, London.

Beauchamp, P., 1983. 'The Role of the Old Testament in the Process of Building up Local Churches' in Beauchamp *et al.*, pp. 1–16.

Beauchamp, P., *et al.*, 1983. *Bible and Inculturation*, Rome.

Bede, the Venerable. *A History of the English Church and People*, tr. L. Sherley-Price 1955 (Penguin ed.), Harmondsworth, Middx.

Berger, P., 1980. *The Heretical Imperative*, London.

Bettenson, H. (ed.), 1956. *The Early Christian Fathers*, Oxford.

Blomjous, J., 1980. 'Development in Mission Thinking and Practice 1959–1980: Inculturation and Interculturation' in *AFER*, Vol. 22, No. 6, pp. 393–8.

Boff, L., 1986. *Ecclesiogenesis: The Base Communities Reinvent the Church*, London.

Brown, R. E., 1985. *Biblical Exegesis and Church Doctrine*, New York and London.

Bwana, S., 1986. 'L'effet produit par le nouveau code en Afrique' in *Concilium*, 205, pp. 133–40; (= 'The Impact of the New Code in Africa' in *Concilium*, Eng. edn, 185, pp. 103–9).

Carrier, H., 1987. *Évangile et Cultures de Léon XIII à Jean-Paul II*, Rome.

Chupungco, A. J., 1982. *Cultural Adaptation of the Liturgy*, New York.

Churchill, W. S., 1957. *Great War Speeches*, London.

Cohen, R., and Middleton, J., 1970. *From Tribe to Nation in Africa*, Scranton, Pa.

Congar, Y. M. J., 1953. *The Catholic Church and the Race Question*, Paris.

Congar, Y. M. J., 1986. 'Moving towards a Pilgrim Church' in Stacpoole (ed.), pp. 129–52.

Coulbeaux, J. B., 1928. *Histoire Religieuse et Politique de l'Abyssinie*, paris.

Coulson, J. S., 1981. *Religion and Imagination*, Oxford.

Crollius, A. R., 1984. 'What is so new about Inculturation?' in Crollius and Nkéramihigo, pp. 1–18.

Crollius, A. R., and Nkéramihigo, T., 1984. *What is So New About Inculturation?*, Rome.

Crollius, A. R., *et al.* (eds), 1986. *Creative Inculturation and Unity of Faith*, Rome.

Cruz, M. de la, *et al.* (eds), 1987. *Effective Inculturation and Ethnic Identity*, Rome.

Dahood, M., 1978. 'Ebla, Ugarit and the Old Testament' in *The Month*, August–October.

Daly, G., 1980. *Transcendence and Immanence: A Study in Catholic Modernism and Integralism*, Oxford.

Daly, J., 1975. 'Incarnation of Christianity in a Local Culture' in *AFER*, Vol. 17, No. 6, pp. 328–36.

Davis, C., 1970. *Christ and the World Religions*, London.

Dawson, C., 1950. *Religion and the Rise of Western Culture*, London.

de Dinechin, B., and Tabart, V., 1986. *Un Souffle venant d'Afrique: Communautés Chrétiennes au Nord Cameroun*, Paris.

de Gasperis, F. R., 1983. 'Continuity and Newness in the Faith of the Mother Church of Jerusalem' in Beauchamp, P., *et al.*, pp. 19–69.

Dickson, Kwesi A., 1984. *Theology in Africa*, New York.

Dorotheos, Metropolitan, 1985. 'The Influence of the Moravian Mission on the Orthodox Church in Czechoslovakia' in *IRM*, Vol. 74, No. 294, April, pp. 219–29.

Droogers, A., 1977. 'The Africanization of Christianity — An Anthropologist's View' in *Missiology*, Vol. 5, No. 4, pp. 443–56.

Duchêne, P., 1950. *Le Cardinal Lavigerie: Instructions aux Missionnaires*, Namur.

Dulles, A., 1978. *The Resilient Church*, Dublin.

Ela, J.-M., 1985. *Ma Foi d'Africain*, Paris.

Endo, S., 1971. *Silence*, Tokyo.

Erivwo, S. U., 1979. 'Traditional Culture and Christianity: Rivals or Partners?' in *AFER*, Vol. 21, No. 4, pp. 216–22.

Fabella, V. (ed.), 1980. *Asia's Struggle for Full Humanity*, New York.

Fabella, V. and Torres, S. (eds), 1983. *Irruption of the Third World — Challenge to Theology*, New York.

Fashole-Luke, E., *et al.*, 1978. *Christianity in Independent Africa*, London.

Fiedler, K., 1974. 'Attempts to Reach an Integration between African Culture and Christianity in German Protestant Missionary Work in Tanzania, 1900–1940' (mimeographed), Limuru Conference Paper.

Fisher, E., 1980. 'Ebla and the Bible' in *The Bible Today*, Vol. 18, No. 3, pp. 171–9.

Flannery, A., 1975, *Vatican Council II: The Conciliar and Post Conciliar Documents*, Dublin.

Fransen, P., 1967. 'How can Non-Christians Find Salvation in their own Religions?' in Neuner (ed.), pp. 67–122.

Geertz, C., 1966. 'Religion as a Cultural System' in Banton (ed.), pp. 1–46.

Geertz, C., 1975. *The Interpretation of Cultures*, New York.

Gilbert, M., 1984. 'Le Livre de la Sagesse et l'Inculturation' in Gilbert *et al.*, pp. 1–12.

Gilbert, M., *et al.*, 1984. *L'Inculturation et la Sagesse des Nations*, Rome.

Gilli, A., and Chiocchetta, P., 1977. *Il Messagio di Daniele Comboni*, Bologna; (part tr. as *Daniel Comboni: the Man and his Message*, Bologna, 1979).

Gremillion, J. (ed.), 1985. *The Church and Culture Since Vatican II*, Notre Dame.

Hake, A., 1977. *African Metropolis: Nairobi's Self-Help City*, Falmer, E. Sussex.

Hastings, A., 1986. *A History of English Christianity 1920–1985*, London.

Healey, J. G., 1981. *A Fifth Gospel*, New York and London.

Hearne, B., 1980. 'Christology and Inculturation' in *AFER*, Vol. 22, No. 6, pp. 335–41.

Hebblethwaite, P., 1984. *John XXIII, Pope of the Council*, London (= *Pope John XXIII: Shepherd of the Modern World*, New York, 1985).

Hebblethwaite, P., 1986. *Synod Extraordinary*, London.

Hengel, M., 1983. *Between Jesus and Paul*, London.

Hickey, R., 1982. *Modern Missionary Documents and Africa*, Dublin.

Hutton, J. E., 1922. *A History of Moravian Missions*, London.

Jeremias, J., 1958. *Jesus' Promise to the Nations*, Naperville, Ill.

John Paul II, Pope, 1979. *Catechesi Tradendae*, London.

Kalilombe, P. A., 1984. *From Outstation to Small Christian Communities*, Gaba Spearhead 82–83, Eldoret, Kenya.

Kavanaugh, J. F., 1985. 'Capitalist Culture and the Christian Faith' in *The Way*, Vol. 25, No. 3, pp. 175–85.

Kraft, C. H., 1979. *Christianity in Culture*, New York.

Kuhn, T. S., 1970. *The Structure of Scientific Revolutions*, Chicago.

Küng, H., 1967. 'The World Religions in God's Plan of Salvation' in Neuner (ed.), pp. 25–66.

Lamont, D., 1986. '*Ad Gentes*, A Missionary Bishop Remembers' in Stacpoole (ed.), pp. 270–82.

Lash, N., 1983. 'Marxism' in Richardson, A., and Bowden, J., *A New Dictionary of Christian Theology*, pp. 349–51.

Latourette, K. S., 1937–45. *A History of the Expansion of Christianity*, 7 volumes, London.

Lonergan, B., 1973. *Method in Theology*, London.

McCabe, J., 1985. 'The Challenge of Inculturating the Liturgy' (mimeographed), AMECEA Liturgy Colloquium.

McNamara, M., 1983. *Palestinian Judaism and the New Testament*, Good News Studies 4, Dublin.

Masson, J., 1962. 'L'Église ouverte sur le monde' in *NRT*, Vol. 84, pp. 1032–43.

Metz, J. B., 1980. *Faith, History and Society*, London.

Metz, J. B., 1981. *The Emergent Church*, London.

Meyendorff, J., 1985. 'Christ as Word: Gospel and Culture' in *IRM*, Vol. 74, No. 294, April, pp. 246–57.

Milingo, E., 1984. *The World in Between*, London and New York.

Montesquieu, C. L. de Secondat, Baron, 1748 (1949 edn). *The Spirit of the Laws*, New York.

Neckebrouck, V., 1971. *L'Afrique Noire et la Crise Religieuse de l'Occident*, Tabora, Tanzania.

Neill, S., 1986. *A History of Christian Missions*, Harmondsworth, Middx.

Neuner, J. (ed.), 1967. *Christian Revelation and World Religions*, London.

Newman, J. H., 1868. *Parochial and Plain Sermons*, 8 Vols, London.

Newman, J. H., 1870 (1947 edn). *An Essay in Aid of a Grammar of Assent*, London.

Newman, J. H. (ed. J. S. Coulson), 1986. *On Consulting the Laity in Matters of Faith*, London.

Ngugi wa Thiong'o and Micere Mugo, 1976. *The Trial of Dedan Kimathi*, Nairobi.

Niebuhr, R., 1952. *Christ and Culture*, London.

Paul VI, Pope, 1975. *Evangelization in the Modern World (Evangelii Nuntiandi)*, London.

Pelikan, J., 1985. *Jesus Through the Centuries: His Place in the History of Culture*, New Haven and London.

Pénoukou, E.-J., 1984. *Églises d'Afrique Propositions pour l'Avenir*, Paris.

Pobee, J. S., 1984. *The Word Became Flesh*, CAMEC, London.

Propaganda Fide, Sacra Congregatio de, 1907. *Collectanea*, 2 Vols, Rome.

Rahner, K., 1976. *Theological Investigations*, Vol. 14, London.

Rahner, K., 1978. *Foundations of the Christian Faith*, London.

Rahner, K., 1980. 'Towards a Fundamental Theological Interpretation of Vatican II' in *AFER*, Vol. 22, No. 6, pp. 323–34.

Rahner, K., 1981. *Theological Investigations*, Vol. 17, London.

Ranger, T. O., 1972. 'Missionary Adaptation of African Institutions: The Masasi Case' in Ranger and Kimambo (eds), *The Historical Study of African Religion*, London, pp. 221–51.

Ratzinger, J. (with Messori, V.), 1985. *The Ratzinger Report*, Leominster.

Rocarés, A., 1967. *Robert de Nobili ou le Sannyasi Chrétien*, Toulouse.

Rossano, P., 1978. 'Interfaith, Its Importance and Implications, An Analytical Study from a Catholic Theological Point of View' in *Bulletin of the Secretariat for Non-Christians*, Vol. 13, No. 1, pp. 29–39.

Rossano, P., 1980. 'Lordship of Christ and Religious Pluralism' in *Bulletin of the Secretariat for Non-Christians*, Vol. 15, No. 1, pp. 17–30.

Russell, H., 1981. *Africa's Twelve Apostles*, Boston.

Sanon, A. T., 1972. *Tierce Église ma Mère*, Paris.

Sanon, A. T., and Luneau, R., 1982. *Enraciner l'Évangile*, Paris.

Sarpong, P. K., 1975. 'Christianity Should be Africanized, not Africa Christianized' in *AFER*, Vol. 17, No. 6, pp. 322–8.

Schillebeeckx, E., 1980. *Christ, the Christian Experience in the Modern World*, London.

Schineller, P., 1983. 'Ten Summary Statements on the Meaning, Challenge and Significance of Inculturation' in Zuern *et al.*, pp. 1–14.

Schönenberger, P., 1961. 'Names for God known and used by the Wanyamwezi' in *Anthropos*, Vol. 56, No. 5/6, pp. 947–9.

Schreiter, R., 1985. *Constructing Local Theologies*, New York.

Schurhammer, G., 1977. *Francis Xavier, His Life, His Times*, Vol. 2, New York.

Senior, D., and Stuhmueller, C., 1983. *The Biblical Foundations for Mission*, London.

Shorter, A., 1972. *Theology of Mission*, Theology Today No. 37, Cork.

Shorter, A., 1973. *African Culture and the Christian Church*, London.

Shorter, A., 1977. 'Liturgical Creativity in East Africa' in *AFER*, Vol. 19, No. 5, pp. 258–67.

Shorter, A., 1983. *Revelation and its Interpretation*, London.

Sobrino, J., 1986. 'Conflict within the Church' in *The Way*, Vol. 26, No. 1 (January 1986), pp. 33–43.

Soyinka, W., 1976. *Myth, Literature and the African World*, Cambridge.

Sperber, D., 1985. 'Anthropology and Psychology: Towards an Epidemiology of Representations' in *Man*, Vol. 20, No. 1, pp. 73–89.

Stacpoole, A. (ed.), 1986. *Vatican II By Those Who Were There*, London and San Francisco.

Standaert, N., 1985. 'L'Inculturation et la Mission en Chine au 17ième Siècle' in *Église et Mission*, No. 240, pp. 2–24.

Stott, J., 1975. *The Lausanne Covenant: Exposition and Commentary*, Minneapolis.

Sybertz, D., and Healey, J., 1984. 'A Narrative Theology of Inculturation' in *AFER*, Vol. 26, Nos. 1 and 2, pp. 70–74.

Theissen, G., 1982. *The Social Setting of Pauline Christianity*, Philadelphia.

Thomas, R. S. (ed.), 1971. *A Choice of Wordsworth's Verse*, London.

Thornton, J., 1984. 'The Development of an African Catholic Church in the Kingdom of the Kongo, 1491–1750' in *JAH*, Vol. 25, No. 2, pp. 147–68.

Timiadis, E., 1985. 'Unity of Faith and Pluralism in Culture — A Lesson from the Byzantine Missionaries' in *IRM*, Vol. 74, No. 294, pp. 237–45.

Torres, S., and Eagleson, J. 1981. *The Challenge of Basic Christian Communities*, New York.

Torres, S., and Fabella, V. (eds), 1978. *The Emergent Gospel*, New York and London.

Toynbee, A. J., 1961. *A Study of History*, Vol. 12, 'Reconsiderations', London.

Turner, V. W. and E., 1978. *Image and Pilgrimage in Christian Culture*, Oxford.

Tylor, E. B., 1891. *Primitive Culture*, 2 Vols, London.

Uzukwu, E. E., 1982. *Liturgy Truly Christian, Truly African*, Gaba Spearhead 74, Eldoret, Kenya.

Voulgarakis, E., 1985. 'A Lesson in the Lives of Cyril and Methodius' in *IRM*, Vol. 74, No. 294, April, pp. 230–36.

Waliggo, J. M., *et al.*, 1986. *Inculturation, Its Meaning and Urgency*, Kampala-Nairobi.

Wenger, A., and Gallay, P. (eds), 1964. *Paul VI: Pèlerinage en Terre Sainte*, Paris.

Wilson, B. (ed.), 1970. *Rationality*, Oxford.

Wilson, M., 1971. *Religion and the Transformation of Society—A Study in Social Change in Africa*, Cambridge.

Winch, P., 1970. 'Understanding a Primitive Society', in Wilson, B. (ed.), pp. 78–111.

Zuern, T., *et al.*, 1983. *On Being Church in a Modern Society*, Rome.

Bible quotations are from *The New Jerusalem Bible*; Vatican II documents are from Flannery 1975; Papal addresses and encyclicals—apart from those listed in the bibliography—are from *AAS* or Hickey 1982.

Index

231, 233, 235, 236, 247,
248, 263, 268, 269
Greek language, culture 116,
139, 148, 227, 232, 256;
see also Hellenism
Gregory I, Pope St 141–2,
172, 184, 186
Gritti, J. 37
Guadalupe, Our Lady of 157
Guatemala 156
Gutmann, B. 175

Hake, A. 254
Halle Society 173
Hastings, A. 242
Hauser, H. 123, 126
healing 251, 268
Hebblethwaite, P. 187, 235
Hebrew (Aramaic) 143, 232
Hegelianism 229
Heiler, F. 98
Hellenism 108, 112, 114–7,
119, 123, 124, 125, 126,
127, 128, 130, 131, 132,
138, 139
Hengel, M. 132
Henrique, Bishop of
Kongo 147
Hinduism 100–1, 160, 168,
173
Hobbes, T. 20
Holland 143; *see also*
Netherlands
Holy Ghost, Congregation of
the 168
Holy Spirit 63, 84, 85, 86,
94, 97, 125, 198, 214
Homer 139
Hosea 110–1
Hume, D. 20
Hungary 141

Ignatius, St, of Antioch 92
imagination 24
incarnation 11, 78, 79–83,
85, 113, 195, 196, 197,
213, 224, 225, 226, 232,
255
inculturation 4, 6, 7, 10–13,
14, 15, 16, 29, 35, 37, 43,
46, 48, 51, 56, 59, 62, 63,
64, 70, 71, 75, 76, 77, 79,
80, 87, 96, 102, 105,
109–14, 115, 116, 119,
130–1, 137, 158, 160, 163,
166, 171, 172, 173, 174,
179, 181, 183, 189, 194,
197, 198, 199, 202, 208,
211, 214, 217, 219, 222,
223, 224, 225, 226, 227,
231, 233, 234, 236, 241,
242, 245, 246, 247, 248,
250, 251–4, 256, 257, 258,
259, 261–70
India 42, 140, 160, 168,
173, 194, 206, 243, 244,
245
Indo-China 43
infallibility, papal 166
interculturation 13–14, 29,
63, 211, 257
Iran 118, 140; *see also* Persia
Iraq 140
Ireland 141, 246
Irenaeus, St 92
Isaiah 104–5, 109, 138
Islam 41, 42, 49, 90, 100,
101, 140, 160, 206
Israel, ancient 105–17
Italy 21, 116, 141, 246

Jacobs, D. 35, 36
James, St 128, 129